**Key to Japan's
Economic
Strength:
Human Power**

Key to Japan's Economic Strength: Human Power

Rosalie L. Tung
The Wharton School
University of Pennsylvania

LexingtonBooks
D.C. Heath and Company
Lexington, Massachusetts
Toronto

Library of Congress Cataloging in Publication Data

Tung, Rosalie L. (Rosalie Lam), 1948–
    Key to Japan's economic strength.

    Bibliography: p.
    Includes index.
    1. International business enterprises—Personnel management.
2. Japanese—Employment—Foreign Countries.   3. Americans—
Employment—Foreign countries.   I. Title.
HF5549.5.E45T86   338.8′8952′00683   82-48172
ISBN 0-669-06039-9 (alk. paper)

Copyright © 1984 by D.C. Heath and Company

Published simultaneously in Canada

Printed in the United States of America

International Standard Book Number: 0-669-06039-9

Library of Congress Catalog Card Number: 82-48172

To Michele

Contents

Tables and Figure

Preface and Acknowledgments

In an earlier study (Tung 1982a) that compared the selection and training procedures for expatriate assignments of U.S. compared to Japanese multinational corporations, I found that Japanese multinationals consistently outperformed their U.S. counterparts by a wide margin. Although some U.S. multinationals experienced failure rates as high as 30 percent (30 percent of the people sent overseas are dismissed or recalled home because they cannot perform effectively in a foreign environment), the failure rates among the Japanese multinationals studied nowhere exceeded 15 percent. In fact, the majority of Japanese multinationals had recall rates of below 5 percent. Although this lower rate could be attributed partly to the different criteria used by Japanese firms in defining failure on the job, much of the success of Japanese multinationals in this regard is due to the more comprehensive criteria used for selecting expatriates and the more rigorous programs for training candidates for overseas assignments.

The book compares and contrasts the selection and training procedures for expatriate assignments among a sample of U.S. and Japanese multinationals; analyzes the reasons for the success of the Japanese multinationals; and shows how U.S. multinationals can learn from their Japanese counterparts in this regard. Specifically the book is concerned with studying and/or identifying: (1) the criteria used by both U.S. and Japanese multinationals in selecting candidates for overseas assignments; (2) the kinds of training programs sponsored by U.S. and Japanese multinationals to prepare candidates for managing, working, and living in a foreign country; (3) the failure rates of U.S. and Japanese multinationals; (4) the factors that are responsible for the expatriate's inability to perform successfully in a foreign assignment; and (5) case studies of how a number of Japanese multinationals select and prepare personnel for overseas assignments. The case studies describe and analyze the criteria Japanese multinationals use in selecting candidates for overseas assignments and the kinds of training programs used to prepare them for living and working in a foreign country. Training programs include those held in Japan prior to actual assignment overseas and the ongoing programs conducted in the host country. These programs are designed to sensitize the candidate to the pressures and problems of working and living in a foreign environment and to provide them the skills they needed to interact with customers, colleagues, and subordinates in a different cultural environment. The case studies are based on interviews with senior executives in the international divisions and those in charge of training and development programs in the respective companies. Japanese expatriates in the United States were also interviewed.

The findings of the book are important to both practitioners and academicians. The knowledge gained from Japanese multinationals regarding expatriate assignments will assist practitioners in restructuring their existing programs. This will improve the rate of success of future assignments and also the overall performance of the overseas subsidiaries because they would then be staffed by individuals trained to live and work in a foreign environment. Although the book compares the practices of U.S. and Japanese multinationals, the information presented can be applied to multinationals headquartered in other parts of the world.

A comparative analysis of the selection and training procedures of expatriate assignments of U.S. and Japanese multinationals has implications for theory and research in the field of international management. The results will assist our understanding of the relationships between antecedent (in this case, selection criteria and training programs) and outcome variables (in this case, the success/failure of expatriate assignments) and other extraneous factors. Such understanding will assist in the development of more appropriate and comprehensive selection procedures and training programs, which will increase the efficiency and effectiveness of expatriate assignments.

I thank all those who have given their time willingly and generously to enable the successful completion of this project. Because respondents to the questionnaire surveys were not required to disclose the names of their organizations, I cannot cite them here by name.

I am particularly grateful to those who gave their time unsparingly by taking part in the interviews to provide a more comprehensive picture of their companies' human resource development programs. Specifically I thank the following individuals: Yoshikazu Hanawa, general manager, Technical Services, Nissan Motor Co., Ltd., and a vice-president of Nissan Motor Manufacturing Corporation U.S.A.; Makoto Haya, manager, Personnel Department, Nippon Steel Corporation; Ichiro Horide, director and general manager, International, Suntory Limited; Namiji Itabashi, chairman, board of trustees, International Education Center; Yashuiro Iwata, assistant general manager, Personnel Development, A, Mitsubishi Corporation; Tsuneo Iyobe, Personnel Development Section, Mitsubishi Corporation; Masaki Kobayashi, general manager, International Operations, Headquarters, Canon Inc.; Hiroshi Kurata, manager, administration, Marubeni America Corporation; Hiromichi Matsuka, deputy general manager, Dai-Ichi Kangyo Bank Ltd.; Henry S. Miyazaki, vice-president and assistant corporate secretary, Marubeni America Corporation; Masakazu Mizutani, general manager, General Planning, Overseas Operations Division, Furukawa Electric Co., Ltd.; Shigemitsu Morita, director and general manager, Daicel Chemical Industries Ltd.; Tadanori Nakaoka, Second Personnel Section, Personnel Department, Toray Industries Inc.; Shoichi Ohmagari, director, overseas programs, Institute for International Studies and Training; Ken-ichi Ozawa, general manager, planning, International Department,

Bank of Yokohama; Toshihide Nakajima, manager, First Primary Aluminum Section, Light Metals Division, Mitsui and Co., Ltd.; Yoshiro Sasaki, general manager, Personnel Department, Nippon Steel Corporation; Katsuhiko Satoh, senior staff personnel, Nissan Motor Co., Ltd.; Nakao Tawara, manager, compensation, Sony America Corporation; Yoshio Terasawa, chairman and chief executive officer, Nomura Securities International, Inc.; Jiro Tokuyama, executive director and dean, Nomura School of Advanced Management, Nomura Research Institute; Chisato Uematsu, personnel manager, Olivetti Corporation of Japan; and Susumu Yamada, deputy general manager, Planning, International Department, Bank of Yokohama.

I would like to thank the Office of the Dean at The Wharton School and The Wharton Center for International Management Studies for providing partial funding for the research project. I wish to express my gratitude to Professor Yasuo Okamoto, professor of economics at the University of Tokyo, for arranging some of the interviews on my behalf. I would also like to thank Yoko Horio, a doctoral candidate in Oriental studies at the University of Pennsylvania, for translating some of the materials provided me by the aforementioned Japanese executives.

As usual, I am deeply appreciative of and grateful to my family for their moral support and understanding throughout the entire project.

1 Human Resource Development: A Key Ingredient to Success in International Business

Since the industrial revolution, nations have focused on technological innovations and developments to gain superiority in the world economic arena. While technology is essential to a firm's international competitiveness, the successful operation of a multinational corporation is contingent on the availability of additional resources, among them include capital, know-how, and manpower. This book argues that manpower is a key ingredient in the efficient operation of a multinational corporation (MNC). Without a highly developed pool of managerial and technical talent, all the other resources could not be effectively or efficiently allocated from corporate headquarters to subsidiaries. Given this premise, it is essential that MNCs pay greater attention to human resource planning and development within the organization. As Peter Drucker stated in his seminal work, *The Practice of Management* (1954), the function of management is to combine human power, capital, and technology to attain a desired level of performance in the organization.

Although U.S. MNCs have emphasized the traditional aspects of human resource planning, such as the selection of people who possess skills in the various functional disciplines of administration, accounting, finance, marketing, and so on, they have by and large assumed that an effective manager in the United States will also be a high performer in a foreign country. This is not necessarily true. Earlier (Tung 1981) I found that the failure rates among U.S. expatriates were high (failures are defined here as expatriates who had to be recalled to headquarters or dismissed from the company because of their inability to perform effectively in a foreign country). More than half of the firms surveyed (n=80) had failure rates of between 10 to 20 percent, and some 7 percent of the respondents had recall rates of 30 percent. This is consistent with the findings of other researchers. Henry (1965), for instance, showed that approximately 30 percent of overseas assignments in

Portions of this chapter appeared in R.L. Tung, "Selection and training of personnel for overseas assignments," *Columbia Journal of World Business,* Spring 1981, pp. 68–78, reprinted with permission; and R.L. Tung, "Selection and training procedures of U.S., European and Japanese multinationals." Copyright (1982) by the Regents of the University of California. Adapted from *California Management Review,* Vol. XXV, No. 1, pp. 57–71 by permission of the Regents.

U.S. MNCs had been mistakes. Furthermore, the country in which U.S. expatriates appear to have the greatest difficulty in adjusting to is Japan, a market yet largely untapped by U.S. manufacturers but with huge potentials for large profitability. Seward (1975), for example, found that nine of ten expatriates were significantly less productive in Japan compared to their performance back home. Adams and Kobayashi (1969) similarly reported that four out of five expatriates in Japan were deemed as failures by their headquarters. These failures are costly in time, money, and human resources to the companies. Because of their inability to operate effectively abroad, the company's foreign operation may stagnate and, worse, lose its market share to competitors. Besides lost opportunities and revenues for the company, these failures often constitute a heavy blow to the expatriate's self-esteem and ego. Many who were sent abroad were star performers and had good records in the home office prior to overseas assignment. Hence, even if they are accepted back by corporate headquarters, it may take some time before they can regain confidence in their own abilities. For these reasons, multinational corporations should devote more attention to the area of human resource planning and development to maximize efficient performance overseas.

This chapter compares the human resource development programs of a sample of U.S. and Japanese multinationals. In general, it appeared that the Japanese multinationals sent abroad individuals who were more adept at living and working in a foreign environment. Although the international competitiveness of U.S. multinationals may be weakening because of the narrowing technological gap between the United States and Japan, a more important reason perhaps could be attributed to the fact that since Japanese multinationals traditionally place heavier emphasis on international markets, they devote considerably more attention to selection and training of their people for overseas assignments, which in turn translate into more effective performance abroad. In the United States, because of the large size of its domestic market, international sales have often been relegated a secondary position in the company's overall corporate picture. This is often reflected in the assumption that what sells well in Peoria, Illinois, for example, will also have a ready market abroad. This attitude is also manifested in its staffing policy; it is believed that an effective manager in the United States will perform well in a foreign environment. This strategy does not always work.

In contrast, Japanese multinationals appeared to have done an admirable job in this regard—all the more remarkable considering that the Japanese, by culture and history, do not readily mix with *gaijins* ("foreigners"). Due to the homogeneity of Japanese society and its relative isolation from the outside world (with the possible exception of China) until the mid-nineteenth century, its people are less adept at living and working in a foreign environment. As Hill (1977, p. 15) noted, "The natural insularity of this homogeneous island race, with its distinctive ethos, does not make it easy for the Japanese to absorb other cultures and become truly 'international.'" Furthermore, as compared to the United States and Western Europe, multinational corporations are only a fairly recent phenomenon in the Japanese industrial scene. Although the Japanese have engaged in international trade for centuries, such activities have been largely confined to importing and exporting. The trend toward foreign direct investment overseas and the practice of establishing wholly owned subsidiaries abroad gained popularity only in the 1970s, for a variety of reasons, such as the desire for expansion, diminishing returns on exports, and pressures from host governments. By the end of 1980, there were only 213 manufacturing concerns in the United States with majority ownership by Japanese investors. In 1979, U.S. foreign direct investment in Japan reached $192.7 billion, compared to $52.3 billion in foreign direct investment by Japanese firms in the United States (*Yearbook of U.S.–Japan economic relations*, 1980, pp. 66–70).

The Japanese multinationals have performed extremely well within a relatively short time. Through self-discipline and meticulous preparation, the Japanese who were sent abroad to establish foreign subsidiaries have succeeded in making Japan a formidable economic force. Although much of this success could be attributed to the quality and competitiveness of its products, the ingenuity of its work force has also played a major role in ensuring that its products are effectively marketed abroad. Jiro Tokuyama, executive director and dean of the Nomura School of Advanced Management, a division of Nomura Research Institute, noted, organizations are "collections of people," and the key factor behind Japan's industrial strength is the way in which its people are harnessed to pursue organizational goals (*Newsweek*, January 25, 1982, p. 4). Thus, much of the success of the Japanese economy in the global arena, or Japan's economic miracle as many describe it, could be attributed to the conscientious and meticulous human resource planning and development programs adopted by many of its companies. Given the high failure rates experienced by U.S. multinationals and the often negative image of U.S. expatriates overseas, U.S. multinationals could certainly learn from the Japanese in this regard.

This chapter presents the results of a survey research comparing the human resource programs for international assignments among a sample of U.S. and Japanese multinationals.

Questionnaire Survey Findings

Instrument Development

A questionnaire was developed for studying the following characteristics:

1. The extent to which affiliates of U.S. and Japanese MNCs in different regions of the world are staffed by parent country nationals.

2. The criteria used for selecting personnel to fill positions in different categories of overseas job assignments.
3. The procedures undertaken to determine a candidate's suitability for the foreign position.
4. Types of training programs used to prepare candidates in each of the job categories for overseas work.
5. The failure rate and reasons for such failures.

The questionnaire was pretested with a sample of twelve personnel administrators of U.S. MNCs. As a result of the pilot study, certain terminologies and items in the questionnaire were revised to improve readability and to facilitate responses on the part of the administrators (see the Appendix). The questionnaire was translated from English to Japanese by a bilingual researcher. The translated questionnaire was then translated back into English by a separate bilingual researcher. Comparison of the original English questionnaire against the back-translated version facilitated the identification of problem phrases and terminologies, which were subsequently modified.

Sample and Data Collection

The English-language questionnaires were sent to a sample of 300 of the largest U.S. MNCs listed in Angel's *Directory of American Firms Operating Abroad*; 105 questionnaires were returned, of which 80 were usable. The Japanese-language questionnaires were sent to 110 of the largest Japanese multinationals listed in Fortune's "Directory of the 500 Largest Industrial Companies Abroad"; 35 usable questionnaires were returned. The questionnaires for both samples were completed by the vice-president of foreign operations (or some similar designations) of the firms.

Locations of overseas affiliates were categorized into one of eight regions: Western Europe, Canada, Eastern Europe, Middle and Near East, Latin and South America, Far East, Africa, and the United States. Respondents were asked to identify the regions in which they had affiliate operations. Table 1-1 presents a breakdown of the percentage of firms with affiliate operations in each of these eight regions of the world.

Few or none of the Japanese MNCs included in this study had affiliate operations in the Middle and Near East, Eastern Europe, and Africa. This could reflect the early stage of development of Japanese MNCs. Furthermore, as evident from the case studies presented in subsequent chapters, Japanese expatriates have the greatest aversion to working in the Middle East.

Table 1–1
Percentage of Firms in Different Parts of the World

	Western Europe	Canada	Middle and Near East	Eastern Europe	Latin and South America	Far East	Africa	United States
U.S. MNCs	95	86	66	19	91	88	71	NR[a]
Japanese MNCs	62	39	29	0	86	81	29	57

[a]NR = Not relevant.

Analysis of Findings

Staffing Policies

Respondents in both samples were asked to identify whether management personnel at three different levels (senior, middle, and lower) in each of the eight regions were primarily staffed by parent country nationals (PCNs refer to personnel who are citizens of the home country of the MNC), host country nationals (HCNs refer to personnel who are citizens of the country of foreign operation), or third country nationals (TCNs refer to personnel who are neither citizens of the home country of the MNC nor citizens of the country in which the foreign operation is located).

Table 1–2 presents a breakdown of the responses by regions at the three different management levels for both samples. Frequency distributions in the table show that for the U.S. sample, HCNs are used to a much greater extent at all levels of management in developed regions of the world as compared to the less developed countries. This is logical; one would expect the more developed nations to have a larger pool of personnel who would possess the necessary manpower and technical skills to staff management-level positions. Japanese multinationals, on the other hand, employ considerably more PCNs in their overseas operations at the senior and middle management levels. This is consistent with a 1978 survey by the Japan Society of 1,200 U.S. subsidiaries of Japanese multinationals, which found that most of the senior management positions were occupied by Japanese nationals. The ratio of Japanese managers to U.S. workers in these enterprises was 10,500 to 81,000 (Matsuno and Stoever 1982). The Japanese MNCs do not use TCNs at any level of management in their overseas affiliate operations except in Africa.

Table 1–2
Extent to Which Foreign Affiliates Are Staffed by
PCNs, HCNs, and TCNs
(percentage)

	U.S. *MNCs*	Japanese *MNCs*
United States		
Senior management PCN	NR[a]	83
Senior management HCN	NR	17
Senior management TCN	NR	0
Middle management PCN	NR	73
Middle management HCN	NR	27
Middle management TCN	NR	0
Lower management PCN	NR	40
Lower management HCN	NR	60
Lower management TCN	NR	0
Western Europe		
Senior management PCN	33	77
Senior management HCN	60	23
Senior management TCN	7	0
Middle management PCN	5	43
Middle management HCN	93	57
Middle management TCN	2	0
Lower management PCN	0	23
Lower management HCN	100	77
Lower management TCN	0	0
Canada		
Senior management PCN	25	33
Senior management HCN	74	67
Senior management TCN	1	0
Middle management PCN	1	33
Middle management HCN	99	67
Middle management TCN	0	0
Lower management PCN	3	17
Lower management HCN	96	83
Lower management TCN	1	0
Middle/Near East		
Senior management PCN	42	67
Senior management HCN	34	33
Senior management TCN	24	0
Middle management PCN	27	83
Middle management HCN	63	17
Middle management TCN	10	0
Lower management PCN	9	33
Lower management HCN	82	67
Lower management TCN	9	0
Eastern Europe		
Senior management PCN	15.5	NR[b]
Senior management HCN	69	NR
Senior management TCN	15.5	NR
Middle management PCN	8	NR
Middle management HCN	92	NR
Middle management TCN	0	NR
Lower management PCN	0	NR
Lower management HCN	100	NR
Lower management TCN	0	NR

Table 1-2 continued

Latin/South America		
Senior management PCN	44	83
Senior management HCN	47	17
Senior management TCN	9	0
Middle management PCN	7	41
Middle management HCN	92	59
Middle management TCN	1	0
Lower management PCN	1	18
Lower management HCN	96	82
Lower management TCN	3	0
Far East		
Senior management PCN	55	65
Senior management HCN	38	35
Senior management TCN	7	0
Middle management PCN	19	41
Middle management HCN	81	59
Middle management TCN	0	0
Lower management PCN	2	18
Lower management HCN	96	82
Lower management TCN	2	0
Africa		
Senior management PCN	36	50
Senior management HCN	47	33
Senior management TCN	17	17
Middle management PCN	11	0
Middle management HCN	78	100
Middle management TCN	11	0
Lower management PCN	5	0
Lower management HCN	90	100
Lower management TCN	5	0

[a]Data were collected on staffing policies of foreign affiliates only. Hence, no statistic was gathered for home country of MNC.

[b]None of the Japanese MNCs included in this study has affiliate operations in Eastern Europe.

Respondents were asked to identify the reasons for staffing overseas operations with PCNs, HCNs, and TCNs. For the U.S. sample, the most important reasons mentioned for staffing with PCNs and the relative frequencies with which the reasons were cited were

1. foreign enterprise is just being established (70 percent) and
2. technical expertise (68 percent).

The most important reasons for staffing with HCNs and the relative frequencies with which the reasons were cited were

1. familiarity with culture (83 percent),
2. knowledge of language (79 percent),
3. reduced costs (61 percent), and
4. good public relations (58 percent).

The most important reasons for staffing with TCNs and the relative frequencies with which the reasons were cited were

1. technical expertise (55 percent) and
2. TCN is the best man for the job, all things considered (53 percent).

For the Japanese sample, the most important reason for staffing with PCNs and the relative frequency with which the reason was cited was, PCN is the best man for the job, all things considered (55 percent). All the other reasons were considered relatively unimportant. The same held true for staffing with HCNs. The most important reason given for staffing with HCNs and the relative frequency with which the reason was cited was, HCN is the best man for the job, all things considered (68 percent). Since Japanese MNCs used TCNs hardly at all in their foreign affiliates, no reason was given under this category.

Criteria for Selection

Overseas managerial assignments were classified into four major categories: (1) the chief executive officer (CEO) whose responsibility is to oversee and direct the entire foreign operation, (2) functional head whose job is to establish functional departments in a foreign subsidiary, (3) troubleshooter whose function is to analyze and solve specific operational problems, and (4) operative. Jobs in each of these categories involve varying degrees of contact with the local culture and varying lengths of stay in a certain country. For instance, one would expect a CEO to have more extensive contacts with members of the local community than would a troubleshooter. Also, one might expect the troubleshooter's job in a certain country to be of a shorter duration than that of the CEO. Given these differences, it would be interesting to study whether there were variations in criteria used for selecting personnel in each of the job categories.

Analysis of variance showed that for the U.S. sample, the criteria used for selecting candidates in each of the job categories were significantly different at the .005 level. For the U.S. sample for each job category, certain criteria were considered more important than others. In jobs that require more extensive contacts with the local community (such as those of the CEO and functional head), attributes like "adaptability, flexibility in new environmental settings" and "communication" were more frequently identified as being "very important" compared to jobs that were more technically oriented (such as that of troubleshooter). For the Japanese sample, the pattern was slightly different. The most important criterion for selecting candidates in the CEO category was "managerial talent", the most important criterion for selecting candidates in the functional head, troubleshooter, and operative categories was "technical knowledge of business." Besides "technical knowledge of business," most of the Japanese firms considered "experience in company" as a very important criterion for jobs in three of the four job categories; 89 percent of the respondents identified this as a very important criterion for jobs in the CEO category, 71 percent of the respondents cited this as a very important criterion for jobs in the functional head category, and 53 percent of the respondents mentioned this as a very important criterion for jobs in the troubleshooter category. This perhaps reflects the system of employment and the attitude toward business education in Japanese society. U.S.-type business schools are rare in Japan because corporations believe that management principles cannot be adequately taught in a classroom setting; rather they must be acquired through on-the-job training and experience.

"Adaptability, flexibility in new environmental settings" was also cited as a very important criterion for each of the four job categories by a majority of the firms although not as frequently as the other criteria. The findings here are consistent with a survey conducted by the Industrial Research Group in 1978, which found that the criteria used by Japanese multinationals in selecting personnel for overseas assignments since the mid-1970s were (presented in descending order of importance): administrative and managerial skills, technical and specialized organizational skills, aggressiveness and ability to empathize and relate with members of a foreign culture, and language proficiency (*Basic skills required of employees in international undertakings,* July–August 1978). Professor Tanaka at Chuo University has found that 52 percent of the Japanese multinationals surveyed used adaptability as an important criterion for selecting candidates for overseas assignments. A similar percentage cited language skills and "mental strength" to endure and tolerate different cultural settings as criteria for selection. A possible explanation for the identical percentages in these three criteria is perhaps best summarized by Mr. Mizutani, general manager for General Planning of Furukawa Electric Co.: "The concept of adaptability is comprehensive and consists of various components. Adaptability could be closely tied to language ability and personality." In Professor Tanaka's study, 48 percent of the firms indicated that the criteria of "physical health" and "good judgment" were also used (*Human resource development in industry,* 1983, p. 32). Dr. Tokuyama, executive director and dean of the Nomura School of Advanced Management, made a similar observation: "First of all, we select people with a knowledge of the substantive issues in business. This is priority number 1. In the past, language abilities took precedence over technical competence, but a mere linguist proved to be inefficient in many cases. Of course, language is an important criterion, but it is no more than a means to achieve the objectives. The second but not the least factor is one's psychological makeup. An extrovert person who is free from culture shock is ideally suited to overseas assignments."

"Sex (or gender) of candidate" was mentioned by over half of the Japanese multinationals as a criterion used in all four job categories. Gender of the candidate was not mentioned as a criterion by any of the U.S.

multinationals surveyed. This is probably due to differences between the countries in terms of equal employment requirements. Besides the traditional status relegated to women in Japanese society, the Japanese multinationals were less inhibited in acknowledging that there are problems in assigning women as expatriates because of the attitude toward working women in some societies. The latter reason held in the case of European multinationals (Tung 1982a).

Selection Procedures: Tests, Interviews

The study then examined procedures undertaken by the firms to determine a candidate's suitability for the overseas position. In response to the question, "Are tests administered to determine candidate's technical competence?" 3 and 5 percent, respectively, in the U.S. and Japanese samples replied in the affirmative. In response to the question, "Are tests administered to determine the candidate's relational abilities?" 5 percent of the U.S. firms replied in the affirmative. None of the Japanese firms administered any formal test to determine the candidate's relational abilities. The U.S. firms that did test the candidate's relational abilities described such assessments to include judgment by seniors, psychological appraisal, and interviews by a consulting psychologist with both candidate and spouse.

An overwhelming majority of the U.S. firms in the study failed to assess the candidate's relational abilities, yet they clearly recognize that human relational skills are important for overseas work, as evidenced by their responses discussed under the "criteria for selection" section and when research (Hays 1971, 1974; Ivancevich 1969; Miller 1972) shows relational abilities to be crucial to success in overseas assignments. Given the increasing demand for personnel who can function effectively abroad and the relatively high failure rate, there certainly appears to be room for improvement in this area.

Although none of the firms administered any formal test to determine the candidate's relational abilities, the Japanese MNCs clearly recognized the importance of such skills to success in an overseas environment, as evidenced by the fact that 57 percent of the firms had special training programs to prepare candidates for overseas work. Given the Japanese preference for implicit control procedures, formal tests are generally not administered. However, given the system of personnel management characteristic of most Japanese organizations, there is ample opportunity for superiors to assess attitude and aptitude. Perhaps the apparent absence of formal procedures to determine a candidate's suitability is best represented by a remark made by Mr. Satoh of Nissan Motor Co., Ltd.: "Mr. Hanawa [his immediate supervisor] has interviewed me for a long time, ever since I joined Nissan fifteen years ago. Every day is an interview." Thus, although there is no formal assessment, the evaluation is carried out implicitly, on a continual basis.

The respondents were asked to indicate whether interviews were conducted with the candidate only or both candidate and spouse in management-type and technically oriented positions. In the U.S. sample, 52 percent of the firms conducted interviews with both candidate and spouse for management-type positions; 47 percent of the companies conducted interviews with only the candidate; and 1 percent did not conduct any interviews. For technically oriented positions, 40 percent of the companies conducted interviews with both candidate and spouse; 59 percent of the companies conducted interviews with candidate only; and 1 percent did not conduct interviews altogether. These figures suggest that in management-type positions characterized by more extensive contact with the local community as compared to technically oriented positions, the adaptability of the spouse to living in a foreign environment was perceived as important to performance. However, even for technically oriented positions, a sizable proportion of the firms did conduct interviews with both candidate and spouse. This lends support to the contention of other researchers (Borrmann 1968; Harris and Harris 1972; Hays 1974) that MNCs are becoming increasingly cognizant of the importance of this factor to effective performance abroad. The study did not examine the nature of questions asked during these interviews. In general, these should be more probing than interviews for the average domestic position. Questions pertaining to the candidate's "marital relationships, prejudices, interpersonal relationships, and many characteristics related to adjustment abroad" should be asked to determine the person's suitability for an overseas position (Sieveking, Anchor, and Marston 1981, p. 201).

For the Japanese sample, 71 percent of the firms conducted interviews with candidates only for management-type positions, and 62 percent of the firms conducted interviews with candidates only for technically oriented positions. None of the firms included the spouse in interviews, a striking difference from the U.S. sample. This difference could be attributed to the fact that Japanese culture and society have a very different view of the spouse's (in this case, the wife's) role and status in the family. It should be noted, however, that given the unique characteristics of the Japanese system of personnel management, even though official interviews are not conducted with the candidate's spouse, the company is usually very familiar with the details of the person's family situation. Hence, the employer already has information about personal data, which may be sought in interviews in U.S. multinationals. Consequently the family situation is indirectly taken into consideration in the selection decision.

Training Programs

The analysis will focus on those problems which are designed to prepare personnel for cross-cultural encounters. These are presented in ascending order of rigor with which the program seeks to impart on the candidate knowledge and understanding of a foreign country.

Area Studies Programs: These include environmental briefing and cultural orientation programs designed to provide the trainee with factual information about a particular country's sociopolitical history, geography, stage of economic development, and cultural institutions.

Culture Assimilator: This consists of a series of seventy-five to one hundred episodes briefly describing an intercultural encounter. The culture assimilator is based on the critical incidents method—incidents judged (by a panel of experts, including returned expatriates) to be critical to the situations between members of two different cultures are included. Studies designed to test the validity and effectiveness of this training device have shown that in general "these programs provide an apparently effective method for assisting members of one culture to interact and adjust successfully with members of another culture" (Fiedler and Mitchell 1971, p. 95). The technique, however, was designed specifically for people who had to be assigned overseas on short notice. Consequently, where time is not a major factor and in assignments that require extensive contact with members of the local community, this technique should be supplemented by more rigorous training programs.

Language Training: The candidate is taught the language of the country to which he is assigned. It often takes months, or sometimes years, before a candidate can master a foreign language.

Sensitivity Training: These programs focus on learning at the affective level and are designed to develop an attitudinal flexibility within the individual so that he can become aware of and eventually accept that unfamiliar modes of behavior and value systems can also be valid ways of acting in a different culture. Although the effectiveness of sensitivity sessions has been questioned, there is some indication that they "may well be a powerful technique in the reduction of ethnic prejudice, particularly among those who are low in psychological anomie" (Rubin 1967, p. 30). The Peace Corps is by far the most ardent advocate of this type of training program. To increase the effectiveness of sensitivity training, the Peace Corps developed a strategy whereby such sessions were supplemented with field experiences.

Field Experiences: Candidates are sent to the country of assignment or microcultures nearby (such as Indian reservations or urban black ghettoes) where the trainees may undergo some of the emotional stress that can be expected while living and working with people from a different subculture. Research indicates that although differences in cultural content exist between these microcultures and the country to which the trainee is assigned, trainees seem to benefit from an encounter with people whose way of life is different from their own since "the process problems that grow out of confrontation are similar" (Harris and Harris 1972, p. 9).

In the U.S. sample, only 32 percent of the respondents indicated that their company had formal training programs to prepare candidates for overseas work; 68 percent had no such training program. The reasons, and the relative frequencies with which the reasons were cited for omitting training programs, were (1) trend toward employment of local nationals (45 percent), (2) temporary nature of such assignments (28 percent), (3) doubt effectiveness of such training programs (20 percent), and (4) lack time (7 percent).

In contrast, 57 percent of the Japanese MNCs sponsored some form of training to prepare candidates for overseas work. This is consistent with the survey findings of *Japan Economic News* (June 24, 1982), which reported that 70 percent of the 267 largest Japanese multinationals provided some formal training programs to their expatriates prior to overseas assignment. Another survey of Japanese firms found that over the ten-year period 1965 to 1975, 50 percent of the companies provided formal training to their expatriates prior to departure overseas. A breakdown of the contents of these programs is as follows: 79.3 percent of the firms provided language training, 48.3 percent sponsored environmental briefing, and 13.8 percent conducted courses designed to improve the Japanese expatriates' relational skills with foreign nationals. Until the mid-1970s, the emphasis was on language training. Since 1975, there has been a greater recognition on the part of most Japanese multinationals that in order to be truly competitive in the global arena, language skills alone are inadequate. Thus, the emphasis since then has been on the development and training of internationally minded employees (*Basic skills required of employees in international undertakings,* July–August 1978). For firms that did not provide any training, the reasons and the relative frequencies with which the reasons were cited for omitting training programs were lack of time (63 percent) and doubt effectiveness of such training programs (37 percent).

The firms that sponsored training programs were asked to identify the procedures they used to prepare candidates for cross-cultural encounters in each of the four job categories. Table 1–3 presents the relative frequencies with which a particular program was used for each job category in both samples. Results indicate that for the U.S. sample, most of the firms that sponsored training programs recognized the need for more rigorous sessions for the CEO and functional head job categories, as compared to the troubleshooter and operative job categories. In contrast, the Japanese firms that sponsored training programs appeared to provide slightly more rigorous training programs for personnel in the operative category. This could arise from the fact that since people occupying CEO positions have more extensive and longer records of overseas work experience, the need to subject

Table 1-3
Frequencies of Training Programs Used for Each Job Category in U.S. and Japanese Samples
(percentage)

Training Programs	CEO United States	Japan	Functional Head United States	Japan	Troubleshooter United States	Japan	Operative United States	Ja
Environmental briefing	52	67	54	57	44	52	31	6
Cultural orientation	42	14	41	14	31	19	24	2
Culture assimilator	10	14	10	14	7	14	9	1
Language training	60	52	59	57	36	52	24	7
Sensitivity training	3	0	1	0	1	5	0	
Field experience	6	14	6	10	3	10	1	3

personnel in this category to the more rigorous programs was perceived as less important.

The firms that provided formal training were asked whether they evaluated the effectiveness of their programs and, if so, to identify the types of evaluation procedures used; 32 percent of the U.S. firms and 33 percent of the Japanese companies adopted some form of evaluation. For both samples, the procedures included trainees' and supervisors' subjective evaluation of the effectiveness of the training programs.

Failure Overseas

Respondents were asked to identify the most important reasons for an expatriate's inability to function effectively in a foreign environment. For the U.S. sample, the reasons given, in descending order of importance, were:

1. Inability of the manager's spouse to adjust to a different physical or cultural environment.
2. Manager's inability to adapt to a different physical or cultural environment.
3. Other family-related problems.
4. Manager's personality or emotional maturity.
5. Manager's inability to cope with the larger responsibilities posed by the overseas work.

6. Manager's lack of technical competence for the job assignment.
7. Lack of motivation to work overseas.

These findings are in line with Hays's (1974) assertion that the "family situation" and "relational abilities" factors were responsible, in the main, for failure or poor performance abroad. In the light of these findings, it appears all the more surprising that although most personnel administrators recognize the importance of these factors, a majority fail to take appropriate actions by developing rigorous methods and procedures for assessing and developing the relational abilities of their expatriate personnel.

For the Japanese sample, the reasons for failure, in descending order of importance, were:

1. Inability of the manager to cope with the larger responsibilities posed by the overseas work.
2. Manager's inability to adapt to a different physical or cultural environment.
3. Manager's personality or emotional maturity.
4. Manager's lack of technical competence for the job assignment.
5. Inability of the manager's spouse to adjust.
6. Lack of motivation to work overseas.
7. Other family-related problems.

This rank ordering of reasons for failure contrasts with that for the United States and reflects the differences in management systems between the two countries. In Japan, decisions are usually arrived at through consensus. There is a strong sense of group cohesion, or groupism, among Japanese managers. Overseas managers, however, find themselves fairly isolated from corporate headquarters. Although they still maintain daily contact through the telephone or other means of telecommunications, they lack the close interaction that they were accustomed to back home. They also are suddenly burdened with added responsibilities as overseas representatives, a status or role they are generally not used to performing on a singular basis. In the words of one executive some expatriates experience a "status shock."

Another salient difference is the relatively low significance assigned to the family. The family, however, does influence an overseas assignment because of children's education. This theme was echoed in virtually all the cases. The finding with respect to the spouse should not come as a surprise because of the role and status that Japanese culture and society relegate to women in general.

Respondents were asked to indicate the percentage of expatriates who have had to be recalled to their home country or dismissed because of an inability to function effectively in a foreign country. For the U.S. sample, 7 percent of the respondents indicated that the recall or failure rate was between 20 and 40 percent; 69 percent of the firms had a recall rate of between

10 and 20 percent; and the remaining 24 percent had recall rates below 10 percent. For the Japanese sample, 76 percent of the firms had failure or recall rates below 5 percent; 10 percent had failure or recall rates of between 6 and 10 percent; and the remaining 14 percent had failure rates of between 11 and 19 percent. There are two possible explanations for this finding. First, the Japanese expatriates by selection and training are more adept at living and working in a foreign environment. Furthermore, because of the system of lifetime employment, Japanese employees have a strong sense of loyalty and commitment to their company. Hence they tend to endure even when the overseas assignment imposes hardship and requires personal sacrifice. Second, Japanese multinationals use different criteria for judging whether a person can work effectively in a foreign country. This could arise from the more paternalistic role assumed by the firm and also the practices of lifetime employment and promotion based on seniority rather than merit. In evaluating the performance of employees, attitudes are considered more important than actual performance in the short term. Furthermore, given the employer's total concern for the employee, the supervisor tends to consider such difficulties in the initial period of assignment overseas.

The study then sought to analyze the relationships of selection criteria, training programs, and the incidences of failure. Given the rather qualitative nature of the responses with respect to selection and training procedures, it was not possible to use advanced statistical techniques. Consequently less sophisticated assessment devices were used. Each respondent firm received an overall score of 1 to 5 on the degree of rigor of its selection and training procedures. A low score indicates that the MNC did not use rigorous procedures in its selection and training; a high score indicates that it adopted very rigorous selection and training procedures. An overall score for each respondent was arrived at through the raters' assessment of the appropriateness of the criteria used in selecting candidates for the different job categories, the procedures (tests and interviews) undertaken by the firm to determine the individual's suitability for the foreign position, and training programs used (types of program and evaluation of effectiveness of such programs). Thus, a firm that received a high score was one that used appropriate criteria for selecting candidates in each of the four categories (for example, emphasizing relational abilities for management-type positions and technical competence for the more technically oriented positions); adopted rigorous procedures for determining the candidate's suitability for the position (for example, by administering tests to determine the candidate's relational abilities for management-type positions and by conducting interviews with both candidate and spouse); sponsored appropriate training programs to prepare the candidate for the overseas assignment (for example, for a CEO position, more rigorous techniques, such as sensitivity training and field experience, were used); and evaluated the effectiveness of the training programs.

Two raters were used. Each independently evaluated the procedures and criteria used by each firm and assigned a score. The two raters' assessments were correlated as an indicator of interrater reliability. The r was .78, which meant that there was agreement between the raters in their assessments of the degree of rigor of the selection and training procedures used by the firm. These overall scores were then correlated with the failure rates of the respective firms. For the U.S. sample, the r was −.63. This means that the more rigorous the types of selection and training procedures used, the lower the failure rate. For the Japanese sample, the r was −.34. The lower correlation in the Japanese sample may be attributed to the fact that the scoring procedure used to determine the rigor of selection and training is more appropriate for the North American sample, which was used to test empirically the validity of the contingency framework for selection and training of personnel for overseas assignment developed by Tung (1981).

Cross-tabulations showed that for both samples, the use of rigorous training programs significantly reduced the incidences of an expatriate's inability to function effectively in a foreign environment ($p \leqslant .005$). For the U.S. sample, the adoption of appropriate criteria for selecting candidates and the use of interviews in management-type positions significantly reduced the incidences of expatriates' inability to function effectively in a foreign environment ($p \leqslant .01$). For the Japanese sample, the relationships between the last sets of variables were not statistically significant.

Summary of Findings and Implications for Management Practices

Sources of Manpower

The Japanese multinationals surveyed used parent country nationals more extensively in their top and middle management positions in all their foreign operations. This finding could be attributed to one of several reasons:

1. Stage of evolution of Japanese multinationals. In the startup phase of overseas operations, it is common to rely on parent country nationals to establish the business abroad.
2. The Japanese system of management requires constant consultation and interaction between the parent headquarters and the overseas subsidiary. Hence it may be difficult for foreigners to operate within the system.
3. Since many of the senior executives in Japanese corporations do not speak English and, conversely, most foreigners do not speak Japanese, there is a language barrier. Besides, the control mechanisms in Japanese organizations are usually implicit rather than explicit (Pascale and Athos 1981). Hence it may be difficult for foreigners to have an implicit

understanding of the company's philosophy, which is central to smooth operations in industrial organizations. Even when local nationals are used, it is common practice for Japanese multinationals to assign a senior Japanese executive to serve in the capacity of coordinator and thus "solve communication and coordination problems" between the parent headquarters and the foreign operation (Matsuno and Stoever 1982, p. 47).

4. Until recently, Japanese multinationals had problems in recruiting competent local nationals to work for their overseas subsidiaries.
5. Because of the systems of lifetime employment and seniority, there may be a psychological reluctance among the Japanese to hire foreigners.

The Japanese are beginning to see advantages associated with the use of host country nationals, and many of the manufacturing companies have embarked on a policy of localization. However, there are still problems in implementing such policies. Many of these pertain to the difficulty of incorporating local nationals into the Japanese industrial system. According to Matsuno and Stoever (1982), some of the major problems associated with using U.S. employees, as indicated by the Japanese executives interviewed for their study, are differences in time perspectives, expectations, employment relationships, and control systems. In general, Americans are more short-term oriented and demonstrate a greater concern for immediate profitability. The Japanese, on the other hand, place a heavier emphasis on market share and growth, both of which take time to develop (Tung 1984). As Akio Morita, chairman of Sony Corp., contended, the real reason behind the lower rates of growth in productivity in U.S. firms could be attributed to the shorter-term orientation of U.S. managers. In his words, "Real professional executives are those who can take proper steps for long-term planning for the firm, even if the business declines in the short run" (Matsuno and Stoever 1982, p. 47).

The difference in expectations refers to the employment relationship between employer and employee, a contractual relationship that extends beyond office hours. Hence, a Japanese career staff is generally willing to assume organizational responsibilities beyond those specified in his job. With regard to control systems, the Japanese are accustomed to more implicit control procedures. As an executive at Dentsu, the largest advertisement agency in Japan and the world, noted, the Japanese favor communication in almost "telepathic" means, such as "gesture, nuance, inflection. They would rather infer than listen" (*Fortune*, November 11, 1982, p. 66). Americans, on the other hand, generally prefer more explicit control procedures (Pascale and Athos 1981). Many of these themes are echoed by the Japanese executives interviewed in this book.

In contrast, most of the U.S. multinationals used host country nationals to a much greater extent at all levels of management in developed regions of the world as compared to the less developed countries. Most of the U.S.

multinationals surveyed appeared to realize the advantages associated with hiring host country nationals: familiarity with local culture, good public relations, knowledge of the language, and reduced costs. Although this policy is commendable and should be continued, there are two reasons why U.S. multinationals should not rely solely on this source for staffing their overseas operations. First, although local nationals can effectively manage their fellow countrymen and relate well to domestic clients, they might have problems in communicating with corporate headquarters because of an inability to comprehend overall corporate goals and objectives. Hence many U.S. multinationals recognize the need to send over a number of expatriates who can serve as liaison persons between the foreign subsidiary and corporate headquarters in the United States (Tung 1984). Second, with the increasing cooperation among nations in the fields of commerce, the absolute number of individuals who will be sent overseas in the years ahead will rise. Consequently, U.S. multinationals should try to improve their present selection criteria and training programs for expatriate assignments.

Failure Rates and Reasons for Failure

The statistics for U.S. multinationals were fairly dismal. The principal reasons for failure are lack of relational skills (the inability of the individual to deal effectively with clients, business associates, superiors, peers, and subordinates in a foreign environment) and the family situation. This points to the need for U.S. multinationals to include an assessment of the candidate's spouse to determine the individual's suitability for overseas work and the need to include spouses in training programs to prepare them for living in a different environment. Given the importance of relational skills, efforts should be made to assess and develop the candidate's relational abilities.

The rank ordering of reasons for failure by Japanese multinationals was very different from the ones given by their U.S. counterparts. The manager's inability to cope with the larger responsibilities posed by the overseas work emerged as the most important factor for failure. This stems from the unique characteristics of the Japanese management system.

Selection Criteria

Despite the recognition among U.S. personnel administrators that the family situation and lack of relational skills are often responsible for the expatriate's inability to function effectively in a foreign environment, they failed to place sufficient emphasis on these criteria. Many based their selection decision primarily on technical competence. There are two possible reasons for this phenomenon. First, since it is difficult to identify and measure attitudes appropriate for cross-national interaction, it is easier to focus on the task-related variables. Second, Miller (1972) found that almost all of the personnel administrators he interviewed adopted a minimax decision strategy, one that would minimize the personal risks in selecting a candidate who might fail on the job. Since technical competence almost always prevents immediate failure on the job, the selectors play safe by placing a heavy emphasis on technical qualifications. This practice of basing the selection decision on technical competence alone, regardless of country of foreign assignment, may account for the high failure rate among expatriates in U.S. multinationals (Hays 1971; Howard 1974, Tung 1981).

Although the Japanese multinationals did not administer a specific test to determine the candidate's relational abilities, these were clearly taken into consideration. Furthermore, most Japanese MNCs recognize the importance of such skills to success abroad, as evidenced by the fact that 57 percent of the firms studied here and 70 percent of the 267 largest Japanese multinationals surveyed by the *Japan Economic News* (June 24, 1982) had specialized training programs to prepare candidates for overseas work.

Training Programs

In the U.S. sample, only 32 percent of the respondents indicated that their company had formal training programs to prepare candidates for overseas work. Most of these firms used environmental briefings designed to provide the trainee with information about a particular country's sociopolitical history, geography, stage of economic development, and cultural institutions. The assumption behind this approach is that "knowledge will increase empathy, and empathy will modify behavior in such a way as to improve intercultural relationships" (Campbell 1969, p. 3). Although there is some indication that increased knowledge will remove some of the fear and aggression that tend to be aroused by the unknown, the evidence that knowledge will invariably result in increased empathy is sparse and usually not the result of rigorous experimental control. Besides, some evidence indicates that understanding and endorsement of a different culture are not necessarily linked (Useem, Useem, and Donoghue 1963; Deutsch 1970). When used alone, environmental briefings are inadequate in preparing trainees for assignments that require extensive contact with the local community overseas (Textor 1966; Harrison and Hopkins 1967; Lynton and Pareek 1967). Furthermore, since there can be numerous cultural differences between two countries, training programs of this nature cannot possibly pass onto trainees all the knowledge that they will require over the duration of their assignments. These should be supplemented with more rigorous kinds of training programs. Given the financial resources available to international corporations and the ready accessibility to microcultures at home, MNCs could introduce their candidates for overseas assignments to such types of training programs. The field experience of living and working with members of a microculture need not mean prolonged absence from the company. Often a week-long live-in experience will expose candidates to the emotional stress of living with members of a different culture. Many of the other training programs designed to improve technical or human relations skills are week-long sessions.

The five types of training programs outlined focus on different kinds of learning—cognitive versus affective—and vary in terms of medium of instruction, information content, and time and resources required. These five types are by no means mutually exclusive; rather, they should be complementary and seen as part of a continuum ranging from low rigor (environmental briefing) to highly rigorous training programs (sensitivity training and field experiences). Depending on the job and the country of foreign assignment, the individual should be exposed to one or several of these programs.

In contrast, 57 percent of the Japanese multinationals studied had training programs to prepare candidates for overseas work. Besides environmental briefings, most of the Japanese firms emphasized language training. (In the case of U.S. multinationals, language training is less important since English is the universal language of international business transactions.) Indeed most Japanese multinationals mentioned language skills as one of the most important criteria in selection, for if the expatriate cannot converse with people in the host country, it is impossible for the individual to adjust to the foreign country, much less perform his job. Most Japanese multinationals also sponsor programs to prepare the candidate for interaction with members of a foreign culture, such as studying the host country's history and social traditions, and sponsoring exchanges in which Caucasians are brought in to live under the same roof as the Japanese trainees, and hence allow the trainees ample opportunity to practice their language skills and learn foreign ways.

Relationship between Selection, Training, and Incidences
of Success

For the U.S. sample, it was found that the use of appropriate criteria for selecting candidates, as identified in the contingency framework for human resource planning in Tung (1981), significantly reduced the incidences of an expatriate's inability to function effectively in a foreign environment ($p \leqslant .01$). The contingency model essentially states that given the differences in degrees of contact required with the local culture, varying durations of stay in the foreign country, and the varying degrees of differences between the home and other foreign cultures, no one selection criterion should be emphasized and no one training program should be used regardless of the task and environment. Rather, the contingency framework allows for the systematic analysis of variations in task and environmental factors. Due to the variability of each situation in terms of country of foreign assignment and the task to be performed, constant weights applicable to all instances could not be assigned to each of these factors. A more feasible strategy is to adopt a contingency approach to the selection of personnel for overseas assignments.

This approach requires a clear identification of the task, the environment, and the psychological characteristics of the individual under consideration. A first step in the selection process is to identify the job. Here the administrator should assess the amount of interaction with the local community called for by the position. Jobs in the CEO and functional head categories generally call for more extensive contacts with the community. Hence jobs in these categories rank high in terms of degree of interaction required with the local community. A second set of factors relates to the environment. In considering the environment, the magnitude of differences between the political, legal, socioeconomic and cultural systems of the home country and those of the host nation should be assessed and rank ordered. Data on such differences are readily available from research and educational institutions in the United States, such as the International Data Library and Reference Service at the University of California at Berkeley, and the Cross-National Data Archive Holdings at Indiana University, Bloomington.

The multinational should ascertain whether a candidate is willing to serve abroad. If the individual is opposed to serving abroad, no training program can change this attitude. If the individual is willing to live and work in a foreign environment, an indication of the extent to which he is tolerant of cultural differences and his ability to work toward intercultural cooperation should be obtained. Howard (1974, pp. 140–141) presents a list of appraisal methods (including psychometric devices) that could be used for assessing such personality traits. These include the Minnesota Multiphasic Personality Inventory, the Guilford-Zimmerman Temperament Survey, the Allport-Vernon Study of Values, the F-test (a psychiatric evaluation), and evaluations from superiors, subordinates, friends, and acquaintances to determine the individual's ability to be tolerant of foreign customs, cultures, and business practices.

In addition, personnel administrators should consider an alternative source of worker supply—local nationals. Most of the eighty U.S. multinationals surveyed appeared to realize the advantages associated with staffing overseas subsidiaries with local nationals. There were, however, variations in the extent to which local nationals were used at various levels of management. They were used to a much greater extent at all levels of management in developed countries than in LDCs. This is not surprising; the more developed nations have a larger pool of personnel with the necessary skills to staff executive-level positions. The countries staffed by a smaller percentage of local nationals at management levels of U.S. subsidiaries tend to be the ones whose culture, values, and business practices are more different from those in the United States. For example, one would expect the culture, values, and business practices of the United States to be more similar to those of the United Kingdom (both evolved from the Protestant-capitalist ethic) than to Thailand. Consequently the issue of selecting a candidate who is able to live and work in a dissimilar cultural environment still constitutes a pressing problem for U.S. international corporations.

The selection-decision process can be illustrated by means of a flowchart (see figure 1–1). Before headquarters launches a search at home for an appropriate individual to fill an overseas position, it should consider if the job could be filled by a local national. If the answer is yes, this alternative should be considered. If the position cannot be filled by a local national, a search must be conducted among those with domestic operations or within competing industries.

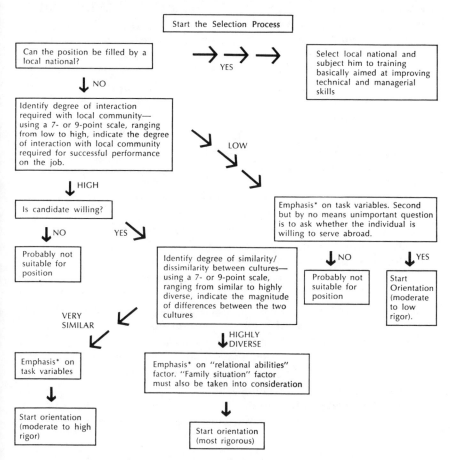

* "Emphasis" does not mean ignoring the other factors. It only means that it should be the dominant factor.

Figure 1–1. Flowchart of the Selection-Decision Process

The first step in the decision process is to identify the degree of interaction with the local community that is required by the job. In positions with extensive contact with the culture and an understanding of the local value system, relational abilities and environmental variables should be dominant factors in the selection decision. The selector should then examine the degree to which the foreign environment differs from the home country. If the differences are insignificant, the selection should be primarily on the basis of task variables. Where the differences are great, the selection decision should focus on relational abilities and the family situation. In figure 1-1, the family situation factor is categorized with the relational abilities factor. Although these are distinct categories, research is still needed to determine how much effect the spouse has on the employee's performance.

The rest of the flowchart is self-explanatory. Training programs to prepare candidates for cross-cultural encounters vary according to the degree of rigor with which the program seeks to inculcate within the individual the ability to relate to foreigners. If the job requires a great deal of interaction with the local community and if the differences between the two cultures are great, the candidate should be subjected to all five kinds of training programs, with particular emphasis on types 4 and 5. If contact with the local community is minimal, such as in a troubleshooter's job and where the differences between cultures are small, the area studies program would probably be sufficient. Between these extremes is a continuum of situations requiring varying degrees of contact with the local culture and involving varying magnitudes of difference between the cultures. Personnel administrators should locate the job under consideration along this continuum and determine a suitable training program.

No significant relationship was found between the use of appropriate criteria and incidences of success in the Japanese sample. This finding could be attributed to the different system of human resource planning used in Japanese multinationals.

Although the relationship between selection and incidences of success was insignificant in the Japanese sample, in both U.S. and Japanese multinationals, it was found that the use of rigorous training programs could significantly improve the expatriate's performance in an overseas environment. Thus it appears all the more important for U.S. multinationals to provide comprehensive training for their expatriates.

In an attempt to gain a better understanding of the reasons for the lower failure rates of Japanese multinationals, interviews were conducted with a sample of eighteen Japanese multinationals engaged in different industries. For the eighteen multinationals, the failure rate nowhere exceeded 5 percent. In addition, interviews were conducted with personnel in two educational institutes that train expatriates for overseas assignments: the Institute for International Studies and Training, which operates under the auspices of the Japanese Ministry of International Trade and Industry (MITI), and the International Education Center. These studies provide a better understanding of the human resource planning and development programs among a sample of Japanese multinationals.

2

Characteristics of Japanese Personnel Management

Many of the differences in practices, procedures, and outcomes between U.S. and Japanese multinationals with regard to selection and training of expatriates for overseas assignments can be attributed to the unique characteristics of Japanese personnel management.

Emphasis on Education

Historical Development

Education was emphasized in Japan even before the onset of modernization in the mid-nineteenth century. During the feudal era of the Tokugawa Shogunate (early 1600s to 1868), approximately half of the male population received some formal schooling (Patrick and Rosovsky 1976). During this period, there were essentially two types of schools. The first category was the elite or *han* schools, where the children of the warrior class *(samurai)* learned culture, ethics, and martial arts to prepare them to be military and political leaders. The second category of educational institutions was the *terakoya* or temple schools. There were approximately 20,000 such schools throughout the country during feudal times. These were established to teach the farmers and urban dwellers the skills essential to manage their business affairs, such as reading, writing, and mathematics. Although the majority of the population depended on agriculture for their livelihood, feudal Japan was already fairly urbanized, with three of the largest cities in the world: Edo (or Tokyo), Osaka, and Kyoto. Attendance at the temple schools was on a voluntary basis, and there was no age restriction. It is estimated that approximately 40 percent of the farmers and urban dwellers attended such schools (*Nippon: The land and its people,* 1982).

In 1868, when power was restored to the royal house of Japan, Emperor Meiji embarked on a series of reforms designed to strengthen and modernize Japan. Meiji's formula for converting Japan from an essentially backward agricultural country to an economically advanced and militarily strong nation was embodied in his five principles for modernization and industrialization. One principle was to upgrade the educational levels in the country, expressed clearly in the charter for the reform of the educational system: "We look forward to a time when there will be no illiteracy in any village house, no illiterate in any home" (*Nippon: The land and its people,* 1982, p. 147). Meiji was aware that without a fundamental upgrading of the level of educational and technical skills among its people, Japan's efforts toward modernization and industrialization would prove futile. Japan was virtually devoid of any natural resources. Its greatest asset lay in its people.

In 1872, the government established an integrated educational system, extending from elementary school to the university level. In 1900, the government mandated that all children who have reached the age of six must undergo four years of education. In 1907, the number of years of compulsory education was extended to six. In 1947, this figure was increased to nine years (*Nippon: The land and its people,* 1982). These efforts bore fruit. Today the literacy rate in Japan is almost 100 percent as compared to 96 percent in the United States (Richardson and Ueda 1981, p. 327). A recent report by the U.S. National Commision on Excellence in Education (1983) disclosed that the average Japanese high school graduate receives an equivalent of four more years of education than his or her U.S. counterpart. There is every indication that this emphasis on education will continue in Japan. Between 1975 to 1978, for instance, expenditures on education increased 52 percent and those for education-related items (such as text and reference books) expanded by 59 percent. These rates of increase are substantially higher than that for real consumption (*The Japanese consumer,* 1980).

Education and Employment

In Japan, status in society is determined largely by one's company. For example, when Japanese children are asked about the occupation of their father, the usual response is not, "He is an accountant" or "He is an engineer." Rather the typical response is, "My father works for Mitsubishi Heavy Industries" or some other company (Tung 1984). Candidates for executive-track and technical positions (referred to as career staff) in the well-established, prestigious companies are generally recruited from elite universities. Consequently there is fierce competition to gain admission to one of these universities. The chances of being accepted by one of these elite universities are largely determined by the secondary and primary schools (including kindergarten) one has attended. In Japan, there is a "generally recognized hierarchy of high schools and universities" (*Japanese corporate decision making,* 1982, p. 10). Given this extremely competitive environment, which begins in early childhood, the individuals who are recruited into the well-established companies have a record of academic excellence.

A person's formal education does not end with graduation from college. Although U.S.-type business schools are rare in Japan, administration skills are acquired through experience, on-the-job training, and in-house educational programs tailored to suit the needs of the particular enterprise. Thus, the "premanagement phase of the Japanese employee's career cycle is ... devoted to education and development, as well as to the office work at hand" (*Japanese corporate personnel management*, 1982, p. 6). Most Japanese companies have a career development program designed to develop skills needed by the respective enterprise. "The program is not confined to training employees for everyday tasks but extends to areas such as detecting and developing special skills held by employees" (*Human resource development in industry*, 1983, p. 22). According to a survey of 592 companies by the Japan Recruitment Center, 52.2 percent of top management perceived training to be of "utmost importance" for new employees (*Summary of recruitment survey: Personnel training within a corporation*, 1980).

In most Japanese companies, an individual is promoted to the level of assistant manager approximately eight to ten years after joining the company. This means that the initial period of employment is largely devoted to education and development, with emphasis on the particular company's long-term goals. This system is implemented in some of the Japanese subsidiaries of foreign-based multinationals.

The education of employees, however, does not end with promotion to the managerial level. Rather the career development program at most Japanese companies extends over the person's entire career. According to statistics compiled by the Japan Recruitment Center in 1982, 55.8 percent of the firms surveyed provided follow-up education for their employees on promotion to the managerial level. The percentage is higher among larger-sized organizations, probably because the larger companies have more resources and facilities to provide continuing education for their employees at all levels. In firms with 3,000 or more employees, 75.5 percent of the companies surveyed sponsored training for their management personnel; 61.3 percent with 1,000 to 2,999 employees provided training for their managers; and 61.5 percent of the organizations with 500 to 999 employees sponsored follow-up education (*Human resource development in industry*, 1983, p. 21).

A second reason for the emphasis on continuing education is *nemawashi*, which literally translates as "carefully uprooting and transplanting the seedling into a new environment." A Japanese is always identified as a member of a group. When a person graduates and joins a particular company, he is "transplanted," so to speak, from an academic to a corporate environment. Each company has its own corporate culture; thus, the recruit must be imbued with the company's corporate philosophy and culture, which are essential to the smooth operation of a Japanese organization because the individuals comprising the team or group must share a common ethos and perspective. This explains, to a large extent, why Japanese companies hire employees directly from college and carefully groom the individual to conform to corporate expectations. Thus individuals are seldom recruited because of their expertise in a particular field; rather they are generalists whose innate abilities and intelligence can subsequently be "trained and molded" to suit the needs of the company (*Japanese corporate decision making*, 1982, p. 9). To borrow the terminology used by Mitsui & Co., Ltd., college graduates are hired as "raw material" (Material provided by Mr. Nakajima of Mitsui).

A third reason for the emphasis on continuing education can be attributed to the system of lifetime employment. Under this system, career staff are employed on college graduation to their retirement at age fifty-five. (Because of the aging of the Japanese work force, the government plans to extend the official retirement age to sixty by 1985.) Since job turnover among the career staff is virtually zero, the company can afford to provide extensive training to employees so that they in turn will render useful service to the corporation. The company often spends a considerable sum of money on each career staff's educational development because these are considered safe investments for the firm's future since these new recruits will remain with the company until retirement. A principal purpose of the career development program is to promote the overall growth of the company (*Human resource development in industry*, 1983).

In most large Japanese companies, one's first major promotion does not come until many years after induction. The first several years in a company typically are spent on intensive in-house training. One of the publications of the Japan External Trade Organization describes in detail the educational program provided by a manufacturer of food products, a company with approximately 4,000 employees. In the past, promotion in that company was based on seniority. Now the minimum seniority required for promotion to the position of low level management has been reduced to five years, and the pace of one's promotion is determined primarily by one's performance in written examinations administered after each of the thirty-nine correspondence courses offered by the company. Each employee is required to take courses in his area of specialty, conducted outside of company time (*Japanese corporate personnel management*, 1982, p. 9). Similar programs have been established at many other Japanese companies.

Besides formal education provided by the company, many employees engage in self-development or self-enlightenment programs undertaken on a voluntary basis in the employee's spare time. These may be correspondence courses or simply reading literature to improve one's knowledge. According to a survey by the Furukawa Electric Co., Ltd., 70 percent of the employees engage in self-development programs, including in-house study groups, correspondence courses, television and radio courses, and language schools (material provided by Mr. Mizutani of Furukawa Electric). In the same study, it was found that managers spend an average of 9.76 hours per week on reading literature related to their job outside office hours; departmental managers spend an average of 9.59 hours per week; heads of clerical workers read an average of 8.4 hours per week; and engineering and clerical staff spend an average of 7.34 hours in reading. In general, the higher the level within the organizational hierarchy, the more time spent on reading outside material. According to Jiro Tokuyama, executive director and dean of the Nomura School of Advanced Management, "Many of the Japanese executives not only follow a number of Japanese magazines and newspapers, but read at least a few of the following periodicals: *Newsweek, Time,* the *London Economist,* the *Wall Street Journal,* the *New York Times,* the *Financial Times.* We are making such an effort to understand the global market. As you know, we live in an information-oriented era when countries with valuable pieces of information or intelligence win. So-called industrial policy is not necessarily the cause of our competitive position in world markets. The economic 'miracle' of Japan is attributable in part to our eagerness to gather and analyze the available information on world markets. I would recommend that American executives do the same if they want to remain intact in the highly competitive global market."

Job Recruitment

In Japanese organizations, virtually all the career staff are recruited directly from college. The academic year in Japan coincides with the fiscal year of business corporations. Students graduate at the end of March and join the company on April 1. Given the quality of graduates from the elite universities, there is strong competition among companies to attract them. Every year *Nikkei Business* conducts a survey requesting the graduating seniors in the nation's top seventeen universities to rank order the one hundred most desirable companies to work for, based on criteria the students perceive as important, such as "work is worth doing," challenge, international atmosphere, and desire for stability. The order of these criteria changes from year to year. In 1982 the desire for stability emerged as the second most important criterion (*Nikkei Business,* May 17, 1982, pp. 59-60), perhaps reflecting a greater concern for job security in recessionary times.

Companies usually begin recruiting in July of the preceding year and intensify their efforts in September and October because the universities are closed over the summer. According to Mr. Terasawa, chairman and chief executive officer of Nomura Securities International Inc. (whose parent company is the largest investment banker in Japan), jobs are not advertised in newspapers. Rather, the company approaches the universities, particularly professors who teach business and economics. In Mr. Terasawa's words, "We donate to the universities, with the understanding that they will give us good students," The recruiting is also done through the old boys' network or *gakubatsu,* pervasive in Japan (Haitani 1976). Mr. Terasawa believes the network is an effective means of recruitment because "students who see the old boys feel close to them."

Given the fact that one's status in society is largely determined by one's company, the graduate chooses the prospective company very carefully. According to Mr. Terasawa, the decision to work for a particular firm is perhaps one of the most crucial decisions in a college graduate's life. Once he joins, it is "very difficult to leave the company and join another, unless one sacrifices himself, both financially and status-wise." This explains the low turnover rates in Japanese companies and, more important, the dedication and loyalty employees demonstrate toward their employer because once they decide to join a particular firm, they have implicitly made a lifetime commitment. The recruitment process is usually completed by the end of October.

Lifetime Employment

The practice of lifetime employment has no legal basis. It is a moral or psychological contract entered into between the employer and the employee at the time of recruitment. The fact that the agreement is not entered into on a legal basis may stem from the general aversion to law and litigation in Japanese society. According to the Japanese view, to negotiate the terms of one's employment contract would change the relationship into an "adversarial one and destroy the basis of mutual trust between employer and employee" (Matsuno and Stoever 1982, p. 47). Approximately one-third of Japan's labor force is covered by this system (Cole 1981). This protection is usually provided by the large and well-established companies to the career staff only, primarily male college graduates employed by the company in technical and executive-track positions.

The system of lifetime employment has a number of advantages. The employees become completely committed to organizational goals. Given the internalization of corporate objectives, the career staff can thus focus on activities beneficial to the company in the longrun instead of pursuing courses of action designed to promote one's selfish interest only. As Mr. Morita of Sony Corp. contended, the higher growth rate in productivity among Japanese companies can be attributed in the main to the longer time perspective adopted by their executives. A career staff's promotion within the company is determined largely by his potential for contributing to the organization in the long run. U.S. executives, on the other hand, are usually evaluated on their performance in the short term, which may lead them to adopt courses of action detrimental to the long-run profitability and success of the company. A second reason is that given the low job mobility among the career staff because of the reluctance of well-established companies to take in people who have previously worked for another Japanese firm, the employee knows that he must not make waves since he will be spending the rest of his career in the organization. Consequently the career staff will tend to endure whatever job assignments the company gives him, even though they may entail temporary hardship and self-sacrifice. This explains, in part at least, the more positive attitude of Japanese expatriates in their overseas assignments. Finally, because of low turnover, Japanese companies can afford to invest considerable time, money, and resources in educating their employees, including training for overseas assignments.

Company Loyalty

Company loyalty stems from the system of lifetime employment and the strong tradition of groupism that pervades all aspects of Japanese society. The family system constitutes the core and fabric of Japanese society (Haitani 1976, p. 14). All other social entities are modeled after the hierarchical patterns in the family, which involve loyalty, responsibilities, and obligations on the part of all its members. This phenomenon is deeply rooted in Japanese society. In feudal times, urban dwellers were organized into merchant houses, corporate entities that transcended the members of one's biological family. The members of a house did everything in the name of and for the good of the house, which was the "embodiment of the achievements and honors of the ancestors" (ibid., p. 13). Some merchant houses later evolved into the giant *zaibatsus,* which were subsequently disbanded in 1945. In the early 1950s, however, the member firms of the former *zaibatsus* were once again reorganized into its present form, with the major difference being that the companies in the group are no longer majority owned by a particular family but by the general public. Although the management of all the companies that belong to a group is separate, the members share an esprit de corps and demonstrate a marked affinity in philosophy, values, and attitudes.

This strong tradition of groupism explains why the staff identify so closely with the achievements of the company and work section and why they are willing to endure assignments that may entail temporary hardship and self-sacrifice. This loyalty to one's company is perhaps best described in a news article that recounted the death of the wife of a MITI official. The official's wife died alone of pneumonia because her sickness coincided with budgetary time at the ministry. Since her husband's first loyalty was to MITI, he could not attend to her failing health. The magazine article ended with a quote from the vice-minister of MITI saying that the woman died a "tragic death on the battlefield as the wife of a government bureaucrat" (Bartholomew 1981, p. 331).

This attitude of placing one's company above one's family may be changing. A 1979 survey by the Public Opinion Research Institute found that 45 percent of the work force was promotion oriented and 51 percent was not. For the former group, work and company were considered most important. The nonpromotion-oriented employees desired to strike a "balance between work and private life." However, even among the nonpromotion-oriented group, the desire to strike a balance took precedence over the objective of "private life first" (*Human resource development in industry,* 1983, pp. 9–10).

Although the attitude among the younger generation may be changing, many senior executives interviewed for this study believed that because of the extremely competitive environment in Japanese organizations, as the younger people take on positions of responsibility, their attitude will more closely resemble that of their forefathers. Competition for promotion to higher positions in the organizational hierarchy is expected to intensify in the years ahead. According to the Japanese Ministry of Labor, 60 percent of the college graduates reached the positions of departmental head and divisional head by age fifty to fifty four in 1978. By 1988, the percentage is expected to decrease from 60 to 30 percent (*Human resource development in industry,* 1983, pp. 5–7). Given the fact that the Japanese are accustomed to competition from a very early age, it is unlikely that this ethos will slacken in the future.

Given the familial structure of business organizations and the high premium placed on loyalty, an employer will often evaluate the performance of an employee based on the latter's "dedication to the company and ability to cooperate with co-workers" rather than the typical Western attributes of initiative and self-motivation (*Keys to success in the Japanese market,* 1980, p. 22). As a Japanese proverb goes, "The nail that sticks up is hit" (Van Zandt, 1970, p. 47). In Japanese organizations, the ability to conform and work with others on a team are valued attributes because decisions, and hence activities, are generally carried out within the context of a group.

An intrguing and often misunderstood aspect of Japanese management practice is the dual emphasis on homogeneity and competitiveness, two principles that may appear contradictory. On the one hand, Japanese corporations adopt policies that engender homogeneity and conformity among employees, such as subjecting all new recruits to the same orientation and in-house training programs. This accounts for the slower rates of promotion in Japanese organizations and explains why there are seldom distinctions in status and basic wages among employees in the first eight to ten years of employment. On the other hand, given the pyramidal structure of the organizational hierarchy and the intensely competitive environment, only a few will eventually be promoted to top management. Consequently the company simultaneously embarks on policies and procedures designed to foster a spirit of competitiveness and striving for excellence over one's peers. In the case of a food products company, after the fifth year of employment, promotion is based primarily on scores attained in examinations administered after each of the thirty-nine courses offered by the company.

A key to understanding this apparent contradiction in the Japanese management system lies in the time horizons adopted by most Japanese companies. In general, Japanese firms tend to view objectives ten or twenty years hence. In terms of corporate goals, this is often translated into a greater concern for market share and growth, which often take years to develop and may mean operating in the red for a couple of years (Tung 1984). Similarly employment matters are viewed in the long term. Employees who excel are placed on an elite track. Given this longer-term orientation, the rewards in Japanese companies in the early years are not so much in the form of promotion or increases in basic wages but rather in the guise of additional responsibility and recognition of ability, which includes special bonuses. Thus the payoff for the elite tracker is further off than that for U.S. organizations (*Japanese corporate decision making*, 1982, pp. 8–9). Hence, instead of rewarding an employee for short-term accomplishments, the individual expects to reap the fruits of his labor "within the context of his length of service within the company" (*Nippon: The land and its people*, 1982, p. 119).

Employer's Concern for the Total Person

Japanese organizations are modeled after the family pattern with its responsibilities and obligations. In return for the employee's unquestioning dedication and loyalty to the company, the employer (as head of the corporate household) is obligated to assume responsibilities for all aspects of the worker's livelihood and well-being. Like children in a family, the employees are protected and cared for by their parents, the employer. This phenomenon is called *amaeru* (Van Zandt 1970).

Japanese employers are concerned not only with the employee's work life but also with all aspects of private and family life. Thus, besides paying the wages, an employer is expected to arrange social events for the employees and their families on weekends and major festivities throughout the year. Many firms provide company housing, which they rent to employees at low rates. For example, Nippon Steel Corporation, the largest steel manufacturer in Japan, provides dormitories for single employees and company housing to approximately 35 percent of its married employees. Many firms that do not offer similar arrangements provide financing for the purchase or construction of the employee's home (*Nippon: The land and its people*, 1982, pp. 239–241). Besides housing allowances, most companies offer comprehensive fringe benefits.

The employer's concern for the total person contributes to the lower failure rate in expatriate assignments among Japanese multinationals in at least four important ways. One, since the employer is concerned with the employee's private and family life, the company generally will not make unreasonable assignments. For example, an employee who has aged parents who need to be taken care of may be excused from an overseas assignment without negatively influencing his chances of future promotion in the organization. Two, the employer tends to make allowances for poor performance in the first one or two years of foreign assignment to allow sufficient time for adaptation and adjustment to a new environment. Hence, if the individual is not performing up to his usual standard in the initial years overseas, his supervisor generally would not evaluate him too harshly. Furthermore, if the expatriate has to leave his family in Japan because of his children's education, the employer will try to find business excuses for the person to visit Japan often during the course of his overseas assignment. Given the tough entrance requirements to the elite universities, children who are educated in high schools abroad have difficulty gaining admission to Japanese universities. Consequently expatriates with children (more specifically boys) in junior or senior high school will usually leave them behind in Japan for education purposes. Given the mother's overwhelming dedication to her children's education, she often remains in Japan. Three, many Japanese multinationals have special divisions whose sole function is to take care of the needs of the expatriates. These include match-making arrangements for single employees, delivery of correspondence in countries with inefficient postal systems, and the sending of gifts to expatriates during the traditional gift-giving seasons of July and December every year. Four, in U.S. multinationals, expatriates are often reluctant to work overseas for extended periods of time for fear of isolation and estrangement from corporate headquarters; they fear being passed up for promotion in the organizational hierarchy back home. These fears are often justified and add to the worries that an expatriate has to contend with overseas. In contrast, the superior-subordinate (*senpai-kohai*) relationship in Japanese organizations is strong. Besides acting as a mentor to couch the subordinate's career development when the latter is working in Japan, the superior will continue to take care of the subordinate's interests and speak on his behalf when the latter is overseas. The superior generally assumes the role of mentor for the rest of the subordinate's career. Consequently the expatriate can usually rest assured that somebody in corporate headquarters will look after his interests when he is away. This system alleviates the tension and stress that the expatriate may experience otherwise and thus allow him to focus on the pressing responsibilities of an overseas assignment.

Performance Evaluation and Promotion

Evaluation Criteria

Japanese organizations generally have a fairly complex and detailed set of procedures for evaluating employee performance. The criteria used in assessing performance vary, depending on the employee's position. In a detailed study of the personnel evaluation system in a high-technology firm that employs 1,000 people, the eleven ranks below the level of the president were divided into three general categories; junior employees, senior employees, and managers (*Japanese corporate personnel management,* 1982, pp. 11–13). Personnel in each category are evaluated twice a year by a group of superiors (including one's immediate supervisor) on a set of criteria specific to that particular level. At the junior employee level (or the premanagement phase), the emphasis is on the ability to obey orders from superiors, team spirit or cooperation, and general aptitude. Thus the junior employee is evaluated on work attitudes, including "obedience, cooperation, and responsibility"; basic and conceptual abilities; and performance of work as measured by "quality, volume, originality, and leadership." The ability to attain specific quantitative goals is deemphasized. Evaluation of volume of output is defined not in quantitative terms but subjectively as to whether the output is "efficient and punctual." The employee receives a score on each of these criteria based on a four-point scale ranging from superior to inferior.

At the senior employee level (the advanced level of the premanagement phase), the person is evaluated on the same three criteria, but here performance is specified in quantitative terms. At this stage of career development, the employee is expected to develop skills in "judgment and negotiation." Because of the indirect approach to issues and a desire to avoid confrontation, the development of such skills is paramount to effective performance at the managerial level. Thus, the senior employee is assessed on ability to develop "a subtle, perceptive, diplomatic" approach to "resolving problems through discussions with peers and superiors" (*Japanese corporate personnel management,* 1982, p. 15). These skills are considered essential for eventual promotion to management level. As a manager, the individual will have to evaluate the performance of his subordinates and to work closely with members of other departments to arrive at decisions important to the overall organization. Most decisions at the junior and middle management levels are made through the process of consensus (*ringi-sho*), which requires subtle probing of the positions favored by other people, and diplomatic negotiations on issues with members from other divisions in the organization.

Besides the written evaluation, the senior employee is interviewed for ten minutes and requested to engage in self-appraisal. Interviews are common in Japanese organizations. The Bank of Yokohama conducts a forty- to forty-five-minute interview with each employee every year to allow the employee ample opportunity to voice his feelings, aspirations, and any grievance. This stems from the employer's concern for the total person. In Ouchi's *Theory Z* (1981), he argued that this was one of the characteristics conducive to organizational effectiveness. This mechanism has been found to be effective in American organizations as well. In the case of Delta Airlines, for instance, top management schedules regular meetings (once every 18 months) with employees in groups of 25 to 30. Besides these regularly scheduled meetings, the company maintains an open-door policy, whereby employees can arrange to discuss problems with top management on a one-on-one basis. These practices, coupled with other policies designed to treat employees as members of a family have contributed to Delta's success, and have won the company the enviable distinction of being the "world's most profitable airline" (*Business Week,* August 31, 1981, pp. 68–72). This is all the more remarkable in light of the problems of declining productivity and sagging morale that appear to plague many of its competitors in the airline industry.

Self-appraisals by employees are common in Japanese organizations. Besides asking the employee to assess himself on specific criteria, the individual is requested to describe his aspirations in terms of career development and the actions he intends to take to attain these goals. The employee is also asked to indicate the types of jobs he would like to undertake and why. These are generally combined with any suggestion the employee may have for improving organizational procedures and constitute part of the dossier kept on each employee.

At the manager level, the focus of evaluation is on the person's ability to motivate and develop the skills of subordinates. The superior-subordinate relationship is pervasive in Japanese organizations. These camaraderie relationships are developed not only during office hours but in the context of after-hours socializing. In Japan, most male workers tend to fraternize with each other in restaurants and bars after office hours. Most aspiring Japanese businessmen do not go home until 10 or 11 o'clock every evening. Through these intensive contacts, one's superior is usually familiar with details of the subordinate's family and personal life and hence does not generally make unreasonable job assignments. Mr. Terasawa, chairman and CEO of Nomura Securities International has said, Japanese employees "talk and talk after work. So each person knows the other very well—they know what the other person's mother looks like, etc. It is very different in America. I don't know whether my colleague has a girlfriend or not—it is none of my business. In Tokyo, they know. In Tokyo, the boss knows your family situation. So he does not make any ridiculous decision. If I know a person has a sick mother, I do not recommend him to the board of directors for an overseas position."

There is a general belief among Japanese executives that administrative skills are learned not through textbooks but rather through practice and experience. Consequently the onus is on the superior to develop these skills in his subordinates. The Japanese subscribe to the saying that "One can lead a horse to water, but one cannot make it drink." A basic task of the manager is to "foster initiative and ambition" within his subordinates to learn and fully benefit from comprehensive career development programs (*Human resource development in industry*, 1983, p. 21). The manager is expected to understand the strengths and limitations of his subordinates and encourage them to capitalize on their attributes and minimize or correct their weaknesses. Upper management is usually less preoccupied with establishing goals and running the day-to-day affairs of the company; rather his function is primarily to serve as a figurehead whose responsibility is to motivate workers to pursue organizational goals and to provide an organizational environment conducive to raising productivity and enhancing efficiency within the company (*Doing business in Japan*, 1981, pp. 30–31). As Chie Nakane (1972, p. 65), a distinguished authority on Japanese culture, noted, "It is not essential for the superior, including the man right at the top, to be intelligent. In fact, it is better if he is not outstandingly brilliant" because if he were, he may distinguish himself too much from his subordinates and hence become too independent of them. According to the Japanese superior-subordinate relationship, there must be a symbiotic interdependence between the leader and the led. While providing guidance to his subordinates, the leader must depend on his followers for the fulfillment of organizational goals and tasks.

In summary, although the criteria for evaluation are different at the various levels within the organizational hierarchy, the attributes emphasized in Japanese organizations are primarily threefold: the ability to work as members of a group, proficiency at personnel development, and general aptitude and achievement (*Japanese corporate personnel*, 1982, p. 2).

A distinguishing feature of the system of personnel evaluation in Japanese organizations is the emphasis on attitude rather than performance in the initial stages. In the context of overseas assignments, in the first one or two years abroad, the expatriate is evaluated on general attitude rather than actual peformance. Consequently although the individual may not be performing up to his usual standard, as long as he possesses the appropriate attitudes and demonstrates progress and potential, his work is considered acceptable.

Another salient characteristic of Japanese personnel evaluation is the tendency to assess on the basis of subjective criteria (Harrari and Zeira, 1978). As Pascale and Athos (1981) noted, a distinguishing feature of Japanese management is the emphasis on implicit rather than explicit control. It is virtually impossible to use explicit evaluative procedures "without running the risk of permanently damaging relationships," which are paramount in Japanese organizations. Even among Americans, where face is apparently less of an issue, most respond more favorably "to helpful face-saving hints than to sledgehammers" (Schein 1981, pp. 60–61). Consequently, when U.S. multinationals dismiss or recall expatriates on the basis of the individual's inability to fulfill certain organizational goals (usually measured in quantitative terms) within a relatively short period after being stationed abroad, these may constitute a severe blow to the person's ego and might destroy self-confidence. In comparison, the Japanese method of evaluating an expatriate on the basis of the person's potential and attitudes in the initial phase may strengthen the individual's self-confidence and thus contribute to effective performance in the long run.

Promotion

In most Japanese organizations, promotions are based on seniority and ability. These may appear contradictory since the most capable people may not necessarily be the most senior in terms of age, tenure, and rank. To overcome this apparent contradiction and to preserve organizational harmony, many companies have adopted a double standard: the employee will be given a title and salary based on his age and years of service in the company, but the responsibilities he performs may not be commensurate with his title. Thus, a younger employee who has demonstrated marked competence and talent may be assigned duties normally performed by a person occupying a more senior position.

The reward in Japanese companies in the early years is not so much promotion or salary increases but rather the guise of "additional responsibility and recognition of ability" (*Japanese corporate decision making,* 1982, pp. 8–9). Thus, promotion on the basis of seniority can often be a facade. As one Japanese executive put it, "Promotion of local personnel is a 'cosmetic' practice in the sense that the title does not [always] carry the authority and power" commensurate with the position (Inohara 1982, p. 35). This is what the Japanese refer to as *tatemae* or "the truth for public consumption." The real truth (*honne*) becomes evident when major decisions are made. In these instances, top management chooses those most capable of making the decisions (*Doing business in Japan,* 1981, p. 30). Thus talent in Japanese organizations is recognized and rewarded in a manner more subtle and different from that generally practised in the West. However, increasingly more Japanese organizations are beginning to adopt the practice of promotion on the basis of merit. In the case of the manufacturer of food products, a person may be promoted to a low-level management position after five years on the basis of merit (*Japanese corporate personnel management,* 1981, p. 4). This was almost unheard of in the past. Similarily, in the case of Kobe Steel (Yamanoue 1982), adequate performance on aptitude tests is a prerequisite for promotion to section manager and departmental manager. This trend toward promotion on the basis of merit is expected to gain ground in the near future. According to the Japanese Ministry of Labor, while most of the departmental heads and divisional managers were in the fifty to fifty-four age bracket in 1978, this is expected to decline to the forty to forty-four age group by 1988 (*Human resource development in industry,* 1983, pp. 5–7).

Another distinguishing feature of promotion is the criteria for promotion to top management. Although promotion is primarily on the basis of seniority, at least in the initial years, achievement and talent are also important. A recent survey conducted by the editors of a leading Japanese economic journal found that most employees who have risen through the ranks to the board of directors' level had "good records of achievement." However, this criterion alone is inadequate to guarantee advancement to the top. In other words, achievement is necessary but insufficient for promotion. In the opinion of the company presidents interviewed, "The social capacities to understand, communicate with and cooperate with other leading managers were considered indispensable criteria in the selection of a top manager" (*Japanese corporate personnel management,* 1982, p. 11). This emphasis on human relational skills perhaps explains why Japanese expatriates are usually more adept at working in a foreign environment. My study found that lack of relational skills was a primary factor responsible for the failure of U.S. expatriates abroad. This area is precisely the forte of Japanese managers. Although relating to members of a foreign culture is quite different from associating with others in a domestic context, the dynamics of interaction are essentially similar. Furthermore, with proper and adequate training, these skills could be transferred to an alien environment.

Compensation

Remuneration policies in Japanese organizations are comprised of several components: a basic wage, bonuses, and numerous allowances. The starting wages of college graduates are relatively uniform, regardless of educational institution attended. However, a survey of salaries among top management of well-established Japanese companies indicated that education from the elite universities does pay off in the long-run (*Japanese corporate decision making,* 1982, p. 10). The wage differentials between employees at the entry level and those in top management positions are usually less marked than in the United States. In general, the ratio between starting salary and that on retirement for the average employee is 1 to 3.5.

Significant increases in salary are generally not made until the employee's seventh year of employment with the company, when the person is about to embark on the transition from premanagement to management. A national survey of salaries paid by private enterprises that employ 100 or more people found that as of March 1981, the average monthly wage scales were as follows: high school graduate, 94,530 yen ($378.12); university graduate, 117,170 yen ($468.68); chief or *kakaricho,* 273,840 yen ($1,095.36); section head or *kacho,* 358,270 yen ($1,433.08); department head or *bucho,* 448,660 yen ($1,794.64); and branch or plant manager, 462,880 yen ($1,433.08) (*Doing business in Japan,* 1982, p. 26). The basic wage is highly correlated to the age of the employee; the more advanced in years, the higher the basic salary. For example, a person graduates from college at the age of twenty-two or twenty-three and is not normally promoted to the position of *kacho* until age thirty-two, but no later than age forty-two. The average age for a *bucho* or department head is thirty-nine to forty-eight; and that for directors *(torishimari yaku)* is forty-five years of age and over (*Japanese corporate decision making,* 1982, p. 10).

Most companies provide generous bonuses. These are given twice a year, in July and December, and may average between two and six months of the employee's basic wage. The amount of bonus is determined by a variety of factors, including the company's profitability and the individual's performance. The company's profitability provides an incentive for the employee to cooperate with team members to accomplish organizational goals and thus foster a spirit of homogeneity and uniformity. Individual performance is designed to encourage individuals to compete with others and to excel. After the initial two to three years of employment, the brightest recruits are singled out for promotion on the elite track. Although the person may not be informed officially of the selection, an indication that he has been thus favored is in the form of his semiannual bonus (*Japanese corporate personnel management,* 1982, pp. 19–20).

Many Japanese companies provide numerous kinds of allowances to their employees, among them the following (the figures in parentheses indicate the percentage of Japanese/enterprises that pay these allowances): rank (80.6 percent; these are commensurate with the position held by the person in the organization; for example, the department head is given a sizable allowance as compared to the chief clerk); special assignment (30.9 percent); special skill (38.2 percent; these are given employees who are licensed to perform specific tasks); zero rate of absenteeism from work (58.7 percent); transportation to and from work (88.5 percent); family (22.4 percent; allowances are made for the spouse, the first three children, parents, and other family members); housing (22.4 percent); and miscellaneous (48.1 percent). The family allowance is comprehensive. According to an all-industry survey, the average monthly family allowances paid were 11,257 yen ($45.03) for the spouse, 3,628 yen ($14.51) for the first child, 3,294 yen ($13.18) for the second child, 2,635 yen ($10.54) for the third child, 2,844 yen ($11.37 for parents, and 2,346 yen ($9.38) for other family members (*Japanese corporate personnel management,* 1982, p. 21). Other fringe benefits include subsidized cafeterias and recreational facilities. Most of the Japanese multinationals interviewed for this book provided a cost-of-living adjustment for overseas assignments and a premium for hardship positions. Thus, although the basic wage of a Japanese employee may not appear high, when it is considered in conjunction with the bonuses and special allowances, the real wage of an average Japanese worker compares favorably with that in the United States and is estimated to be higher than those in the United Kingdom (Abegglen et al. 1980). In the main, wages increased at an annual rate of 15 percent in the 1960s, 17 percent in the first half of the 1970s, and 8.4 percent in the later half of the 1970s (*Doing business in Japan,* 1982, p. 27).

With the increased standard of living in Japan, younger employees have shown a greater reluctance to undertake overseas assignments. In a survey of 100 employees at Mitsubishi Electric Co. recruited since 1965, half were reluctant to go abroad for three primary reasons: increased standard of living in Japan, children's education, and spouse's opinion (Kawaji 1982). In the past, because of limited travel opportunities abroad and the premium wages paid for overseas work, an assignment abroad was considered prestigious. According to Yamanoue (1982), an overseas assignment in the early 1960s was usually greeted with enthusiasm by family and friends. Nowadays, a not uncommon reaction is "What! Being exiled overseas?"

Attitude toward Work

The rapid growth of the Japanese economy over the past three decades has been phenomenal. From the ruin of World War II, Japan has emerged as one of the strongest industrialized nations. Between 1966 and 1970, the GNP in the country increased at an average annual rate of 12.3 percent, the highest growth rate for any other industrialized nation over the same period (*The Japanese consumer,* 1980). Between 1973 and 1978, the country's GNP almost doubled, making Japan the second most prosperous nation in the free world (*The Japanese market in figures,* 1980). The rapid expansion in GNP can be attributed in large part to increased productivity rates. Between 1970 and 1977, the labor productivity rate in Japan's automobile industry increased 44 percent compared with 29 percent for the United States. For the same period, labor productivity in the steel industry increased 27 percent compared with 10 percent in the United States. In the area of electrical machinery, labor productivity in Japan increased by an astounding 90 percent between 1970 and 1979, compared with 27 percent in the United States. According to statistics presented in the *Bentsen Report* prepared by the U.S. comptroller general, labor productivity increases in the United States were less than one-third of Japan's for the eighteen-year period 1960 through 1977 (Abegglen et al. 1980, p. 17). These concur with statistics reported by Japanese sources. For the twenty-year period between 1960 and 1979, the Japanese estimated that their labor productivity increased at an average annual rate of 8.2 percent, approximately two and one-half times higher than that in the United States (*White paper on international trade,* 1981, p. 50).

A key to understanding this phenomenal increase in labor productivity rates lies in an examination of the workers' attitude toward work.

Diligence

If one were asked to identify a single national trait of the Japanese, the response could very well be *diligence.* In a 1953 survey conducted by the

Institute of Statistical Mathematics of Japan, 55 percent of the respondents selected diligence as the most dominant characteristic of its people. A similar survey conducted some twenty years later reported that approximately 66 percent of the respondents again identified diligence as the most representative trait. In the same year, the Office of the Japanese Prime Minister conducted a survey comparing and contrasting the attitude toward work among young people in ten industrialized nations. Respondents were asked to identify their reasons for working; 34.5 percent of the Japanese youth indicated they work "as a means of self-fulfillment." This compared with a similar response by 30.3 percent of the respondents in the United States, 15.3 percent in West Germany, and 13.8 percent in Great Britain, countries supposed to be steeply ingrained with the Protestant work ethic (Bartholomew 1981, p. 249).

This positive attitude toward labor is reflected in the longer hours worked per week and in the fewer days spent on vacation annually as compared with other industrialized nations. In 1973, both U.S. and West German industrial workers averaged 38.3 hours per week on the job, as compared with 42 hours among their Japanese counterparts. The number of hours worked are decreasing, however. A survey of 371 Japanese firms by the Private Industry and Labor Research Institute in 1983 found that approximately 90 percent of the companies practiced some form of two-day weekend system, enforced on a biweekly or monthly basis (Treece 1983, p. 28). In 1970, it was estimated that the average U.S. worker spent 130 days on vacation, as compared to 120 and 70 days, respectively, by West German and Japanese counterparts. In Japan, workers are discouraged from taking paid vacations as an indication of their dedication to their employer. A 1970 study found that only 20 percent of the Japanese industrial workers used up all their paid vacation; 40 percent took half or less of their annual paid holidays (Bartholomew, 1981, pp. 249–250). According to the latest statistics, a second-year worker is entitled to a maximum of 20 days paid vacation annually. Only 46.3 percent of the career staff used all their paid holidays (Treece 1983, p. 28).

This strong work ethic has its roots in the tradition of rice cultivation and zen philosophy. Rice cultivation is rigorous work. In the past, fields were small so it was physically impossible to use cattle to plow the fields; most of the work had to be done by manual labor. To add to the burden of the rural population, the farmers during feudal times had to pay high land taxes to their overlords. To survive under this system, the farming population worked hard. Although the Meiji Restoration in 1868 put an abrupt end to feudalism, this tradition of hard work was continued under the system of meritocracy implemented by the new government. Anybody, regardless of origin, could achieve high status in the government and society based on his efforts. As such, employees of the various sectors—government, military, and business—had to work hard in order to be promoted. Even today when the

Labor Standards Law restricts the number of working hours, many employees voluntarily put in extra hours to meet company deadlines (*Nippon: The land and its people,* 1982).

A second source of this emphasis on hard work stems from the teachings and practice of zen. Zen is more of a social philosophy and a way of life than a religion in the Judaic-Christian tradition. A primary goal of zen is for the follower to realize his potential as a human being. The effort applied to improving oneself, rather than the actual result, is central to the practice of zen (Musashi 1982, pp. xix, xxiii). This explains why Japanese firms often evaluate employees on their attitude and potential instead of actual performance.

Given this emphasis on self-improvement and striving for excellence, progress is a paramount concern. With the opening of Japan to Western commerce in the mid-nineteenth century, a principal goal of the Meiji Restoration was to match and surpass the industrialized West (Naitoh 1980, p. 73). While its dreams of supremacy appeared to be shattered by its defeat in World War II, the Japanese never abandoned their desire for attaining excellence. According to Johnson (1982, p. 241), while the military war effort had formally ended in 1945 with Japan's defeat, the country had "remained on a war footing", wherein the goal had changed from one of military conquest and victory to an economic one. In order to excel, the Japanese people have to work hard. After all, the country is virtually devoid of natural resources. The country's major asset is its people. Consequently, these must be trained and developed, and directed toward the pursuit of national objectives. This attitude toward work and striving for excellence explains why Japanese employees are willing to work overtime without pay, and why many of them engage in study outside of office hours for purposes of self-enlightenment.

Although the younger people tend to value leisure time, given the highly competitive environment and strong need to adhere to group norms in Japanese society, it is unlikely that this work ethic will be easily discarded.

Discipline

Another national trait of the Japanese people is their general observance of discipline, fostered through the strong tradition of groupism. A person's status or position is always defined in relation to the group. As a member of a group, the individual is expected to conform to prescribed norms, assume given responsibilities, and dispense certain obligations in accordance with his hierarchical position in the group. This strong sense of discipline has enabled most expatriates to endure whatever hardships may go with the overseas assignment since they must not fail the company or the group. This theme was echoed by many of the executives interviewed for this study. In the words of Miyamoto Musashi (1981, p. 26), a samurai of the late sixteenth and early seventeenth centuries—whose preachings on how to gain the upper hand in any kind of combative encounter (whether military or economic) are still widely read and followed by people from different walks of life in Japanese society—"If one disciplines one's spirit sufficiently, it is possible to be psychologically superior. If one can achieve this, how could one lose?"

Job Satisfaction

Although the average Japanese worker demonstrates a positive attitude toward work, a comparative study of job satisfaction among 400 employees in three industrialized nations found that the level of worker dissatisfaction among Japanese employees was higher than that for the United States and Britain. Only 70 percent of the Japanese employees expressed satisfaction with their jobs, as compared with 86 and 92 percent, respectively, in the U.K. and U.S. samples (*Japanese corporate personnel management,* 1982, p. 3). There are two possible explanations for this finding: the objective constraints of the labor market in Japan and the questionable validity of the survey findings.

Some of the distinguishing characteristics of the Japanese personnel system are slower rates of promotion and increases in salary in the early years of employment, longer working hours, and fewer paid vacations. According to the study, the two most important sources of work dissatisfaction were low wages, cited by 58.3 percent of respondents, and long working hours and short vacations, mentioned by 34.4 percent of the subjects. Despite this apparent dissatisfaction, Japanese employees remain in the company and contribute to organizational goals for at least two primary reasons. One is low job mobility. When asked about the reasons for remaining in the firm, 33.3 percent of the respondents indicated that there is "no difference between this and other companies"; 34.4 percent indicated that there was no alternative; and 35.8 percent indicated that the "job was worthwhile." This last factor constitutes a powerful incentive for the person to stay. A second and perhaps more compelling reason for the individual to remain in the company is the reaction of family and friends to any job change. Face is very important in Japanese society; there is still a stigma associated with anyone who leaves a company. As Mr. Terasawa noted, a person cannot quit his job and join another company "unless he sacrifices himself, financially and status-wise." Since most of the large companies practice the system of lifetime employment and promotion is invariably from within the ranks of the company, resigning one's present position and joining another would mean starting all over again from the bottom of the organizational hierarchy in another Japanese firm. Given the strong correlation between age and rank in a company, the job mobility for the individual is virtually nil beyond a certain point. Furthermore, relatives and friends would relentlessly query one's parents and spouse as to why the individual had forsaken his career. Most Japanese do not wish to subject their loved ones to such humiliation. In addition, leaving the company would mean alienating colleagues, who would be "offended at such disloyalty." Given the fact that bonds of friendship are often strongest among one's colleagues and given the camaraderie relationships that often prevail among them, most people are unwilling to jeopardize these cherished ties (*Japanese corporate personnel management,* 1982, pp. 24–31).

A second possible explanation for the lower job satisfaction found among the Japanese sample may be attributed to the questionable validity of the survey findings. In most instances, attitudinal survey questionnaires are developed in the United States for a U.S. audience. Although extreme care may have been exercised in the translation of the questionnaires, some of the items used may be irrelevant in the Japanese context because of the vast differences in social and cultural systems between the two countries. For example, although there is a definite correlation between job satisfaction and productivity in most U.S. organizational settings, this relationship is virtually nonexistent or highly insignificant in Japanese companies (Robinson 1978). Consequently while Japanese employees may voice dissatisfaction with certain aspects of their jobs, this attitude has little or no impact on their level of performance, as evidenced by the rapid increases in labor productivity rates in the country. The employees' dissatisfaction perhaps may be mitigated by their overall dedication or loyalty to their employer and the strong work ethic in the country. Besides, most Japanese companies are trying to remove sources of dissatisfaction. Real wages in the country have risen substantially since the 1950s, and many companies have reduced the work week. In addition, as part of the annual or semiannual evaluation, most companies request the employee to state his preferences about particular jobs. Given the supervisor's familiarity with the subordinate's private life and the employer's concern for the total person, most companies take these opinions seriously and generally do not make unreasonable job assignments (*Japanese corporate personnel management,* 1982, p. 31).

Job Rotation

Another distinguishing feature of the Japanese industrial system is the practice of job rotation, with overseas assignments considered as part of the career development process in many multinationals. Prior to the early 1970s, Japan's international economic involvement was largely confined to import and export trade activities. Since the 1970s, Japanese foreign direct investment overseas has more than doubled. This means that contacts with foreign firms and countries can no longer be relegated to the import and export units within the company, as was the case. Since the 1970s, the companies have needed employees who can supervise the operation of their overseas subsidiaries. Even individuals who are not stationed abroad need an adequate understanding of overseas business and the world economy in order to make correct investment decisions (*Human resource development in industry,* 1983).

Over the lifetime of one's employment with the company, the employee is rotated through various departments and divisions so that an employee who may be destined for a top management position can be exposed to the various areas of the company. This practice has arisen because of the general belief that management or administrative skills could not be taught in the classroom setting; rather it must be learned on-the-job. Zen, which is a guiding philosphy in Japan, preaches that "the senses cannot grasp reality from one viewpoint" (Musashi 1982, p. xxii). Consequently job rotation is central to the process of career development. According to Mr. Terasawa, on the average, a person experiences ten to fifteen different positions within the company before becoming a director. In his words: "In Japan, we still believe that it is necessary to give the person a total perspective on the business, rather than be too specialized in one field." Rotation is also important because one of the goals of Japanese organizations is to breed homogeneity and conformity. This cannot be attained if an individual has little or no understanding of the activities and functions performed by colleagues in other departments and divisions. Since most decisions in Japanese organizations are arrived at through consensus, which often requires subtle probing of the positions favored by others and diplomatic negotiations of issues with personnel from other departments and divisions, it is imperative that the person has close personal ties with people throughout the organization, which can be realized through rotation. Rotation also provides an opportunity for employees to experience some of the more unpleasant jobs and thus help them develop greater humility and ability to understand the plight of their subordinates at a future time. According to Mr. Terasawa of Nomura Securities International, college graduates, including those from elite universities, who join the world-renowned Hotel Okura start with bedmaking. They are then rotated through laundry or room service in the following years, altogether serving as an apprentice for five years. This rotation enables them to have a better understanding of hotel management and a greater empathy for the feelings and plight of their subordinates at a later date.

In some instances, job rotation may include assigning the employee to work in another company for a year or two. This process of *shukko* (special assignments) has two purposes: to transfer technology from one company to the other (common between a nucleus firm and its satellite companies and/or subcontractors) and to acquire knowledge from another advanced company. In the early years after World War II, it was common to send Japanese to companies in advanced nations (such as the United States) to serve as apprentices for a year or two and thus acquire advanced technology and knowledge. Even today, when Japanese management techniques are hailed as a key to the country's economic success, many Japanese firms send employees to foreign companies to learn a foreign language and culture so as to develop a more global outlook or orientation, and/or sharpen their skills.

Consensus Decision Making

Another salient characteristic of Japanese management practices is the consensus decision-making process, referred to as the *ringi-sho*. Under the *ringi-sho* system, a proposal must receive the endorsement of all concerned individuals. Although some decisions in certain organizations are made through the edict of top management (which in the Japanese context is referred to as *tsuru no hitoke* or "one screech of the crane"), approximately 90 percent of the decisions at the lower- or middle-management levels are made through the process of consensus. The "one screech of the crane" mechanism is most widely used where the chief executive officer is also the owner or founder of the company (*Japanese corporate decision making*, 1982).

The consensus style of decision making has several implications for human resource planning and development with regard to expatriate assignments. This method requires frequent caucusing, subtle probing, and delicate negotiations of issues among members at different levels of management in various departments. In many instances, this may extend beyond the bounds of one's immediate organization and could involve close cooperation with members of the government sector and other firms in the industry. Consequently, in order to make the system work, managers have to develop close personal ties with people in other departments and divisions and other external sectors and sharpen their human relational skills.

Even in the overseas operations of Japanese multinationals, expatriates maintain constant contact with corporate headquarters because decisions that pertain to the subsidiary are usually arrived at through consensus. By maintaining almost daily contact with corporate headquarters, the expatriate is still very much a part of the group in Japan and does not feel left out from the mainstream of the corporate organization. But even with frequent communication, the interaction cannot be as intense or extensive as it was back home. Thus a number of Japanese expatriates may experience difficulties—status shock—in coping with the larger responsibilities of overseas work. This phenomenon is not unique to Japanese multinationals, although it may be more marked given the unique practices of the Japanese industrial system. According to Sieveking, Anchor, and Marston (1981, p. 198), expatriates generally experience some discomfort because they are expected to "assume much more than the accustomed load of decision making in a foreign setting because of work which is often solitary, or which may be performed without the accustomed support of peers and superiors."

Given the constant interaction required with corporate headquarters coupled with the fact that members of senior management in Japan may not speak English or other foreign languages, it is difficult to staff overseas subsidiaries with local nationals. Most of the senior- and middle-management positions in the overseas operations of Japanese multinationals are occupied by Japanese. Although there are advantages to staffing overseas subsidiaries with parent country nationals, there are also many limitations, such as higher costs, increasing reluctance of Japanese to serve overseas, pressures from the local governments to hire host country nationals, and possible problems of adjustment in a foreign environment. While there is an increasing trend toward localization (use of host country nationals) among firms in the manufacturing sector, given the present stage of evolution of Japanese multinationals and the uniqueness of Japanese management practices, most senior positions in foreign operations will continue to be staffed by parent country nationals, at least in the near to medium future. Hence, there is a continuing need to select and train personnel appropriate for foreign assignments.

The Personnel Department

Given the emphasis placed on education and training, development of human relational skills, and the importance assigned to personnel evaluation, it is not surprising that the power structure in most Japanese organizations is vested in the hands of the executive vice-president responsible for personnel affairs and his staff. Talent and technical competence alone do not warrant promotion to top management; rather, those who are selected for the upper echelons of the organizational hierarchy are invariably those who possess good human relations skills. Since the personnel department provides the focal point for the development of such skills, its members are often regarded as the "trusted personal staff" of the company's president who will organize the human relations needed to implement the chief executive's plans (*Japanese corporate personnel management,* 1982, p. 23).

This is a marked difference from U.S. firms where personnel managers are often relegated a more inferior status, and in many instances are regarded as "glorified file clerks" who simply assist in the hiring function of the organization by screening applications and handling such mundane tasks as the company's payroll and other employee benefits (Richardson and Ueda 1981, pp. 10–11). This difference could perhaps reflect the lower priority that U.S. corporations generally assign to human resource development. This fundamental distinction between U.S, and Japanese companies may account for the greater success attained by the latter in the past decades.

While technology, capital, and know-how are essential to a firm's competitiveness, a principal catalyst to the efficient operation of an enterprise is its people. Without a highly developed pool of managerial and technical talent, its resources cannot be effectively and efficiently allocated or transformed into marketable outputs. Furthermore, increasingly a company's products and/or services are marketed in the international arena. Without a contingent of highly trained personnel skilled in relating to people from a different culture, a firm's competitiveness and, hence, chances of economic success are jeopardized.

3

Training Institutes for International Management

A principal characteristic of Japanese personnel management (indeed that of Japanese society as a whole) is its emphasis on education as a means of assisting individuals to realize their fullest potentials as human beings to facilitate the attainment of corporate and, ultimately, national objectives. Japan is virtually devoid of natural resources; hence the country's survival and continued prosperity depend on foreign commerce. Given this high dependence on trade and the general insularity of its people, the country places a high premium on the development of a contingent of internationally minded Japanese who are able to market Japanese products and services in the global arena. This international orientation is fostered through several mechanisms, such as the in-house training programs sponsored by many of the large Japanese multinationals, and the establishment of educational institutions that serve the needs of the government, business, and finance sectors in this regard.

This chapter examines two of the more widely used programs offered by educational institutions for international management: the Institute for International Studies and Training (IIST) and the Japanese American Conversation Institute (JACI). The IIST was established by a special act of the Japanese government, and operates under the auspices of the country's powerful MITI, which oversees all aspects of international trade and foreign investment, in addition to its important role of charting out the country's industrial policy. The JACI is a private nonprofit organization authorized by the Japanese Ministry of Education. It has been cited by a number of the Japanese multinationals as an alternative or supplement to their in-house training programs and/or the IIST.

Such an analysis points to the commitment of Japanese corporations, both private and public, to the development of a core of highly trained, internationally minded people vital to the smooth conduct of international trade and investment. Japan could not have attained its present status in the global economy without such a pool of international talent. A Japanese maxim says, "The company is its people." It is through the ingenuity and diligence of its people that Japan recovered from the devastation of World War II to become a world economic power.

In the 1950s and 1960s, the label "Made in Japan" was virtually synonymous with shoddy workmanship. Within two decades, this image has been completely reversed. Today the same label is often equated with quality

(*Productivity and quality control, 1981*). This revolutionary change has been accomplished not only through meticulous design and engineering of Japanese products but also through aggressive international marketing and promotion.

Institute for International Studies and Training

The information on the history and types of educational programs offered by the IIST was obtained from an in-depth interview with Shoichi Ohmagari, director, Overseas Programs, IIST, unless otherwise stated.

History and Objective

To some, a striking characteristic of the Japanese industrial scene appears to be the common objectives and ethos shared by the government, big business, and labor so as to give the impression that the threee sectors move in unison as one giant monolith. James Abegglen, a long-time observer of Japan, has referred to this characterization as "Japan Incorporated." Although big business may not always comply with the wishes of the government, nevertheless in general business and government tend to share a common set of objectives, one of which is international competitiveness.

Under the protection of the government, the Japanese economy recovered rapidly from the devastating effects of the war, and by the mid- to late 1950s, Japan wanted to assume the status of a leading economic power by playing a major role in the world trade system. Besides seeking and gaining membership to international financial and economic organizations, such as the General Agreement on Trade and Tariffs and the International Monetary Fund, and adopting procedures to liberalize both inward and outward capital investments, the country recognized the need to develop a pool of internationally minded Japanese. Consequently, in 1967 the government enacted special legislation authorizing the establishment of the IIST, whose mission was to "provide graduate-level training for selected qualified persons contemplating careers in the international field" with the ultimate goal of developing "a body of rising young leaders who will eventually play a key role in international affairs" (*IIST Brochure, 1980–1981*).

The establishment of the institute was made possible through initial funding from the government and business sectors in the amount of 3,800 million yen or $15.83 million (at a conversion rate of 240 yen to the dollar). The institute continues to receive financial support from MITI and members of the Japan Federation of Economic Organizations. Tuition fees typically account for only 40 percent of the institute's revenue. The campus is located at the foot of Mt. Fuji, and provides both classroom and dormitory facilities for trainees and faculty. In principle, the trainees live in dormitories, but married trainees usually go home on weekends since the institute does not provide housing for spouses.

Although the institute operates under the auspices of MITI, members of its board of governors are drawn primarily from large business corporations. The trainees are career staff from a diverse range of government agencies and business organizations, which pay their tuition and expenses in addition to their full-time salary.

Every year the institute educates 150 to 200 trainees. All of the participants are college graduates and have approximately five to six years of experience in government or business. The average age of the trainees is thirty. There are two types of programs: the regular program, which runs for the entire year, and the practical trade program, which spans a period of three months. The primary purpose of the regular program is to train generalists and internationally minded business people; the three-month program is designed to train specialists. In the practical trade program, only English and courses in international business transactions are taught. When it was first established, the three-month program was intended for small enterprises; however, since the energy crisis of the early 1970s, many large companies have reduced the number of new career staff hired annually, which has resulted in a tighter work situation in these organizations. Consequently many of the large companies cannot afford to send trainees to the institute for a year since they need the people in the office.

The practical trade program is not necessarily country oriented; the one-year program is country-specific. For example, a trainee in the year-long program assigned to the United States would study English, U.S. management practices, U.S. history, and various aspects of American society. From the time of its establishment in 1967 to the end of the 1980 academic year, the institute has graduated 1,285 trainees from the regular program and 1,537 trainees from the practical trade program (*IIST: Regular Program*, 1982).

The institute sponsors faculty and student exchanges with foreign universities. Besides the fifteen full-time regular faculty members who teach courses in Japanese and foreign languages and Japanese culture, each year the institute invites approximately 200 instructors from various educational institutions, both domestic and foreign, on a part-time basis. Mr. Ohmagari indicated that the institute generally invites eight visiting professors from the United States, Canada, France, United Kingdom, and other developed nations to teach courses in international management and economics. When asked whether the extensive use of part-time faculty from abroad poses problems in terms of lack of continuity and diversity of standards, he said that it should not because the contracts with the visiting professors are signed one year in advance, at which time they are invited on campus to provide them with information about teaching at the institute. Furthermore, most of the visiting faculty are drawn from IIST's affiliate universitities overseas. Consequently, those who have already taught at the center before could share the information with their colleagues who will be teaching at the IIST the following year.

The institute has formal exchange programs with the American University and the American Graduate School of Management in the United States, the Euro-Japanese Exchange Foundation Study Center in the United Kingdom, and Institut Européen d'Administration des Affaires (INSEAD) in France. Besides inviting faculty from foreign universities, the institute schedules student exchanges. Every spring, between forty and fifty exchange students from its affiliate institutes in the United States, Canada, and France spend four months on campus. Given the phenomenal success of the Japanese economy, the interest among foreign students to learn about Japanese management has increased. The reasons for choosing the IIST are primarily two-fold. One, the IIST is one of the few institutions in Japan that teach Japanese management practices. Two, the trainees are different from the average student in U.S. business schools because the Japanese participants are sponsored by government or business corporations and have five to six years of experience. This is the more attractive feature from the foreign students' perspective because they can thus interact with experienced practitioners.

This increased interest in learning about Japanese management practices is reflected in the number of foreign students who have applied for admission to the institute. In 1975 there were only eleven foreign students. This number increased to thirty-nine in 1981 and fifty in 1982. In 1982 these were selected from over one hundred applicants (*Japan Economic Journal,* February 28, 1982). From the Japanese perspective, having foreign students live with the Japanese trainees over a four-month period provides an opportunity to practice foreign language skills and learn more about the culture, values, and attitudes of various foreign countries. In addition, it heightens their sense of awareness to cross-cultural differences and helps them acquire the skills needed to adapt and adjust to people from a foreign environment. The purpose served by the live-in programs is similar to the "field experience" mechanism described in Chapter 1.

Besides promoting an international orientation among its trainees, the institute also fosters friendship ties among members of the government, business, and financial sectors. Because of their age, most of the trainees are on the threshold of promotion to management, where abilities in negotiating with and relating to people from different divisions are considered essential. In the light of the closer cooperation among the various sectors in the Japanese economy, these human relational skills usually extend beyond the bounds of one's immediate organization to interactions with people outside of the company. Thus, the three to twelve months of communal living provide an opportunity for the trainees to develop these bonds and ties that will prove useful when they become managers. In the words of Mr. Ohmagari, "Even after their graduation from our institute, the friendship established here continues for the rest of their lives. This is an asset for doing business."

Developing friendships among employees from a diverse range of organizations is an important by-product of such educational programs. For example, in 1981, Nomura Research Institute (part of the Nomura Group) established the Nomura School of Advanced Management to train Japanese managers at the middle- and senior-management levels. In the first year of operation, the institute conducted a three-week workshop covering courses in business strategy, financial management, and international business. There were sixty-five participants from the Ministry of Finance, MITI, and large corporations. Most occupied positions at the departmental head level, which is equivalent to the senior vice-presidential or vice-presidential levels in U.S. corporations. Eight were members of the boards of directors of several companies. For the three weeks, the participants stayed in the Keio Plaza Hotel, which is approximately five minutes' walk from the school. Jiro Tokuyama, executive director and dean of the school said, "There is no other place in Japan where sixty or seventy department heads get together. Over the three weeks, the Japanese executives develop closer relationships with each other."

Regular Program

The objective of the regular program, which enrolls eighty people annually, is to train future businessmen who will work in the international arena. To accomplish this goal, the program is designed to foster "an international sense," master practical language skills, and improve the trainee's "ability to correctly understand the various phenomena in international society" (*IIST: Regular program,* 1982). The program is divided into four parts: foreign language, international management and economics, area studies, and overseas training.

Many Japanese multinationals consider language an important criterion in the selection of a candidate for overseas assignment, although its rank ordering has decreased relative to technical and administrative skills (*Human resource development in industry,* 1983). Since the Japanese language is seldom used outside of Japan, in order to conduct international business, the Japanese have to speak English. Although Japanese school children study English from grade 7 on, the emphasis is on reading and writing, not conversing. In the opinion of many Japanese, this method of instruction has made them poor linguists and explains why many have difficulty in conveying their thoughts to non-Japanese (*Nippon: The Land and its people,* 1982, p. 153).

For this reason the regular program emphasizes language training. The number of instructional hours on English language has been increased from 240 to 540, excluding the courses in international management and economics, which are conducted in English. English language is taught in the first eight weeks of the program by native speakers; the emphasis is on improving listening and speaking skills. The trainees are divided into small groups based on their competence in English. Besides learning the language through formal lectures and laboratory training, the trainees are given ample opportunity to practice their English with Caucasian exchange students.

The next segment of the program extends for twenty-two weeks and offers courses in international management and economics, area studies, and Japanese studies. The courses in international management and economics are designed to provide trainees with skills in functional disciplines so that they will be prepared to handle the broader duties associated with an overseas assignment. Some Japanese expatriates have difficulty in coping with the larger responsibilities associated with working abroad. Consequently knowledge in the functional disciplines is considered essential.

The area studies program is designed to provide trainees the knowledge required to live in the geographic region to which they may be assigned. The program consists of two parts, and each trainee selects a geographic region from each section. The first section consists of North America and Western Europe, the second section of the socialist bloc nations, the Middle and Near East, Latin and South America, and Southeast Asia. For each region, the trainee learns about the history, culture, socioeconomic, and political characteristics of the country and the country's relationship with Japan. Although the course content is primarily factual, the program stresses adaptation and interaction with members of a foreign culture. As Mr. Ohmagari noted, "This is particularly important for us Japanese people who live in a small, isolated homogeneous society. We do not know how to deal with foreigners who have different cultures. So, the major purpose of our program is to teach the trainees how to adapt to the local environment once they are overseas."

The course content consists of a combination of lectures by overseas instructors, use of foreign case studies, interaction with foreign exchange students, and seminar discussions with invited speakers, among them ambassadors and ministers, foreign businessmen who live in Japan, and overseas researchers. The seminars provide the trainees an opportunity to interact with experienced practitioners from other nations. The seminars are usually conducted in the evenings, after class hours, which run from 9 A.M. to 4 P.M. After the seminars, the trainees have homework and other preparation for the following day's lectures. According to Mr. Ohmagari, most of them study until 2 A.M., reflecting the general diligence and dedication of Japanese employees to their companies. Mr. Ohmagari indicated that although most trainees are not concerned with grades, they nevertheless work hard because of the company's expectations. They do not want to fail their companies, which have invested a considerable sum of money on their future.

The trainees are taught about Japanese society, its position in the world economic system, and how to explain the distinguishing characteristics of Japanese culture and society to non-Japanese. According to a survey conducted by the *Japan Economic News* (June 24, 1982), which examined the problems encountered by 612 expatriates during their overseas assignments, only half of the expatriates (54.3 percent) and 33.9 percent of their spouses had sufficient information about various aspects of Japanese society. Given the increasing interest in Japan by people of other nationalities, many Japanese lack sufficient knowledge to discuss with foreigners the subjects of Japanese martial arts, Japanese life and culture, floral arrangements, and the tea ceremony. According to the survey, only 8.6 percent of the males and 7.5 percent of the females could converse in English on such subjects immediately on arrival in a foreign country. The newspaper lamented this state of affairs and cautioned that if Japanese expatriates do not know enough about their own country to explain them to foreigners, they cannot serve as "roving ambassadors of Japanese culture" and might consequently distort Japan's image in the minds of non-Japanese. Hence the Japanese studies program fulfills a special need in an overseas assignment. The Japanese studies program also provides opportunities for trainees to interact with members of a foreign culture.

Besides the exchange students from the advanced nations, the institute invites fifteen participants from developing countries to study for four weeks, who attend the Japanese studies program. These participants are either professors at universities or members of the government or business communities. Their transportation and expenses are paid by the institute, in return for which they are "required to interact with Japanese students on campus during their stay in Japan." These interactions help develop the trainees' abilities to work with members of a foreign culture, particularly useful since Japanese investments in the developing nations, particularly the Far East, are very extensive.

The third section of the regular program is devoted to eight weeks of another foreign language (such as Spanish and German) or advanced English. The selection of the language is based on the country or region to which the trainee will probably be assigned.

The fourth section focuses on overseas training. Participation in this segment is entirely voluntary and involves four weeks of study in one of following institutions abroad: the American University and the American Graduate School of Management in the United States, INSEAD in France, and the Euro-Japanese Exchange Foundation Study Center in the United Kingdom. This program provides an opportunity for the participants to live in the foreign country to which they may be assigned later and associate with experts and business people there. In addition, according to the terms of the formal exchange program between IIST and the American Graduate School of International Management in Arizona, a trainee may attend two semesters at the latter and obtain a master in international management (MIM) degree from the U.S. university.

Enrollment at the regular program is limited to eighty people annually. The tuition and expenses for the program amount to roughly $26,387, broken down as follows: tuition, 1.5 million yen ($6,250); instructional materials, 100,000 yen ($416.66); room, 492,600 yen ($2,052.50); board, 440,300 yen ($1,834.58); heat surcharge in winter months, 50,000 yen ($208.33); overseas training fee, approximately 1.65 million yen ($6,875); and MIM program at the American Graduate School of International Management, 2.1 million yen ($8,750) (*IIST: Regular program,* 1982).

The tuition fee typically accounts for only 40 percent of the IIST's revenue. The balance of the operating expenses is funded through grants by MITI and business corporations. Although the amount spent on each trainee is high, the company considers this a safe investment because of the system of lifetime employment. The company's willingness to spend large sums on each career staff's education reflects the overall commitment of both the private and public sectors to international development.

Practical Trade Program

The three-month program focuses on the practical aspects of doing business abroad, specifically international business transactions, foreign exchange management, and foreign investment (*IIST: Practical Trade Program,* 1982). In addition, English is taught.

The first six weeks of the program are devoted to English-language training. The objective and medium of instruction are similar to those of the regular program; the difference is in terms of number of hours spent. In the three-month program, every trainee spends 230 hours in learning English as compared to 540 hours for the regular program. The trainees in the three-month program also share the dormitory with foreign exchange students to enable them to practice their English skills and to learn more about foreign cultures. The participants in the three-month program also attend the same evening seminar discussions.

The second part of the practical trade program focuses on developing skills in corresponding in English; the objective is to help trainees write "business English with genuine English expressions rather than Japanese English" (*IIST: Practical Trade Program,* 1982).

The third part of the program concentrates on intercultural communication, fostered through an understanding of the culture behind English expressions. This is a very useful approach because without comprehension of the cultural roots behind the development of certain expressions, a nonnative speaker of English could not hope to acquire a good command of the language.

The fourth part of the program deals with practical training in the areas of international business transactions, foreign exchange management, and other related subjects. These include courses in international trade theory, trade administration regulations, documentation, marketing abroad, and so on, conveyed through lectures, case studies, and seminars.

The practical trade program is not country oriented and does not include an area studies program as does the regular program.

Enrollment in the practical trade program is limited to seventy participants per semester. All trainees are sponsored by their respective organizations, which pay all tuition and expenses, in addition to the person's regular wage. The expenses for the three-month program amount to approximately $3,373, which is broken down as follows: tuition 430,000 yen ($1,791.66); instructional materials, 45,000 yen ($187.50); room, 173,200 yen ($721.66); and board, 161,500 yen ($672.92).

Evaluation of Program Effectiveness

On completion of either program, trainees are asked to evaluate the effectiveness of the program in preparing them for overseas work. In addition, the institute periodically invites personnel managers from major Japanese companies to review the program and offer suggestions for improvement. This information provides help in modifying the program to meet the needs of government and industry better.

When asked about the possible changes that may be made to the program in the future, Mr. Ohmagari indicated that he would like to expand the exchange programs by having more foreign students and visiting professors. He further noted that although the institute would like to include foreign participants with work experience, this may not be possible because it is difficult for foreign companies to grant extended leaves of absence to their employees.

Some General Observations on Expatriate Assignments

Mr. Ohmagari was asked to comment on various aspects of expatriate assignments. When asked to proffer some reasons for the low failure rates among Japanese multinationals, he mentioned three factors. The first is management education programs, such as the ones offered by his institute and other agencies. Second is the long-term perspective adopted by most

Japanese companies. In his opinion, most Japanese firms spend at least three years investigating overseas market opportunities before they enter a particular country. This analysis provides them with a better understanding of consumers' needs and preferences and the nature of competition in the foreign country. This thorough investigation greatly reduces the chances of failure overseas (Tung 1984). Third, given the practice of lifetime employment, employees have a strong sense of loyalty and commitment to the company; in turn, the employers have a total concern for the employees. Mr. Ohmagari noted, "[Japanese] companies do not expect short-term returns. In other words, the company views the market from a long-range point of view. They earn profits over a decade or so. They don't expect to earn profits overnight. This is very different from the American mentality. The most important concern of American firms is profit. In contrast, Japanese firms are most concerned with maintaining their employees."

Mr. Ohmagari was asked to identify the criteria most often used by Japanese multinationals in selecting employees for overseas assignments and the manner in which the criteria were assessed. He noted that although the criteria vary from company to company, in general the two most important ones are language skills and ability to adapt to a local environment. Although Japanese companies may not have any specific mechanism for assessing ability to adapt, because of the strong tradition of groupism in Japanese organizations, the supervisor knows his employees very well. Consequently, he understands the person's strengths and limitations and hence seldom makes poor decisions in this regard.

When asked why Japanese multinationals use parent country nationals more extensively than their U.S. and West European counterparts, he attributed this practice primarily to problems of communication that local nationals may have with Japanese corporate headquarters. In his opinion, "It is very difficult for foreigners to learn the Japanese language. The Japanese economy as a whole is aggressive, but Japanese people are not aggressive in communicating. It is very difficult for Japanese to communicate with foreigners. We have non-verbal communications; it is implicitly understood." Given the overriding concern for face, most Japanese tend to approach issues indirectly. Hence, adequate communication with the Japanese does not entail mere knowledge of the language but understanding of the subtleties associated with the language and how to present them correctly. In the words of a U.S. executive, such communication skills are a "real art" and are rare among nonnative speakers of the language (Tung 1984).

Mr. Ohmagari was asked to comment on the role of the family in terms of expatriate assignments. While Japanese multinationals have traditionally deemphasized the role of the spouse in the training programs, Mr. Ohmagari was asked whether this trend would likely change in the future, given the evolving value system of the younger generation. According to a survey of

100 employees of Mitsubishi Electric Co., Ltd., the increasing reluctance among younger employees to serve abroad stems in part from the spouse's opinion (Kawaji 1982). In response to this query, Mr. Ohmagari noted that more and more Japanese companies are sponsoring programs for the wives prior to departure overseas. According to a survey conducted by *Japan Economic News* (June 24, 1982), approximately 30 percent of the respondent firms provided seminars for the wives of expatriates prior to departure, either in-house or through external agencies.

Mr. Ohmagari noted that there is a general misunderstanding about the role of the family in Japanese society. In reality the family is more important than the company, and wives do play a major role in the family. Japanese husbands are often referred to as "salary men," a designation that stems from a Japanese tradition dating back to ancient times that husbands generally turn their unopened pay envelopes to their wives. In return, they receive a daily allowance from their wives. However, since "wives are generally not interested in company affairs, they would not interfere" with their husbands' work overseas by complaining about the difficulties of adjusting. A Japanese family's overriding concern is the education of the children. According to Mr. Ohmagari, "We are a very democratic country—the single most important factor for promotion is education. So people are crazy about education." In Japanese society, a wife's primary responsibility is to her children. Her life revolves around them. This explains why expatriates with children in high school generally leave them in Japan for education reasons. In many instances, the wives remain behind to supervise their children's education.

Japanese American Conversation Institute

Another frequently used external facility for preparing candidates for overseas assignments is the Japanese American Conversation Institute (JACI). The information presented here is provided by Namiji Itabashi, chairman of the board of trustees of the International Education Center (IEC), the parent organization of JACI.

History and Objective

The JACI was established in November 1945 to service the needs of the Ministry of Finance and other governmental agencies to provide English-language training to young government employees who had to communicate with the Allied Occupation authorities. As Japan began to expand its international role, the demand for people who could speak fluent English increased. Today the institute serves a much broader audience; its student body is drawn from the financial, business, and government sectors. In addition to language training, the institute offers programs to assist trainees in acquiring a broader understanding of the global arena and to "develop their potentials as internationally-oriented, well-educated" representatives of Japan (*International Education Center Brochure,* 1982). In Mr. Itabashi's opinion, the prerequisites for developing an "international person" are primarily threefold. First, the individual must be a trustworthy and respectable Japanese citizen who can present a good image of Japan to the rest of the world. This person must know Japanese history and culture because he has to explain Japan to non-Japanese in foreign countries. If he were ignorant, "we could not be regarded as intelligent Japanese." This criterion is similar to the observation made by the *Japan Economic News* (June 24, 1982) that Japanese expatriates must serve as "roving ambassadors" of Japanese culture. Second, the person must have a "broad, international vision." To promote this objective, the IEC established the School of International Studies (SIS) in 1973, which specializes in international communication, international business, and area studies. Third, the individual must acquire proficiency in at least one foreign language. Since English is the universal language of international business transactions, it should be emphasized. This is offered under the Scholarship School (Itabashi 1978, p. 172).

Although JACI offers other programs, the discussion here centers on the Scholarship School and the SIS. Unlike the IIST, the JACI does not provide dormitory facilities for its trainees. Hence they commute from home.

Scholarship School

The school offers day programs, which meet five hours a day for five days a week, and evening programs, which meet three hours a day. The day and evening programs range from eleven to twenty weeks for the daytime program and up to two years for the evening program.

In Mr. Itabashi's opinion, a principal limitation of the way in which English is taught in Japanese schools is the emphasis on writing. Consequently, many Japanese have difficulty conversing with foreigners. He believes that in order to be fluent in a foreign lanaguage, trainees need a comprehensive understanding of the foreign culture. In his words, "A language has been developed on the soil of a culture while a culture has been advanced with the language as its blood, and the two are inseparable" (Itabashi 1978, p. 173). Consequently, the training in both must go hand in hand. Mr. Itabashi contends that a good method for improving oral English skills is to help students "think in English." Consequently a portion of the program is devoted to a course entitled, "Thinking in English."

This recognition represents a major strength in international development education programs offered by this and other Japanese institutes. In contrast, although some U.S. multinationals may sponsor a crash course in a foreign language for its trainees, the trainees may acquire some familiarity with the foreign language and hence may risk insulting the other party when trying to converse in a foreign language. In the Chinese and Japanese languages, for example, there are various levels of formality in the spoken language depending with whom one is conversing. Consequently inappropriate use of certain terminologies, which stems from an inadequate understanding of cultural norms, may do the American more harm than good when trying to converse in the other language.

The program also seeks to teach business negotiating skills and offers courses in listening, note taking, speech making, debate, and case discussions. At the end of the program, there is a one-week simulation of an international conference, which provides trainees an opportunity to demonstrate their skills in communicating in English and serves as a model for the people who have just joined the program (correspondence from Mr. Itabashi, November 16, 1982).

School of International Studies

The SIS offers a three-month program in international communication, international business, and area studies. The medium of instruction is English, which helps to develop the English-language skills of the trainees. On completion of the program, trainees are expected to understand the political and cultural environment of the United States, "perform with proficiency and confidence" in a foreign setting, and have a good command of the English language (*School of International Studies Brochure,* 1982).

Under this program, over thirty courses in various aspects of international management are taught, mostly by foreign instructors. These include business negotiations, international finance and accounting, U.S. society and culture, politics, and U.S.-Japan relations. A course that is particularly useful from the perspective of international assignments is "Cross-cultural Communication," which offers insights into the "day-to-day psychology of human relations," differentiates between Western and Japanese ways of thinking, and provides hints on "how to handle people (especially foreigners), how to get them to like you (everyone likes to be liked) and how to win people to your way of thinking" (*School of International Studies Brochure,* 1982). While the objectives of the course may sound overly ambitious, the very existence of such a course indicates the importance Japanese educational institutes place on human relations skills in doing business abroad.

Training for Wives

According to the findings of my questionnaire survey, a principal factor for failure among expatriates of U.S. and European multinationals is the inability of the family (more particularly the spouse) to adapt and adjust to a foreign country. When serving overseas, the expatriate spends most of his day in the office and interacts primarily with his coworkers, most of whom speak fluent English and are familiar with American ways. Thus, the expatriate is insulated from the shock and stress of mingling with people who do not understand English or the American way of doing things. The spouse and the children, on the other hand, have the greatest amount of exposure to members of the local community through their everyday life. Hence, they are most susceptible to culture shock.

In contrast, it was found that among the sample of Japanese multinationals surveyed, the family situation did not emerge as an important reason for failure. Where it did have an influence was primarily in terms of the children's education. However, although Japanese wives are generally more subservient and, in the words of one Japanese executive "do not raise much complaints," an increasing number of Japanese multinationals are beginning to see the virtues of providing some training to spouses before departure. One reason is that in Japan, wives do not generally participate in the after-hours socializing activities of their husbands, whereas in foreign countries, they are expected to participate in neighborhood and company parties. According to a survey by *Japan Economic News* (June 24, 1982), approximately 70 percent of the Japanese spouses have greatly increased the amount of time in entertaining, dining out, shopping, hobbies, sports, and other kinds of leisure activities while overseas. Thus most Japanese wives play a more active role in foreign societies. A wife who is capable of interacting with local nationals will experience fewer tensions and frustrations in living overseas. A second reason for providing training is that having a wife who can speak a foreign language and who is at ease in relating to foreigners is an asset to the husband's career abroad. Thus several of the multinationals surveyed have encouraged the wives of expatriates to attend orientation sessions sponsored by outside agencies, such as Japan Air Lines and the Japan Overseas Educational Services.

Japan Overseas Educational Services (JOES) was established in 1971 to provide advice and training to the families of Japanese expatriates. JOES is a private, nonprofit organization that receives funding from the Japanese Ministry of Education, the Ministry of Foreign Affairs, and six hundred business entities. It offers a variety of programs, including orientation sessions and consultation programs. The orientation sessions are divided into two categories. The first category consists of environmental briefings for the spouses offered two mornings a week over a two-month period. The briefings are designed to "psychologically prepare" the spouses prior to departure and thus help alleviate many of the tensions and stress they may experience in anticipation of living abroad. According to the survey by the *Japan Economic News* (June 24, 1982), the average employee had to depart for a foreign country 4.6 months after notification of the actual overseas assignment. Wives generally join their husbands two to three months later. Thus the interim waiting period may be stressful for the spouses.

These courses are conducted by people who have lived abroad and/or those who have the academic qualifications to address such subjects from both theoretical and practical points of view. The content of these sessions is primarily factual; they are designed to prepare wives for their daily chores of shopping, using public transportation, going to the physician, and so on. Wives are also given lectures on Japanese culture. Given the short duration of the program, language training is minimal. Some spouses may supplement these with language training at other institutes. The focus of the two-month orientation offered by JOES is to provide useful information to the spouses on "how to make oneself understood in the English language" and offer correct pronunciations of the most commonly used English words (*Training program for spouses,* 1982).

The orientation program is also a forum for wives to share their feelings about living abroad and discuss why certain traditional Japanese manners and customs have inhibited them from socializing with non-Japanese. Some of the topics offered include discussions on the Japanese attitude toward religion; sense of values; East versus West; hints on dressing; table manners and etiquette; facts about home parties (how to hold parties and how to be invited); and general information on life-styles of foreigners. Tuition for the two-month program is approximately $208.33 (50,000 yen), and many Japanese multinationals pay such expenses.

The second kind of orientation session is entitled, "Preparations for Local Schools in America." Designed for families sent to the United States, it serves a useful function given the overriding concern with education. The orientation session in this category is divided into parents' and children's classes. In the former, speakers provide information on U.S. schools, both public and private. The speakers have previously taught at weekend schools for Japanese children in the United States and are versed in the area of providing bilingual education for Japanese youngsters. Weekend schools are special classes held on weekends and are designed to familiarize the children of Japanese expatriates with various aspects of Japanese culture. In the children's classes, experienced trainees use the team approach to help participants lessen their tension of being educated abroad, including advice on how to make friends with American children. The differences between the U.S. and Japanese educational systems, values, and attitudes are also explained. Both classes are offered three Saturdays every month; the tuition for the entire family is 15,000 yen ($62.50).

Besides the orientation sessions, free consultation is provided to all participants about Japanese weekend schools and problems of readjustment to the Japanese school system on return. These consultations are provided both prior to departure and on reentry to Japan. In addition, the JOES provides a valuable service by sending teachers and instructional materials to the Japanese weekend schools for children of expatriates.

Although such programs are not comprehensive and do not purport to prepare a Japanese wife for all the contingencies that may arise in living abroad, they are better than nothing. Regrettably some U.S. multinationals do not provide similar programs for the expatriates themselves.

4 Japanese Trading Companies

A distinguishing feature of the Japanese industrial scene is the existence of a handful of general trading companies or *sogo shosha,* which collectively accounted for 40.1 percent of Japan's exports in 1979 and 47.4 percent of the country's imports for the same year (*The role of trading companies in international commerce,* 1982).

The history of the *sogo shosha* dates back to the early years of the Meiji Restoration in the 1870s, with some of the merchant houses (which were their predecessors) tracing their origin several centuries back. Mitsui's origin, for instance, goes back to 1673 (Roberts 1973). Known in early twentieth century as the giant *zaibatsus*, they played a major role in Japan's modernization and industrialization efforts through the promotion of foreign investment, trade, and provision of financing for such activities. The *zaibatsus* were disbanded after World War II at the request of the Allied Occupation authorities because of their involvement in the war effort. The former member firms of the *zaibatsus* were once again reorganized into its present form in the 1950s, however. Their groupings remained essentially the same: Mitsubishi, Mitsui, and Sumitomo. A principal difference between the reorganized groupings and the former *zaibatsus* is that the shares of the companies are no longer majority owned by members of the respective families. Rather they are publicly owned. In 1980, there were nine major trading companies, which together had an annual turnover of 72.7 trillion yen ($302.92 billion) for fiscal year ending 1981. The nine *sogo shosha,* presented in descending order of sales volume for fiscal year ending March 31, 1981, are: Mitsubishi, 13.9 trillion yen ($57.92 billion); Mitsui, 12.7 trillion yen ($52.92 billion); C. Itoh, 10.7 trillion yen ($44.58 billion); Marubeni, 10.2 trillion yen ($42.5 billion); Sumitomo, 9.7 trillion yen ($40.42 billion); Nissho-Iwai, 6.6 trillion yen ($27.5 billion); Tomen, 3.3 trillion yen (13.75 billion); Kanematsu-Gosho, 3.0 trillion yen ($12.5 billion); and Nichimen, 2.6 trillion yen ($10.8 billion) (*The role of trading companies in international commerce,* 1982, p. 8).

The *sogo shosha* have a number of important functions. They engage in import and export trade. The nine general trading companies typically account for roughly 40 to 50 percent of the nation's imports and exports. Besides international trade, they serve an equally important function in the domestic economy. Because of their extensive information-gathering and distribution networks both within and outside Japan, they provide valuable services to foreign manufacturers interested in penetrating the Japanese market and smaller Japanese concerns with little or no access to the world market on their own. Because of their extensive importing and exporting functions, they are able to absorb much of the foreign exchange risk associated with international transactions. Hence, they act as a buffer for small Japanese manufacturers in this regard. They help organize new business ventures by putting together capital, financing, and other technological and marketing know-how. They serve as vehicles of Japanese foreign direct investment overseas. And they promote third-country trade (*The unique world of the sogo shosha,* 1978).

With regard to the future of the general trading companies, the authoritative Japan External Trade Organization (JETRO) believes that it will be bright. It notes that the uncertainty over the roles to be performed by the *sogo shosha* in the early 1960s have by and large dissipated. According to JETRO, the *sogo shosha* will develop in three important areas in the years ahead. One, they will continue to internationalize their activities by establishing more overseas operations and recruiting a larger number of local nationals to make further inroads into foreign markets. Two, they will expand their information-gathering and diagnostic facilities. As Dr. Tokuyama of the Nomura School of Advanced Management noted, "The economic 'miracle' of Japan is attributable in part to our eagerness to gather and analyze available information on world markets." Three, they will play an even more active role in promoting third-country trade (*The role of trading companies in international commerce,* 1982). Future developments in these areas add to the demand for people who possess an international outlook and perspective and who are capable of operating in the global arena. Some, however, argue that the *sogo shosha* are a "dying" breed (Abegglen and Stalk 1983, p. 19). They support this contention by citing such statistics as decreasing return on investments and declining income from trade as a percentage of sales. However, both Abegglen and Stalk concede that there are three general directions or areas in which the general trading companies can proceed to regain much of their earlier vitality: greater involvement in third-country trade, "high-risk overseas 'mega' projects," and high-technology industries. Given the phenomenal size and diversity of activities pursued by the general trading companies, coupled with their quest to establish new frontiers, it is difficult to imagine that they will constitute a vanishing breed; however, it is beyond the bounds of this chapter to debate the role of the *sogo shosha* in the future. Rather, the focus here is on how two of the four top general trading companies organize and prepare their people for the task of promoting international commerce. The two companies examined are Marubeni and Mitsui.

Marubeni

The information presented here is obtained from an in-depth interview with Henry S. Miyazaki, vice-president and assistant corporate secretary, and Hiroshi Kurata, Manager, Administration, Marubeni America Corporation.

Overview

In 1872 Chubei Itoh established a store by the name of Marubeni in Osaka, Japan. In 1903, he established a cotton yarn business for his oldest daughter. This became known as the Itoh-Cotton Yarn Office and provided the beginnings for Marubeni's sister affiliate, C. Itoh and Company, which is the third largest *sogo shosha* today (*The unique world of sogo shosha*, 1978, pp. 33–34). Although the general trading companies are engaged in a diverse range of activities, each specializes in a particular field. Marubeni is "the leader in the sales and construction of overseas industrial plants, power stations, refineries, transportation and communication systems," primarily on a turnkey basis (*Marubeni: Annual report*, 1981, p. 4).

In 1981, Marubeni had 50 domestic branches, 212 affiliate companies in Japan, 80 wholly owned subsidiaries and 162 affiliate operations in 178 locations in over 50 nations. One such wholly owned subsidiary is Marubeni America Corporation, which was established in November 1951. In fiscal year 1982, its total volume of transactions exceeded $12,935 million, netting the company over $11.265 million in income. This represented a 15 percent increase over the preceding year (*Marubeni America Corporation: Annual Report*, 1982).

The company employs 9,500 people in Japan and over 4,500 overseas. These are engaged in 366 different kinds of business activities organized around several industrial groupings: metal, machinery, textile, development and construction, energy and chemicals, agri-marine products, and materials and products (*Marubeni: Annual report*, 1981). Of the 4,500 employees abroad, approximately 1,000 are expatriates sent from Japanese headquarters.

Staffing Policies

According to Ichiro Araki, president of Marubeni American Corporation, the company employs local nationals at the senior management level (including the position of president) at some of the subsidiary operations in the

United States *(Marubeni America Corporation: Annual report,* 1982, p. 2). However, with regard to the actual staffing of top management positions in corporate headquarters of Marubeni America Corporation (New York), the president and three of the four vice-presidents are Japanese. (Corporate headquarters of Marubeni America Corporation must not be confused with corporate headquarters in Tokyo. The latter is the parent firm of the former.) There is only one American vice-president. When asked why Japanese multinationals tend to use parent country nationals more extensively than their U.S. and West European counterparts, Mr. Miyazaki posited that there are two primary reasons. One is language. Since the company is Japanese, the president is usually sent from Japan. Given this fact, all the executive meetings are held in Japanese. In his words, "That's one big reason the people at the managerial level are Japanese. Of course, if an American can speak fluent Japanese, he would be able to join us. I think it could be strictly attributed to language." The American vice-president at Marubeni America Corporation does not speak Japanese.

Every Tuesday, an executive meeting is called among the president and vice-presidents of the company. These are conducted in Japanese. Since the American vice-president does not understand Japanese, "there is no need for him to participate." He is, however, informed of all important decisions made at the meetings. In Mr. Miyazaki's opinion, "We can't hire an interpreter just for him. The system has been working. It may be a little bit inconvenient for him, because he may feel that he is not truly participating in the discussions since he was not present. Even if he is there, he could not express himself." Mr. Miyazaki noted, however, that if the American vice-president comes up with valid ideas and suggestions, they are seriously considered by headquarters. The American vice-president is also covered by the system of lifetime employment and has been with the company for twenty-seven years.

A second reason for the more extensive use of parent country nationals in Japanese multinationals could be attributed to the differences in management philosophy between Americans and Japanese. In Mr. Miyazaki's opinion, a local national not only has to understand Japanese but has to be familiar with Japanese management philosophy and practices. The local national, he says, "has to understand Japanese philosophy, because we are not going to change the way we operate. If the head office wants to operate in a certain way, he has to follow suit. Of course, he could always come out and express his feelings, but we could not be sure whether his suggestions will be taken up or not."

The staffing policy for Marubeni Trading Corporation varies from country to country. Marubeni America Corporation employs 675 people, 200 of them Japanese expatriates. Approximately 40 percent of the 475 local nationals employed by the company have been with Marubeni for ten years or more. Although differences in management philosophy may restrict the wider use of host country nationals, Mr. Miyazaki felt that for those who are willing to learn, they could be assimilated into the company: "Once they get settled in the company and do their duties, they more or less have a career with us. It takes time." But because of the fairly rapid turnover rates in U.S. companies, many Americans still have difficulty adjusting to this longer time perspective. According to a survey reported in Ouchi (1981), the average MBA in the United States changed four jobs in the first two years after graduation.

Although it takes the average Japanese career staff twelve years from first entry on graduation from college to promotion to the managerial level, Mr. Miyazaki noted that the promotion rates for American MBAs are faster to accommodate to the American system. In certain positions, such as a tax manager, the company believes that it is better to hire a local national because it would be difficult to send a Japanese here and understand our different tax system and send him to other countries just as he has become familiar with the tax structure in the United States. Other positions that could more appropriately be staffed by local nationals include traffic and sales.

Marubeni's policy is to rotate expatriates from region to region every three to five years. This is atypical, to a certain extent. According to the findings of the *Japan Economic News* (June 24, 1982), three out of four Japanese expatriates surveyed have lived in only one country during their career. There may be multiple assignments to the same country, however; that is, a person may be assigned to the United States, then repatriated to Japan, and later reassigned to the United States.

Mr. Miyazaki was asked whether the different rates of promotion between Americans and Japanese might generate disparity in standards within the company and lead to feelings of inequity among employees. He noted that it should not be a problem because the Americans are hired as employees of Marubeni America Corporation, while the Japanese are recruited as members of Marubeni Trading Corporation, the parent organization. The former's operations are confined to North America, while the latter does business on a worldwide basis. Americans hired at the managerial level are sent to Japan to attend an orientation session. On completion of the program, the Americans return to the United States, where they may be rotated among the branch offices within the United States.

Like many of the other general trading companies, Marubeni has embarked on a policy designed to hire more local nationals. Mr. Miyazaki acknowledges, however, that there are problems in the implementation of such a policy because of language barriers and differences in management and corporate philosophies between U.S. and Japanese companies. However, given the tighter job market in the United States and an increasing interest in the operation of the Japanese economy, there has been a greater willingness in the recent past on the part of Americans to work for Japanese companies. Mr. Miyazaki noted that the number of American students learning Japanese has increased. Many of these go to Japan and live there for a while; some may also work there. After they return to the United States, they may choose to join Marubeni and other Japanese companies here. As of 1982, Marubeni had hired seven or eight American college graduates who speak Japanese. In Mr. Miyazaki's opinion, "If they settle down and stay with us for five or ten years, they will be able to fit into the company. That's how we try to do it." While the rates of promotion for American nationals are faster, there is still a difference in time perspective between U.S. firms and U.S. subsidiaries of Japanese-based multinationals in this regard. As Mr. Miyazaki noted, it takes a foreign national five to ten years before he could be assimilated to the corporate culture of a Japanese firm. Given the shorter time perspective of most Americans, there may still be problems for ethnic Americans to fit into the Japanese management system.

Since the personnel department in Marubeni America Corporation is limited in size, most of the training provided the local nationals is on the job. The company, however, does provide an orientation program for Americans and other foreign nationals who join the firm. They are sent to Tokyo to meet with the various levels of management in corporate headquarters. While in Japan, they also attend seminars sponsored by Japan Air Lines and the Japanese Chamber of Commerce in which the functions of a general trading company are explained and the peculiar characteristics of the Japanese industrial system examined.

Selection Criteria

Since many management positions in the overseas operations of Japanese multinationals are staffed by parent country nationals, it is important to examine the three main criteria Marubeni uses in selecting people for its overseas operations. First is language. Mr. Miyazaki believes that this is the most important criterion because a person could not function, much less adapt to a foreign environment, without speaking the local tongue. A second criterion is overall knowledge of the business. An expatriate has to assume broader responsibilities while abroad. In Japan, there are over 9,500 employees. Hence, there are certain people within corporate headquarters in Tokyo who specialize in accounting, finance, and so on. Once abroad, however, the expatriate could not always depend on Tokyo for guidance and assistance on all matters. In Mr. Miyazaki's words, "When they [expatriates] come over here, it is a small operation and the person cannot just engage in buying and selling and expect somebody else to take care of the rest. The person has to understand accounting and credit, so that they will be able to perform." Consequently the expatriate needs to have knowledge of the various functional disciplines of accounting and finance, in addition to buying and selling. Since corporate headquarters in Japan seldom send an expatriate to tackle one area only, the general training program provided all expatriates prior to departure familiarizes them with information about the overall operation of the overseas office. Although all expatriates participate in the general training program (which includes seminars and on-the-job training) prior to overseas assignment, each person specializes in a particular commodity. This must not be confused with functional specialization in one product group, such as accounting in the textile group. An expatriate works within one product group only. However, within the confines of that particular group, he is expected to be familiar with the various functional disciplines associated with the product.

A third criterion in selection is the person's ability to relate to foreigners. Mr. Miyazaki conceded, however, that "it is very hard to judge unless he actually comes over here and start facing the American people." In the twenty-five years that he has been in the United States, he recalled that there were only three or four Japanese expatriates who were "really not able to get along with Americans, let alone perform." Given the system of lifetime employment in Japan and the close working relationships among members of a departmental unit, the supervisor is generally knowledgeable about the candidate's strengths and limitations in this regard. Furthermore, the person is specifically asked whether he wants to serve abroad. If the company wants to send the person abroad and he likes the overseas position, that is the best possible situation. For some countries that are considered less desirable, the company will simply tell the individual that "there is work there and it has to be done, so you will have to go." In that case, the person will be ordered. In principle, an individual cannot refuse an assignment because under the system of lifetime employment, the employee implicitly agrees to "accept any order given by the company. The person has to endure the hardship." In the words of Mr. Horide, director and general manager, International, Suntory Ltd. (the whisky manufacturer), a person could refuse, "but he would not. In Japan, company orders are almost like military orders." Extenuating circumstances, such as aged parents who need to be cared for, will be considered, however.

In the past, an overseas assignment was considered very attractive because of the opportunity to live abroad; however, with the rising standard of living in Japan, an overseas position is considered less desirable. Mr. Miyazaki indicated that the situation is true in general, "so it is not very appealing for the young ones to live outside of Japan." He attributed the major reason for this reluctance to the education of their children. Furthermore, "they also have to leave their houses, sell their houses and furniture. So they don't enjoy living overseas." However, he added, "While the trend is changing in that direction, I haven't heard of anybody turning down the order or leaving the company." He was asked whether the company was providing any special incentive for the younger people to work abroad. In response, he noted that Marubeni has not because when college graduates join a general trading company, they "expect overseas assignments" since a primary function of a general trading company is the promotion of international trade and commerce. According to the rank-ordering of the most desirable companies to work for by graduates of elite universities, almost all the *sogo shosha* were favorably perceived. From 1979 through 1982, Mitsubishi Trading Company was rated as *the* most popular firm, with Mitsui Trading Co. in second place (May 17, 1982, pp. 59-65). This finding appears to challenge the thesis that all younger people are reluctant to accept overseas assignments.

Given the importance of international trade to a *sogo shosha,* Mr. Miyazaki was asked whether overseas experience was considered necessary for promotion to top management in Marubeni. He indicated that since 60 percent of the company's revenues is generated from international trade, in order to become president of Marubeni, "the person must have overseas experience because in making decisions, he has to know what is going on overseas. International trading is becoming increasingly more important as compared to domestic business. So I think that general managers, vice-presidents and presidents more or less would need to have overseas experience. It is not a must, but it is easier for them to be promoted." The current president and vice-president of Marubeni headquarters in Japan had served in New York. In fact, it is widely believed that among the general trading companies, those people who have worked for a number of years in New York would most likely become the future presidents of corporate headquarters in Japan. This is consistent with the findings of Inohara (1982 p. 46) where the Japanese executives considered an assignment to the United States as a "good omen for promotion" to the very top of the organizational hierarchy. Hence, such assignments are considered very prestigious, and consequently there is an incentive for a career staff to accept an overseas assignment, particularly in the United States.

The length of the overseas assignment for those sent to the less desirable nations is shorter. In the advanced nations, the assignment is generally for five years. In hardship positions, such as the Middle East and Pakistan, the stay is three years. Assignments to Mexico and South America are also for three years. In the shorter stays, the expatriates' families may stay in Japan.

After a person has finished a tour of duty abroad, there is no rule as to how long he will remain in Tokyo before his next assignment. It depends on the division that the individual belongs to. If there are other capable people who can serve abroad, the individual may remain in Tokyo; however, if the division does not have the appropriate person, he may be sent to his next overseas assignment almost immediately. Mr. Miyazaki noted, "We had a controller who was sent directly from London to here instead of going home. That's atypical, however." He furthermore noted that in his twenty-five years with the New York office, some of the expatriates "have been here the third time round."

Mr. Miyazaki did not know whether the company solicits the spouse's opinion about living abroad. Mr. Kurata added that "as a matter of fact, we want to discuss with the wife before we send somebody overseas." However, this is difficult to implement in practice. Mr. Kurata continued, "We do have some experiences where the wife is not able to adjust. In some places where we only have one or two expatriates, the wives experience great difficulties." To alleviate the situation, Marubeni sponsors some environmental-type briefing for the spouse prior to departure.

Mr. Kurata was asked how long a person has to be with Marubeni before he could expect his first overseas assignment. He indicated that it depends on the country to which the individual is sent. If the expatriate were assigned to a very small affiliate abroad, a more senior man will be sent. In the case of the United States where there are over one hundred Japanese expatriates, a person could be sent after he has been with the Japanese headquarters for three or four years. Usually, however, the person has been with the company for ten years before receiving his first assignment abroad. Besides the regular assignments, Marubeni also sponsors an overseas trainee program whereby a college graduate who has just joined Marubeni is sent to the United States or other nations as an apprentice for two years, after which he returns home. This apprenticeship program constitutes part of the training for some of the career staff.

Training Programs

An individual's entire career can be viewed as one long training program. Japanese firms, particularly the large ones, commonly operate according to a written guiding philosophy. In the case of Marubeni, the basic philosophy is as follows: "For a general trading company, human resources are the greatest asset. It is no exaggeration to say that a firm will not develop without excellent human resource. Therefore, training human resource is the most important agenda. In order to achieve this efficiently and permanently, Marubeni adopts and implements a consistent and harmonious training program for new employees, all the way through managers" (*Marubeni: Human resource development system,* 1981, p. 1).

True to its mission, Marubeni provides a comprehensive human resource development program for three levels of employees in the company: assigned, regular, and administrative. These programs are offered under three broad categories: group training, training inside Marubeni, and training outside Marubeni. The assigned training is for female instructors, group leaders, and employees. Since women are generally not considered members of the career staff because they usually resign after marriage, the training provided under this category will not be reviewed. The regular training consists of two levels of seminars for new male recruits (or junior staff) and middle-level employees (or senior staff without title). The administrative program provides training for divisional managers, departmental managers, newly appointed departmental managers, and administrators.

Under group training, there are foreign language seminars, basic training in the various functional areas of business, and special training to prepare people for overseas assignments. Under group training, there is an in-house certified examination system and examination for promotion to the managerial level. Under the training inside Marubeni category, there are special programs offered by the various divisions, and organizational development seminars. Under the category of training outside Marubeni, there is the overseas trainee program (*shukko*) and correspondence education (*Marubeni: Human resource development system*, 1981).

Training Center: Besides on-the-job training, most of the seminars are conducted in the company's own training center, which consists of a four-story building with classroom, dormitory, cafeteria, and recreational facilities. The center is located on the outskirts of the city to provide a quiet and relaxed atmosphere for "lectures, thinking and discussions" (*Marubeni: Human resource development system*, 1981, p. 13).

Mentor System: Besides the formal training programs under the regular and administrative categories Marubeni (like most other Japanese enterprises) has institutionalized a mentor system, considered an important part of an individual's career development. Each new employee is individually tutored and supervised by a mentor in the same division. The people who serve as mentors have worked with the company for three to eight years and act as "educational instructors, both privately and publicly" (*Marubeni: Human resource development system*, 1981, p. 7). Each mentor is expected to coach his subordinate on the following aspects: how to master the various functional skills required to perform one's task, how to behave as a member of Marubeni, how to develop the appropriate mental attitude as an employee of Marubeni (these include the spirits of loyalty, commitment, and dedication to the company, which will enable the employee to accept orders from the company even though they may involve self-sacrifice and temporary hardship), and how to motivate the subordinate to develop his basic knowledge and skills.

Regular Training: The first-level seminar for new male recruits is designed to help them make the transition from academic to corporate life. They are also provided a general orientation on the functions performed by a *sogo shosha*. Since English is the universal language of international business transactions and approximately 60 percent of the company's revenues is derived from international trade, English is also taught. In addition, the trainees are given seminars in accounting, foreign exchange, credit maintenance, and foreign trade. The general orientation program lasts for one month. The objective of the first-level seminar is to provide trainees with sufficient knowledge to pass the third-grade certified examination administered by the Japanese Chamber of Commerce, which is held in June and November. Successful passage through the third-grade certified examination indicates that the trainee has achieved a certain level of competence in the English language.

The second-level seminar consists of a boarding program and is held six months after the employee has joined the company. This four-day seminar is designed to provide a refresher course on business principles, to help new employees understand the current situation at Marubeni and assimilate the proper conduct and protocols as employees of a general trading company, and to heighten group consciousness and strengthen camaraderie relationships through communal living, and thus facilitate teamwork later. Besides lectures, seminars, and group discussions, the participants also engage in athletic sports so as to strengthen them physically and to put into practice the principles of teamwork and cooperation. Because a number of companies use physical health as one of the criteria for selection for overseas assignment, attention is devoted to developing the employee's physique. A full 48 percent of the firms surveyed by Professor Takuo Tanaka at Chuo University used physical health as a criterion in selection for overseas assignments (*Human resource development in industry,* 1983, p. 32).

As the career staff progresses in the organization, the employee attends another set of seminars designed for senior staff without title. Prior to advancement to the level of assistant manager, a career staff is just a regular employee and does not possess any title in the organization. The purpose of the training at this level are fivefold:

1. To help them understand their responsibilities and obligations at this stage of their career development.
2. To strengthen the employee's understanding of corporate goals and objectives.
3. To develop their abilities to solve problems creatively.
4. To promote team spirit and cooperation.
5. Through group discussions, to promote a spirit of mutual enlightenment among the participants (*Marubeni: Human resource development system,* 1981).

It generally takes a college graduate twelve years from first entry to promotion to the managerial level. There are four grades in the premanagement phase. The in-house certified exam tests how much employees have learned from the various seminars. Before the employee is promoted to management level, he has to pass another test, which examines him on a broad range of topics, including company rules. A person who cannot demonstrate his abilities will remain at the clerical level (or premanagement phase) for the rest of his career. According to Mr. Miyazaki, if a person "cannot perform, a college degree is no guarantee that he would become a manager." This policy reflects Marubeni's commitment to the principle of promotion on the basis of merit rather than on seniority beyond a certain level.

Administrative Training: The training program for the newly appointed administrators is given to employees who have just been promoted from regular employee to the position of assistant departmental manager. This program is designed to prepare the individual to take on the added responsi bilities of an administrative role. The objectives of the training are for the employees to acquire a basic knowledge of how to manage; to manage resources, particularly humans in the organizations, effectively; to discover their potential for administrative work; and to establish self-development plans to attain their career goals.

On promotion to the position of departmental manager, the individual has to undergo another set of training in the following areas: methods for managing and motivating subordinates, proper use of personnel evaluation, understanding the operations of personnel systems and policies, and developing general administrative skills. Clearly emphasis is placed on the human relational aspects of management. Technical competence is a necessary but insufficient criterion for rising in the organization. These skills are conveyed in a variety of ways. First, every participant has to undertake the Managerial Aptitude Test, designed to help identify one's strengths and limitations as an administrator, and then pursue self-enlightenment (self-education) programs to remedy one's weak points. Second, the departmental manager has to attend a variety of lectures on personnel management, sales, accounting, and managing overseas operations. These are given by administrators from the respective divisions. Third, the training emphasizes group discussions so that the participants can share their experiences and ideas concerning management in general. Fourth, since communication skills are considered paramount, the participants have to practice and demonstrate their abilities to present ideas to top management. Fifth, guidelines are offered on how to manage one's physical health.

Individuals promoted to the position of divisional manager are provided another set of training to develop their human relational skills, to recognize the various problems that may arise in management, to improve skills in the functional areas, and to draw up strategies in response to changing environmental conditions. Dr. Tokuyama, executive director and dean of the Nomura School of Advanced Management at the Nomura Research Institute, noted that Japanese managers are typically weak in strategic management; hence these skills must be developed. In his opinion, "Japanese department heads excel in practical business affairs because they acquire every imaginable procedure for transactions through the hardships of on-the-job training under the supervision of senior partners. I believe they are analogous to seasoned combat colonels in the sense that they know every inch of their battlefields so that they can easily capture the enemy's bunker if they were told to do so by their division commanders. ... Though they know every conceivable tactic, they are weak in terms of strategy making. Consequently the three-week seminar sponsored by the Nomura School is designed to assist Japanese senior and middle managers to develop and implement corporate strategies (*Marubeni: Human resource development system,* 1981, pp. 11–12).

Basic Training in Business Skills: All employees, particularly the younger ones are provided training in basic business skills: accounting, (duration of program is six months, twice a week), international trade (three months, once a week), foreign exchange (three months, once a week), and credit maintenance (three months, once a week).

English-Language Training: The English-language seminars are divided into several levels. The first level is for all new recruits and is compulsory. This extends for three months. Those who wish may take an extra three months of training. Beyond this there are intermediate-level seminars extending for twelve months, with meetings once a week. Attendance at this level is voluntary. In addition, intensive language training is offered on weekends on a voluntary basis; participants live in dormitories. For advanced management, there is a six-month program that meets biweekly. All individuals who have to use English in business transactions are required to enroll in the program. Another kind of English-language training is offered to employees who have worked with Marubeni for two to three years. The duration of this program is ten months, with lectures once a week. Besides formal lectures, the company encourages employees to improve their English-language skills through self-education (*Marubeni: Human resource development system,* 1981, p. 15).

Language Training Other Than English: Given Marubeni's extensive worldwide operations, its employees are encouraged to learn other foreign languages besides English. Six other languages are taught inhouse: French, Spanish, German, Russian, Portuguese, and Chinese. For each of these languages, courses are offered at the introductory, intermediate, and advanced levels. The introductory program extends for six months and is offered twice a week. The intermediate and advanced programs also run for six months and are offered twice a week. In their annual and semiannual evaluation forms in which employees describe their career aspirations, those who identify an interest in an overseas career in certain countries should take these specific language training programs. Furthermore, employees who require a specific foreign language in their everyday business transactions have to undergo this training. For those who are assigned to a given foreign country, intensive language training is offered prior to departure. The language skills of all the trainees are scored from A+ (excellent) to C– (poor) (*Marubeni: Human resource development system,* 1981, p. 16).

Training for Overseas Assignments: Several programs prepare a person for an overseas assignment: the apprenticeship or overseas trainee program offered to new employees, training provided to candidates prior to departure, and study-abroad programs.

Apprenticeship Program: After completion of the initial orientation session at Marubeni, some career staff are sent abroad for two years to observe and study the operations of the company's overseas business. Since a majority of Marubeni's business comes from international trade, the company needs to develop employees with an international perspective. Consequently just as new recruits are assigned to the various domestic branch offices for on-the-job training, some new employees are sent to overseas subsidiaries.

Norihisa Matsuo, who joined Marubeni in 1979 and spent two years in London, recalled the initial stresses he experienced in living and working abroad: "When I answered the phone, I did not understand what they were saying." After a while, he acquired proficiency in the language and traveled throughout England negotiating with foreign buyers. When asked to summarize his two most significant accomplishments over the two-year apprenticeship progam, he noted that one was traveling 40,000 kilometers throughout England; and two, "I have made friends with the British." This will be a major asset when he is later assigned to work in the London branch (*Marubeni: Human resource development system,* 1981, p. 7).

Training for Expatriates prior to Departure: Individuals who have been selected for an overseas position take courses in international finance, accounting, and management. They are also given environmental briefings about what to expect in the foreign country. In short, the program is designed to prepare them physically and psychologically for living and working overseas.

Marubeni also provides seminars for the spouses of expatriates because of its recognition that the family, particularly the spouse, plays a major role in an overseas assignment. The seminar provides information on procedures for going abroad, environmental briefings, and a forum for spouses to share their feelings and anxieties about living overseas. This program is offered inhouse (*Marubeni: Human resource development system,* 1981, p. 18).

Study-Abroad Program. Young employees under thirty may apply for this program. They must pass a language proficiency test (both oral and written), plus examinations in three other areas: trading, financial accounting, and credit maintenance. In addition, the candidate must be recommended by the office manager of the division to which he belongs. Consequently only high performers are selected. On selection, they are sent to a university in an advanced or developing country to study business administration, language, engineering, or law. The duration of the program varies from one to three years. The company pays their tuition and expenses in addition to their regular salary. In turn, they report their progress to corporate headquarters. Students who take courses related to production and technology engage in factory practicums.

Marubeni currently sends a number of trainees to study law in the United States. On their return to Japan, they will work for the legal department in corporate headquarters. The company also sends approximately twenty to twenty-five employees every year to attend the two-year M.B.A. program in U.S. universities, which continue to attract attendees from virtually all parts of the world. In 1981–1982, 327,000 foreign students attended institutes of higher education in the United States. The reasons for the attraction of U.S. universities are "pioneering research," diverse range of subjects offered, and overall "reputation and prestige." A U.S. university degree remains a "source of upward professional mobility" (Goodwin and Nacht 1983, p. 26).

Organizational Development Seminar: These are provided by the respective divisions and are sometimes referred to as family training or training among employees. Given the emphasis on human relational skills and groupism in Japanese organizations, these seminars are designed to foster an esprit de corps among the people who belong to a particular division. These seminars are attended by employees from all levels.

The objectives of the seminar are to diagnose and analyze problems that hinder growth in the organization specifically from their division's perspective and to foster teamwork, cooperation, and communication among the various levels in the division and between and among divisions. The employees are usually divided into groups of five or six people (*Marubeni: Human resource development system,* 1981, p. 20). This concept is similar to quality control circles where the objective is to identify problems and to solve them creatively.

Shukko: Job rotations in some Japanese organizations involve assigning an employee to work in another company for a period of time. As part of Marubeni's outside training, some employees are sent to the small- or medium-sized companies so that they can be exposed to the problems encountered by such firms. Because one of the functions of a general trading company is to develop domestic trade, a *sogo shosha* often works with and handles the products of the small- to medium-sized manufacturers. As such, the trading company's employees must be aware of the unique problems encountered by firms of these sizes. Prior to their actual assignment to other companies, the candidates are given training in industry diagnosis, tax and legal regulations, labor relations, and credit maintenance (*Marubeni: Human resource development system,* 1981, p. 19).

Correspondence Education or Self-Enlightenment: True to the guiding philosophy behind zen and Marubeni's corporate objective to develop each employee to his fullest, the company encourages employees to take correspondence courses in their spare time to improve themselves. The company pays for half the tuition if the employee completes the course. Some of the courses offered in this area, with the duration of each program indicated in parentheses, are: seminar in management education—commerce (one year), seminar in management education—industry (one year), financial management (six months), corporate law (four months), foreign exchange management (six months), international business (six months), practical accounting (six months), business correspondence (four months), practical English (nine months), labor relations (eight months), and real estate management (one year). Although the payoff for taking these correspondence courses may not be immediate, Japanese companies do award their employees for special talents and efforts in the long run.

Other Programs: The nine *sogo shosha* collaborate with MITI to sponsor a common program for all employees of general trading companies. The instructors are drawn from professors at different universities who lecture on the functions of trading companies. These programs run from one to two weeks.

Success and Factors for Success

The failure rate of Marubeni's expatriate assignments has been very low. During the twenty-five years that Mr. Miyazaki has been with the U.S. operation, only three or four people have had to be recalled to Tokyo. He believes that Marubeni's failure rate throughout the world would nowhere exceed 1 percent. He attributed this low failure rate to several reasons. One is the rigorous selection criteria. Most of the individuals assigned overseas have been with the company for ten years, and therefore their supervisors have had ample opportunity to observe their performance. A second reason can be ascribed to the rigorous training programs. Third is the method of evaluating performance. A number of Japanese multinationals interviewed for this study indicated that a reason for the lower failure rate is that Japanese firms tend to be more patient in terms of evaluation. Mr. Miyazaki concurred and added that "even though [the expatriate's] performance may not be what the company wants, but if he is doing his best (which is 100 percent) we would like to think that way, not that he is just doing 75 percent." The company tries to make allowances for problems of communication and adjustment in the first one to two years abroad. Mr. Miyazaki indicated that his company would usually wait two years before undertaking any drastic action. If it becomes apparent after two years that the individual cannot adapt, he will be sent back to Tokyo. Both Mr. Miyazaki and Mr. Kurata were asked whether the fact that a person were recalled would negatively affect the person's chances of future promotion. Mr. Miyazaki responded that "it all depends on how well he does back in Japan." Mr. Kurata elaborated on the issue by noting that according to the "Japanese way of thinking, since the company sent him, and he doesn't perform well, the company was at fault in sending him to that position." Consequently, if he performs well on his return home, his failure abroad should not have any negative consequences.

While overseas, the expatriate is evaluated three times a year: once for increase in salary, the second time for assessment of performance, and the third for determining the size of his bonus. Bonuses vary from two to six months of the person's regular wage and are closely tied to a person's performance; the better the performance, the larger the bonus. The evaluation is done by a number of people in the overseas branch: the manager, the general manager, the vice-president, and the president. The evaluation reports are then forwarded to Japan. Mr. Miyazaki concedes, however, that there are always problems with the evaluation. He indicated that it is difficult to come up "with an average point. If there is somebody that is above average, then there will be somebody that will be below average. Most of the actual evaluation is done by the immediate supervisor. For smaller-sized operations, the evaluation may be high because there is only one man. The general manager could add his opinion to it that there is only one man, so there is no average point." Given these problems, once Tokyo receives the reports, they try to make some kind of adjustments. Mr. Kurata noted that for this reason, it is imperative that the expatriate maintain "good communications with Tokyo. They try to keep in close touch so that Tokyo will recognize that they exist. Expatriates make an effort to let Tokyo know what they are doing. These are done through phone calls, telexes, trips back home, and so on."

Mr. Miyazaki was then asked to comment on the subject of culture shock and how the Japanese try to cope with it. In response, he indicated that the amount of culture shock experienced by a Japanese on arrival in a foreign country depends on the individual. In his words, "We have heard of housewives with other companies who cannot cope with a foreign country and commit suicide. You can't say that all of them are like that. It depends on each individual. To some extent, it is a very different country and they are not familiar with it. I wouldn't call it shock, but they do have to undergo a certain amount of adaptation." Mr. Miyazaki was asked whether Japanese expatriates tend to cope with cultural differences by forming enclaves in foreign communities. He explained that although Japanese families tend to cluster together, this could largely be attributed to their desire to live close to their place of work. Since most of them work long hours, "convenience to transportation is the major factor. They want to live close to the railroad station. That being the case, all Japanese tend to gather around the same area. If they have children, they are very concerned about their education. Naturally, they tend to live in certain areas." Despite Mr. Miyazaki's explanations for this phenomenon, which certainly sound logical, given the strong tradition of groupism, the homogeneity and general insularity of its people, most Japanese tend to cluster together in foreign communities.

Repatriation

In U.S. multinationals, if an expatriate has been overseas for too long, he may be out of the mainstream of corporate organizational hierarchy and hence might be passed up for promotion. Mr. Miyazaki contends that Japanese expatriates who serve extended periods abroad tend to be concerned about this problem. But because of the mentor system and the practice of lifetime employment, the expatriate's supervisor will continue to be his superior for a long time. Consequently, as long as his superior is around, the expatriate knows somebody will take care of his career path and speak on his behalf in corporate headquarters. This again points to the need for expatriates to maintain constant communication with corporate headquarters. Mr. Kurata noted that in the past, expatriates were concerned about extended durations of overseas assignments, but "now it does not seem to be true because our vice-president spent almost half of his career overseas." He believes that the person's promotion depends on the value and possible contribution of the individual to the company. A talented expatriate will be promoted to top management. He explained that under the system of lifetime employment, the company has to identify an employee's assets and locate him in positions where "he can perform to the utmost," whether at home or abroad. If his talents are needed in domestic headquarters, he will be recalled. Since the strengths of each individual vary, the company will assign its employees to different positions accordingly. Consequently, "If the person spends most of his time overseas, the company thinks that is the best place for the person to be."

Remuneration Policies

The five major *sogo shosha*—Mitsui, Mitsubishi, Sumitomo, C. Itoh, and Marubeni—share information on these matters and come up with an average. Consequently the salaries paid expatriates among the five are comparable. For example, both the president and executive vice-president of Marubeni America Corporation have the use of a company car. The manager of each of Marubeni's branch offices in the United States is provided cars and company housing (the houses belong to the company, and the manager pays a certain percentage of his salary as rent). The president and the executive vice-president do not pay rent, but an equivalent amount in rent is added to their salaries as income.

The company also pays a cost-of-living adjustment. Every year Marubeni conducts a survey of the inflation rates and consumer price indexes throughout the world in order to arrive at a cost-of-living index. In addition, the company pays a premium for hardship positions to compensate expatriates for harsh living conditions in certain regions of the world. The premium varies from region to region. Furthermore, under the system of lifetime employment, an employee has implicitly agreed to accept whatever assignments the company gives him.

Possible Changes

Both Mr. Miyazaki and Mr. Kurata were asked whether they envision any change to Marubeni's human resource development program in the future. Mr. Miyazaki noted that changes will be made in response to evolving environmental conditions. As an example, he cites the current policy of hiring Americans who can speak Japanese. These people have to be sent to Japan for training. Consequently the human resource development system has to include them in the future. The system Marubeni now has "is an accumulation of the past experiences of the company. It is unlike the one that we had in the beginning. It has been gradually changing over the years, and these procedures are updated from time to time."

Mr. Kurata noted that all the divisions and branches of the company work closely with the personnel department in this regard. The personnel division, in conjunction with the training department in Tokyo, is responsible for the human resource development programs within Marubeni. These two departments recruit and train people to meet the needs of the company. Consequently no division or department could make changes "without consulting with the personnel division. It is part of the system." This points to the power wielded by personnel departments in Japanese companies. However, given the emphasis on human relational skills in Japanese organizations, the people in the personnel division work closely with members of other departments and groups, including overseas branches, to design programs that will best suit the requirements of its various constituents.

Mitsui

Mitsui is the oldest merchant house in Japan, dating back to 1673. Today the Mitsui group (Mitsui & Co., Ltd. being one of the over sixty member firms) is the largest economic collective in Japan. A collective refers to a "grouping of independent corporations which operate in a cooperative manner to bring prosperity to the group as a whole" (*Mitsui group: Yesterday, today and tomorrow,* 1982, p. 4). The organizational form closest to an economic collective in the Western world is a conglomerate, although there are important distinctions. The companies that belong to the group do not generally use the Mitsui name but receive cooperation and assistance from members of the group, such as having wider access to the group's financing and technological innovations (*Mitsui group: Yesterday, today and tomorrow,* 1982, p. 9). This spirit of cooperation was embodied in the first and foremost precept of the Mitsui Clan: "A single arrow is easily broken, but many arrows together are very strong. Members of the family must cooperate for the prosperity of the family as a whole" (*Mitsui group: Yesterday, today and tomorrow,* 1982, p. 18).

The three principal policymaking bodies of the Mitsui group are the Second Thursday Club *(Nimoku-kai),* which is made up of the presidents and chairmen of the leading member firms and meets monthly; the Monday Club *(Getsuyo-kai),* which began in 1950 as a weekly luncheon meeting among senior executives of the leading member firms; and the Public Relations Committee *(Koho-iinkai),* comprised of the managers of public relations in the respective member firms. The function of this committee is to coordinate the public relations activities of the group as a whole (*Mitsui group: Yesterday, today and tomorrow,* 1982, p. 7). Thus, although equity ownership and management of the member firms are separate, there is nevertheless a strong sense of team spirit and cooperation among all group members. This explains why they constitute such a formidable economic force in Japan and in the international arena. In fiscal year ended March 31, 1981, the total trading transactions for Mitsui & Co. Ltd. alone (the general trading portion of the group) increased 11 percent, reaching 14,930 billion yen ($70.757 billion). The general trading company is comprised of seventy divisions in the areas of iron and steel, nonferrous metals, machinery, chemicals, foodstuffs, textiles, energy, construction, lumber, general merchandise, and so on. Besides Mitsui & Co., Ltd. (or Mitsui Bussan in Japanese), there are sixty-one other major member companies that belong to the group. In addition, hundreds of other firms constitute secondary or affiliate members of the Mitsui group (*Mitsui & Co., Ltd.: Annual* report, 1981).

The discussion here focuses primarily on the human resource development program at Mitsui & Co., Ltd., the general trading company. The information is obtained from an in-depth interview with Toshihide Nakajima, manager, First Primary Aluminum Section, Light Metals Division, Mitsui & Co., Ltd. In addition, the practices and procedures at two of Mitsui's leading group members, Toray Industries, Inc., and Daicel Chemical Industries, Ltd. will also be introduced for comparison purposes. Toray is the largest manufacturer of synthetic fibers in Japan. The company has four wholly owned subsidiaries in New York, London, Hong Kong, and Singapore and forty joint ventures with local and Japanese partners throughout the world. Its consolidated net sales for fiscal year ending March 31, 1981, were 463,037 million yen ($2,205 million) (*Toray Industries, Inc.: Annual report,* 1980–1981). The information on Toray was provided by Tadanori Nakaoka, Second Personnel Section, Personnel Department of Toray Industries, Inc. Another Mitsui group member, Daicel Chemical Industries, Ltd., is a manufacturer of organic chemicals, cellulosic derivative, plastics, films, rockets, and propellants. In fiscal year ending 1980, its consolidated sales reached 144,097 million yen ($600.4 million) (*Daicel Chemical Industries, Ltd.: Annual Report,* 1980). The information on Daicel was provided by Shigemitsu Morita, director and general manager of Diacel Chemical Industries, Ltd., who is stationed in New York. Mr. Morita first served in the United States between 1968 to 1974, then returned to Japan for three years, and in 1977 was once again assigned to the New York office. He has been working here since then.

Personnel Division

In the case of Mitsui Bussan, the personnel division reports directly to the board of directors of the company. The Personnel Division is made up of ten departments or sections: general affairs, which keeps detailed personnel inventories or profiles; general planning, which oversees the overall human resource system in the company; career development department, which is responsible for the evaluation, promotion, assignment, and retirement of career staff; the personnel development department (where Mr. Nakajima previously served as deputy manager), responsible for the recruiting and training of all staff; overseas department, which caters to the needs of expatriates; employee relations, which engages in collective bargaining with the trade unions (in Japan, labor is generally organized into enterprise unions); employee welfare department, which oversees salaries and other fringe benefits; reemployment and consulting service, which provides advice to retiring personnel; health promotion, which is responsible for the employee's general health; and a clinic.

Clearly the personnel division performs a range of functions and activities that affect the employee's career. This explains in part why it wields so much authority. Of particular interest here is the overseas department, whose primary function is to take care of the needs of expatriates. The existence of such a department shows the overall concern of the company for the well-being of its expatriates and helps to allay many of the tensions that they might experience otherwise.

The prominent role played by the personnel division reflects the importance assigned to human resource development. This emphasis on human resource development is not unique to general trading companies alone but to manufacturing concerns as well. Toray's fundamental principle or guiding philosophy is, "An industry should not only produce goods, but must also create human assets" (*Toray: The corporation that walks with the age,* 1982, p. 42).

Staffing Policies

Mitsui Bussan has a total staff of 13,300, 1,200 of whom are currently serving as expatriates. Approximately 2,300 of the 13,300 are non-Japanese, most hired as clerical staff of the company's overseas operations. The major managerial positions abroad are occupied by Japanese, the "top managers are sent from Tokyo without any exception." Toray has a total staff of 13,600, 200 of whom are expatriates. Daicel, a smaller company compared to the other two, employs 3,083 people, 6 currently serving as expatriates (two each in New York, Los Angeles, and Dusseldorf).

When asked the reasons for the extensive use of parent country nationals by Japanese multinationals, Mr. Nakajima pointed to differences between manufacturers and general trading companies with respect to staffing policies. In his opinion, although there is a trend toward localization, a principal reason for the extensive use of parent country nationals is the nature of the business they are engaged in: "It has some relationship to the training subject. We are not really giving systematized training to our career staff for that kind of business. We use the system of apprenticeship. Without exception, the career staff are college graduates. These are hired at age twenty-two or twenty-three as 'raw material.' " Each career staff is assigned to a certain section and is engaged in a given commodity. He receives on-the-job training over an extensive period of time. For this reason, Mr. Nakajima continued, "It is very difficult to hire local managers and train them. I am afraid we could not give them adequate training overseas." Tsueno Iyobe of the personnel development section at Mitsubishi Corporation (the largest *sogo shosha*) added that a reason for the extensive use of parent country nationals in the general trading companies, as compared to manufacturers, is due to the fact that besides international trade, the *sogo shosha* seeks to promote domestic trade. In his words, "Our business is heavily dependent upon Japanese manufacturers, so the contact with Japanese customers is very important." This observation is similar to one made by another executive at a major general trading company: "Because of the nature of the business, i.e., mostly done with companies related to Tokyo headquarters, local employees are hired mainly to assist the Japanese staff" (Inohara 1982, p. 22).

Even in the case of Toray, a manufacturing concern, all management positions in the wholly owned subsidiaries are staffed by parent country nationals. When asked the reasons, Mr. Nakaoka explained, "The purpose of these companies is primarily for sales promotion, research, and survey. So we don't need many employees." Furthermore, because of language barriers, there may be problems of communication with corporate headquarters in Tokyo, hence the extensive use of Japanese expatriates. Mr. Morita of Diacel, another manufacturing concern, indicated that his company employs local nationals only as secretarial staff; "all the businessmen are sent from Japan." He posited a more important reason for the extensive use of parent country nationals, although he qualified that as being his own opinion. It is his belief that "the Japanese people are not yet internationally oriented. They are rather conservative and they are reluctant to hire foreigners because they do not have sufficient experience to work together with foreigners yet." This may be attributed to the stage of evolution of Japanese multinationals. Perhaps Mr. Morita's description of the Japanese as not being internationally minded should be modified because they are highly dependent on trade; hence they are internationally oriented. However, because of the general insularity and homogeneity of its people, they do not easily mix with foreigners *(gaijins)*. In the minds of many Japanese, even *niseis* and *sanseis* (second- and third-generation Japanese-Americans) are considered as outsiders.

Mr. Nakajima of Mitsu Bussan indicated that his company has tried to hire local nationals for management positions. In the 1970s, the London branch recruited a college graduate from Oxford University. After three years of training in London, the British national was sent to Japan where the company tried to "expose him to the same experience" as the Japanese career staff. He was provided language training and after eighteen months became quite proficient in oral Japanese. In addition, he "mastered the business" of working in the metals division quite well. He was later transferred back to London for further training in the metals division to prepare him for eventual promotion to the managerial level. However, despite all the efforts, the endeavor failed. When asked about the reasons for failure, Mr. Nakajima explained that "there were problems of communication, not necessarily in terms of the language" because the Englishman was quite fluent; however, he "could not understand some of the objectives of the company" or adapt to the "mentality of Japanese in the process of consensus decision making." In order to make the latter process work, there must be a lot of caucusing, implicit understanding, and nonverbal communications. As the executive from Dentsu advertising agency observed, "The Japanese communicate in almost telepathic ways: through gesture, nuance, inflection" (*Fortune,* November 1, 1982, p. 68). As a foreigner with a very different cultural and educational background, the Englishman was unable to operate within the subtleties of the system. Furthermore, there was a problem of credibility. Mr. Nakajima indicated that if a Japanese junior staff were to present a proposal to the finance division about a new business opportunity, it would be considered seriously. However, if the British initiated the proposal, the finance division "will not consider it. This occurred even within the London branch which made such efforts. [The Japanese colleagues] could not eliminate that attitude." Despite that particular failure, Mitsui has continued to hire local nationals with the hope that they could one day be groomed for managerial positions. According to Mr. Nakajima, they trained another foreigner in the steel division in Tokyo in the summer of 1982. "So far, we hired four, and two have left our company. One is working in the Scandinavian office." The latter was also trained in the steel division in Tokyo, and after returning to London, was transferred to Norway because he was a native of Sweden.

Given the smaller size of the training departments in Mitsui's overseas branches, the kind of training program that is provided for local nationals is naturally quite different from that given the Japanese career staff in corporate headquarters. It is nowhere as comprehensive. Consequently, in Mr. Nakajima's words, the local nationals already suffer from "some kind of handicap from the very beginning." However, for those who plan a career with Mitsui, they are sent to Tokyo for two years' training. This is, of course, shorter than the ten-year training program given the Japanese career staff. The training program for the career staff in Japan will be discussed later. Besides language training, the foreign nationals are given on-the-job training where possible. "We tried to give him training that was as close as possible to those given to our own career staff. He experienced the Japanese business. But two years is still very compressed as compared to the ten years. We really learn very slowly. That is one characteristic of career development."

Selection Criteria

Mr. Nakajima was asked to identify the criteria his company used in selecting people for overseas assignments. He noted that the criteria are fairly loose because of the huge demand for people to serve abroad. Of the 1,200 expatriates currently serving overseas, approximately 900 come from the rank below manager (the average age of a manager is between forty to forty-five). In order to be sent overseas, the person must be in grade 3. In Mitsui, as in most other Japanese organizations, the phase prior to the level of assistant manager is divided into three grades. A career staff spends an average of three years in grade 1, four years in grade 2, and four and a half years in grade 3. Consequently, the person must be at least thirty years old before he is sent overseas. Hence, nine hundred expatriates must be selected from the age category of thirty to forty-five. As such, more than 50 percent of the career staff have to serve overseas.

Although the selection criteria are fairly loose, they do exist. These are dictated by the personnel department and circulated throughout the entire company. When an opening for an overseas position arises, the respective divisions draw up plans. The employees apply to their respective divisional managers for approval. On recommendation by the divisional manager, the career development department within the personnel division checks the applicant's qualifications to see if certain minimal criteria are met, such as technical competence and decision-making and language skills. The career development department does not like to "intervene that much. We are just checking whether the person has those criteria." The career development staff also discusses with the supervisors the candidate's relational skills. The career development department asks the respective divisions to nominate candidates who they believe are able to adapt to foreign environments. Although there is no explicit system to test the candidate's relational abilities, Mr. Nakajima noted that they have a built-in mechanism. Since the candidates have a minimum of grade 3 standing, most have been with the company for nearly ten years. Consequently there is ample opportunity for their supervisor to observe their performance. These are reported to the personnel division once a year. The company keeps detailed personnel inventories, including scores on tests administered after the various training programs offered in house.

Given the increasing reluctance of the younger generation to serve abroad, Mr. Nakajima noted that whenever there are transfers within the company (overseas assignments being part of them), the immediate supervisor discusses the possible relocation with the individual and explains why a transfer is necessary. In principle, employees cannot turn down the company's assignments because of the system of lifetime employment. Mr. Nakajima was queried as to whether the spouse's opinion was taken into consideration in the selection process. He responded, "Not really. We have many cases where there is a problem with the wife." In Mr. Nakajima's opinion, the attitudes of Japanese wives are changing and are beginning to more closely resemble that of American women. Some of the wives raise objections, and the husbands relay these to the company. He added, "We believe that most of the employees can persuade their wives that it is an order from the company. As a rule, we cannot disobey the company." If the employee were to raise strong objections, the company would not send him "because we know that he will not work hard." When asked whether that would negatively affect the person's chances of future promotion, he responded, "I think that if I am your superior and you are not persuaded by me, even after I have explained to you how important the overseas assignment is, I am not happy." Under the annual evaluation system, the supervisor assigns a score to each subordinate. These are accumulated over a four-or five-year period and provide the basis for promotion. Thus, refusing an assignment can negatively affect promotion.

Given the importance of international business to a general trading company, Mr. Nakajima was asked whether an overseas assignment was considered a prerequisite for promotion to top management. "I think so. It used to be so," although the younger generation do not necessarily share his sentiments. Mitsui's chairman, president, and many of the people at the second highest level all have international experience; hence, for those who aspire to rise to the top of the organizational hierarchy, there appears to be a real incentive to serve abroad.

This appears to be the case for an increasing number of U.S. multinationals as well. Although there are still problems with repatriation in U.S. multinationals, according to a recent survey by Kenny, Kindler and Hunt, a recruiting firm in New York City, many fast trackers view an overseas assignment as an expedient means to acquire broad management experience. In their study of 125 executives, 37 percent indicated willingness to accept an overseas assignment as compared to 10 percent ten years ago. This finding was supported by Heidrick and Struggles, another recruitment agency. In the past, an overseas assignment was generally described as "two-yeared into oblivion." In the words of Edmund Piccolino, vice-president at PepsiCo's international division, his unit has now become the "primary farm team" for top executive talent (Lublin, 1983, p. 1).

The average duration of an overseas assignment in Mitsui is five years, extended from a previous average of 3.5 years. The reason for lengthening the period of assignment is that three years may be too short for the person to adjust and hence make useful contributions. The duration of the assignment is only two years for hardship positions, such as the Middle East. When asked why most Japanese have an aversion to Middle Eastern countries, Mr. Nakajima noted that there are several factors: general ignorance about the area, which incites fear, strict codes of conduct, and prohibitions on consumption of alcohol. "We have a joke that if we are forbidden to drink alcohol, we cannot live. I think that is one of the big reasons. It constitutes hardship." Shorter durations of assignments in the less developed countries appear to be universal among Japanese multinationals. After completion of an overseas assignment, the individual returns to Japan for three to five years and may then be sent abroad again. There is no fixed pattern, however, and the rotation varies from one commodity group to another. Mr. Nakajima added that he "can safely say that if a person is very capable in the United States, most probably he will be assigned to the U.S. office later when he reaches managerial level." This is consistent with the findings of *Japan Economic News* (June 24, 1982) that three out of the four expatriates surveyed have served in one country only.

In the case of Toray, the criteria used are technical competence, general health, language, and ability to adjust to a foreign environment. When asked how the company assesses the last criterion, Mr. Nakaoka noted that since Toray has a long history of exporting overseas (approximately 40 to 50 percent of its products were exported in the past; this has now dropped to 30 percent), the staff in the export division is good. "Most of these have very extensive contacts with foreigners." The export division staff has acquired expertise in dealing with non-Japanese clientele. In the case of Toray, the average age of an expatriate is forty-two, so most have been with the company for nineteen years, ample opportunity for the company to observe the individual's personality and performance. Toray was the first Japanese company to introduce the system of self-evaluation, whereby each employee is requested to offer a written description of himself on the following dimensions: whether he has fully used his abilities in the past evaluation period, whether his present job is appropriate for him, and what kinds of assignments he would like to undertake (*Toray: The corporation that walks with the age*, 1982, p. 44). These self-evaluations are taken into consideration in the selection decision.

Daicel relies heavily on employee self-evaluations. Based on these self-descriptions, the personnel department selects those who are "very interested in doing business abroad." They then try to asssess the person's suitability by discussing the possibility of such an assignment with the individual's supervisors. Besides language skills, two other criteria are used: overall knowledge of the business and ability to relate to foreigners. In Mr. Morita's opinion, "Japanese tend to be conservative and are modest in talking about their own capabilities and achievements. Americans, on the other hand, in general like to demonstrate their own capabilities. In order to be successful in the United States, the Japanese have to behave like Americans and be outgoing." This second criterion was mentioned by a number of the executives interviewed for this study.

Children's Education

Mr. Nakajima believed that approximately 10 percent of the married expatriates go abroad alone. If the children are over fifteen years of age, most of them (particularly boys) are left behind in Japan to be taken care of by their grandparents if the mother decides to join the husband. Mr. Nakajima lamented that the education system in Japan "is not very international at the moment. Once the children attend high schools overseas, they have a very big handicap in entering the famous universities in Japan." Since status in society is determined by the company to which one belongs, which depends on the university one attended, education is a paramount concern among most Japanese families.

Mr. Morita of Daicel indicated that although his company recognizes the problem, wives are encouraged to join the husbands because in many Western countries, "social activities are usually done as a couple. In order to conform to American society, we prefer the expatriates to go abroad with their families." He added that prolonged periods of separation of husband and wife are not healthy for the family or the company. He described the plight of a number of his friends who are "New York bachelors," married men who go abroad alone because of the problem of their children's education. His sentiment is shared by a number of the executives interviewed for this study. According to another New York–based Japanese executive, as many as 75 percent of his compatriots in New York could be dubbed New York bachelors. Mr. Nakaoka of Toray estimated that approximately 50 percent of their expatriates go abroad alone. Since 170 of their 220 expatriates serve in Indonesia, Malaysia, Thailand, Hong Kong, Republic of Korea, and Taiwan, most Japanese believe that the education systems in these countries are inferior. Hence, generally they do not bring their families along in the case of developing nations.

When asked if the Japanese companies intend to alleviate this situation given the pervasiveness of the problem, Mr. Nakajima indicated that Mitsui is asking the government to estabish special schools for Japanese children who have received portions of their education abroad. The company has been successful to a certain extent because of its political and financial clout. The company has contributed financially to such an effort. The country now has a few private schools that provide special programs for children of returned expatriates. At the beginning of such programs, the classes are conducted in English; however, Mr. Nakajima added that the children who attend these special schools are not treated on an equal footing with locally educated students. After a year at the special program, the student can transfer back to the regular school if he is capable, and only then if his performance is satisfactory would he have the chance to be admitted to an elite university. To alleviate the problem of prolonged separation of families, Mr. Morita indicated that his company will give these individuals all sorts of business excuses to visit Japan more frequently: "The company will say, 'since you have your family and relatives in Tokyo, why don't you go back to Japan on behalf of the company?'"

Training for Career Staff

In the case of Mitsui Bussan, the first three grades of employment in the company are devoted to training of a career staff. Each person stays for a given number of years at each grade before promotion to the position of assistant manager: three years in grade 1, four years in grade 2, and four and a half years in grade 3. In the initial eleven years of employment, promotion is based on seniority alone. Beyond the position of assistant manager, there are the levels of manager of a section, assistant general manager of a department, deputy general manager of a division, and general manager of a division. There is no prescribed number of years that the person must remain at each level because beyond the position of assistant manager, promotion is on the basis of merit or ability. Hence some people may never reach the level of general manager of a division.

There are two types of training programs for employees in Mitsui: according to rank and for special purposes.

Training According to Rank: The Career Development Program (CDP) is provided to employees from grades 1 through 3. The CDP was designed by the Personnel Division but is run by the various divisions. The CDP seeks to develop the technical skills of the career staff to enable them to perform their jobs effectively. Thus, it plays a crucial role in training and development. For grade 1 employees, there is an initial three-year training program, comprised of three components. First is a general orientation, which lasts ten days. To use Mitsui's terms, the college graduates enter as "raw materials" and are exposed to the company. In addition, the orientation is designed to facilitate their transition from the academic to the corporate world. The second is the mentor or "man-to-man leader system." In the first six months of the employee's career with Mitsui, he is assigned to a young staff member who has been with the company for four to five years who provides overall guidance. Third, given the nature of the business performed by Mitsui, the best training is provided on the job. On-the-job training is defined as "being assigned jobs and given responsibilities slightly beyond his capabilities and through accomplishment under superiors' guidance, capabilities are developed" (material provided by Mr. Nakajima). Virtually all Japanese companies place heavy emphasis on on-the-job training. According to Dr. Tokuyama, executive director and dean of the Nomura School of Advanced Management, "this tremendous accumulation of practical experiences [through on-the-job training] explains the surging success of Japanese companies in general."

During the first three years, the person acquires the fundamental knowledge required for conducting business in a *sogo shosha*. Besides on-the-job training, there are in-house lectures, provided in the second or third year of employment. Tests are administered to determine the person's technical knowledge of the business. The test in technical skills is administered in the second year of the career staff's employment with Mitsui. If he fails a certain subject, he can try again the following year.

Mitsui, like most other Japanese companies, emphasizes the importance of self-enlightenment or development. Since international business transactions are fundamental to the functions performed by a general trading company, language training is provided in the first three years. All the career staff are required to reach a certain level of proficiency in a given language. Mitsui provides in-house training facilities in two languages only, English and Chinese. The standard hours of instruction are approximately 100 hours. These are offered at various levels: introductory, intermediate, and advanced. Language training other than English and Chinese is covered under "training for special purposes." The language proficiency test is administered twice a year. Attendance at the English-language lectures is not compulsory, bu all trainees have to pass the proficiency test. The personnel division then collects the scores obtained on the tests and combines these with the data gathered on other aspects of the employee's performance, attitude and behavior to form a huge dossier on each individual. These detailed personnel inventories are used for selection and promotion.

Throughout the eleven years of the CDP, which covers grades 1 through 3, cross-functional rotation is practiced. Each career staff is required to have experience in at least two offices, two commodities, and two types of business (import or export, domestic or international business) during the initial eleven years. Most of this knowledge is acquired on the job. Other channels for learning these skills are self-development, guidance from the superior, and outside training. The company also sponsors in-house seminars on various technical aspects of doing business in a *sogo shosha*.

A person who is promoted to the position of manager attends a three-day intensive training program designed to help him understand the role of a manager, to learn to communicate with top management, and to sharpen his diagnostic and analytic capabilities by means of the Harvard Business School-type method. The three-day program is conducted primarily by people from within Mitsui. The seminars are also attended by other management personnel within Mitsui who share their views on corporate policy with the newly appointed managers. As of summer 1982, Mitsui Bussan was considering developing separate training programs for assistant managers, section managers, and divisional general managers. Besides in-house facilities, Mitsui has also sent one participant to the Nomura School of Advanced Management, which began operations in 1981.

Training for Special Purposes: These refer primarily to training for overseas assignments and special seminars for managers. The focus here is on the former. Mitsui offers two types of programs for overseas assignments, A and B. Under the type A program, some of the younger employees between the ages of twenty-five and thirty are selected to study at foreign universities. This is followed by one year of on-the-job training in an overseas branch. In the past thirty years, Mitsui has sent 550 employees to over thirty countries for type A training. The type A training is area specific and is designed to prepare the employee for eventual assignment to the region. In contrast, the type B program is viewed as part of the cross-functional rotation of employees. Under type B, the employee spends one year in an overseas office where he is engaged in the same product category as he would if he remained in Japan. Since 1963, Mitsui has sent 500 employees overseas for type B training. This category of training is commodity technology oriented rather than area specific as in the case of type A. Every year the company sends approximately 50 to 60 employees for overseas training. In recent years, since the company recruits approximately 170 new career staff annually, roughly 40 percent of the people sent overseas have the opportunity to go through either type of program. The 60 percent who are not given either program are provided simple seminars (one to two days) prior to departure, plus language training. The intensive language training program requires two to three months of full-time study. Besides English and Chinese, Mitsui's employees are trained in other foreign languages. In the case of German, Mitsui sends ten to fifteen employees to the Goethe Institute each year.

Under management training, Mitsui sends one or two employees every year to attend the MBA programs at the Sloan School of Management (MIT), Harvard, and INSEAD in France. In addition, the company sends one employee each year to the one-year program offered by the IIST. When asked why Mitsui does not use such facilities more, Mr. Nakajima noted that although the curriculum offered by IIST is "very good, the feeling of Mitsui and most other Japanese companies is that in order to be trained for an overseas assignment, it has to be conducted overseas. That is the main reason. Besides, for language training, most people prefer to be taught by Americans (in the case of English), rather than Japanese linguists. I think that attitude is the biggest reason."

Program for Wives: The wife generally joins her husband three months after his departure. During this time, Mitsui provides a compulsory one-day (optional three- to four-day) training to the spouse to brief her on such matters as grocery shopping, medical doctors, and so on in the foreign country. The wife is not given any kind of language training; however, if she wishes, Mitsui provides information on which institutes offer training. The company does not pay for such services.

In medium-sized companies like Daicel, there are no in-house language training facilities. Rather, the employees are sent to outside institutes. In addition, given the smaller number of expatriates in each of their overseas branches, the candidate is expected to be familiar with all aspects of the company's operations. For this purpose, the individual is sent to one of the company's six plants and research laboratories in Japan for training for three months. The trainee generally does not engage in production activities during this period but acts as an observer to acquire a better understanding of the company's business. During this period, the person also develops close working relationships with the plant employees, which is essential to his eventual duties overseas. In the words of Mr. Morita, "While abroad, his personal relationship with those who work in Japan is very important in order to do business efficiently and to communicate satisfactorily." Again, the emphasis is on the human relations aspects of doing business. Besides factory practicums, the company also sponsors overnight or two-week seminars on various aspects of the company's operations, put together by the engineering, sales, and finance people in the company. In addition, the company sends people to attend business schools abroad, although not on a systematic basis.

Toray similarly offers special field and language training programs to its expatriates prior to departure. The former is similar to the factory practicum offered by Daicel. The company does not provide in-house language training facilities. The candidates are sent to outside institutes for this purpose. Between 1960 and 1978, Toray sent two to three young employees to attend business schools in the United States annually. After 1978, because of recession in the industry, the company temporarily suspended the program but plans to resume it as soon as business picks up.

Evaluation of Performance

Mitsui's evaluation system is the same for both domestic and overseas employees. Mr. Nakajima acknowledged that there are problems as to who should do the evaluation in the case of expatriates. In Tokyo, the immediate supervisor performs the evaluation. However, if a person were assigned to a small operation overseas, the general manager may not know the individual's particular line of business since each person specializes in one or two commodities. When asked what the company plans to do, Mr. Nakajima indicated that they try to train and educate the general manager in this regard rather than reform the system itself. In his words, "We will maintain the system. The philosophy of evaluation is the same wherever one goes. For example, if a person works for a particular division, but is promoted to the position of general manager in one of the overseas offices, he does not know how to be a general manager. So we try to train him."

In the case of Toray, the evaluation is conducted twice a year by top management in the overseas office. There are apparently no problems here because the product lines of Toray are not as highly diversified as Mitsui's. In the case of Daicel, the evaluation is also conducted twice a year by the immediate supervisor in the overseas office and then forwarded to Tokyo. However, Mr. Morita indicated that the system is quite different abroad as compared to Tokyo: "Once abroad, the employee is treated differently because it is difficult to supervise his work from Japan. In New York, we are not directly engaged in sales and purchasing activities. So the basis for evaluation is neither annual sales nor the amount of profit. It is done on a very subjective basis."

Remuneration Policies

Mitsui has a special section, the overseas department within the personnel division, responsible for implementing remuneration policies. According to Mr. Nakajima, Mitsui's system "was modeled after that of U.S. multinationals." The remuneration policies of the five largest *sogo shosha* are fairly comparable. Premiums for hardship positions are paid for countries such as the Middle East and China. In the case of Africa, the premium is 50 percent for Mitsubishi Corporation. According to Mr. Iyobe of Mitsubishi, for example, the remuneration policy for Japanese expatriates in the United States are quite different because of the EEO guidelines. In his words: "It is very difficult for a Japanese expatriate to have a very large cost-of-living adjustment because we will be sued by local employees if there were big differences in terms of salary." When assigned to the United States, the person's salary is not translated from yen to a dollar equivalent. The wage received is determined by the standard of living in the country. For example, in the case of Beijing, China, where the premium paid by Mitsubishi is 25 percent, the latter is deposited in the employee's Japanese savings account. Besides the salary paid in the foreign country, the employee receives some compensation. Other than hardship premiums, Mitsubishi provides company housing and cars to their expatriates in certain countries. These are provided as "indispensables rather than a premium." In order to maintain the general manager's image and prestige as a representative of a large corporation in a foreign country, he is paid a premium.

Mr. Morita, who currently serves as president of the Japanese Chemical Manufacturers Association in New York, stated that every year the association conducts a survey among its member firms to compare remuneration systems. Although there are variations, in general all expatriates are paid the domestic salary "plus some kind of formula." When asked whether he, as general manager of the New York office, is paid a cost-of-living adjustment to provide him with a standard of living comparable to that of a general manager of a U.S. firm of equal size, he replied that the comparison is made with "other leading Japanese trading companies and manufacturers" and not U.S. corporations. This is not the case in some other companies. Mr. Morita added that "the size and profitability of the company do not necessarily affect the amount of salary paid" because the latter is primarily based on the cost-of-living adjustment index. He noted that although Japanese companies try to provide comparable salaries to their expatriates for positions in their U.S. operations, there are problems. For example, besides being a general manager, Mr. Morita is also a member of the board of directors of his company. "Besides, each person also has his own career, varying educational background, and contribution to the company. Therefore, it is fairly difficult to evaluate what the amount of salary should be."

Repatriation

Mr. Nakajima noted that overseas experience is considered a prerequisite for promotion to top management, although this sentiment may not necessarily be shared by some of the younger generation. He noted that there were instances where some expatriates felt that an international assignment hindered their career advancement because they "were promoted, but not to the highest positions."

In Mr. Morita's opinion, repatriation is increasingly more of a problem. This is the reason why "many employees refuse overseas assignments." There are, of course, other problems that compound to it, such as children's education and housing. Mr. Morita was asked how his company tries to encourage people to serve abroad given this reluctance. In response, he noted, "There are some people who like adventure and are curious to learn about things foreign. We intentionally select those people." In addition, most companies pay a premium for overseas assignment. For example, an engineer in the New York office was paid approximately $1,000 a month (250,000 yen) in Tokyo but earned $2,300 in New York.

In the case of Toray, in Mr. Nakaoka's opinion, overseas experience is considered a prerequisite for promotion to top management. Toray has twenty-five board members, and approximately 50 percent of them have overseas experiences. Consequently there is a real incentive for aspiring candidates to accept an overseas position. However, Mr. Nakaoka admitted that there were some individuals who felt that they were not treated fairly because of an overseas assignment. He attributed this to the victim's "consciousness and lack of information." He added that such fears were totally unfounded.

Success and Factors for Success

Mitsui's failure rate among expatriates is extremely low. According to Mr. Nakajima, "We always have 1,200 people overseas, and we rotate 200 to 300 people every year. I hear of three to five cases per year. These are the reported cases." He attributed the low failure rate to the system of evaluation in which supervisors tend to be more lenient in assessing the performance of expatriates in the first one to two years abroad. In Mr. Nakajima's words, "If I am the general manager in an overseas office, and I find that the individual is not as capable as I expected, but he can do some work (80 percent of the average person's work), if I am generous, I will not send him back to Japan. If he is sent home, it is not good for his future career. If he really cannot do the job (under 50 percent or so), he will be sent back. It is very costly to send a Japanese overseas." Since each of the overseas branches is operated as a profit center, if the individual cannot perform, such failure has to be reported.

Mr. Nakajima attributed the reasons for the few failures to two factors: problems of adjustment and language difficulties. If the expatriate is "sent over as an assistant manager, he has to control the local people. If he cannot communicate with the local people, he cannot do the job properly. So he is frustrated." Mr. Nakajima was asked whether the family situation might have any influence. He said that although he has heard of such incidences, they are extremely rare.

In the case of Daicel, the incidence of failure is below 5 percent. Mr. Morita said that although the family could sometimes pose a serious problem, such as the education of the children, expatriates tried to take care of such matters by leaving the children in Japan and bringing them to the United States only during summer vacations. He attributed the major reason for failure to culture shock. When asked whether the Japanese tend to cope with culture shock by building cultural enclaves, Mr. Morita replied in the affirmative. "I think that we Japanese have a tendency to get together, eat Japanese food, and play golf together. I don't think this is good behavior. As representatives of the company, we have to mix with the local people as much as possible. This is a weak point. The Japanese feel more comfortable if they are with their fellow countrymen. They always try to get together and organize a Japanese society in a foreign country." He recalled that in his student days, he deliberately chose a school that did not have many Japanese so that he could have more opportunities to interact with Americans and thus obtain a better understanding of their way of life. Mitsui appears to share the same philosophy by encouraging employees who are sent abroad to attend business schools in the United States to interact as much as possible with Americans. According to Atsushi Abe, a career staff at Mitsui who is currently enrolled at Stanford University, his company feels that by allowing the wife to accompany her husband during his study abroad, the former is more prone to "remain insular and resist becoming internationalized." There are, of course, debates within the company about the pros and cons of such a policy (Chase 1982, p. 1).

In the case of Toray, Mr. Nakaoka noted that the failure rate was under 1 percent. He indicated that most of the failures could be attributed to language problems. One expatriate could not perform because of poor physical health. Another had to be recalled because of "frictions with the local staff." When asked whether the family situation had any impact, he replied in the negative because, in his words, "Japanese wives are usually more submissive."

Changes

Although the failure rates at all three companies were low, the three men were asked, "If you had the complete freedom to redesign the company's human resource development program with regard to expatriate assignments, what changes would you make and why?" Mr. Nakajima believes that if there were psychometric devices to measure the person's ability to adjust to a foreign environment, he would want to use it. Although such devices are available in the North American context, these may be culture bound; hence, it may be difficult to apply them to Japan. In addition, people who are familiar with the nature and intent of the examination can fake responses. Although he felt that the company has made a "pretty good effort" with regard to language training, he noted that training in the technical aspects could be improved. As noted previously, only 40 percent of the expatriates have the opportunity to undergo either the type A or B programs. The balance are only exposed to a very brief orientation.

Mr. Nakaoka of Toray would like to improve the language training. At present, his company encourages self-development; employees take language training at outside institutes on a voluntary basis. He believes this system is inadequate and that Toray should provide systematized language training for all levels of career staff. He noted that although English is important, since most of Toray's expatriates are assigned to the developing or newly industrialized countries, the expatriates should learn the local languages. "By studying the native language, we could understand their ways of thinking, history, and standard of living." He believes that the training provided by Toray on the technical aspects of doing business is very comprehensive.

While noting the importance of language training, Mr. Morita of Daicel indicated that such training alone is insufficient to prepare the person for overseas work. Those who have a sufficient command of the foreign language may not necessarily be good businessmen. "They need to have a very aggressive, business mind." This explains why an increasing number of Japanese companies are assigning a lower priority to language skills as a criterion for selection in comparison to administrative skills and technical knowledge.

According to the findings of the Industrial Research Group, the most important criteria for selection for an overseas assignment, in descending order, are "administrative and managerial ability, technical knowledge, aggressive attitude to work, and language proficiency" (*Basic skills required of employees,* July–August 1978). Given this observation, Mr. Morita believed that companies should provide a balanced training in language and the technical aspects of doing business. He added that there are good outside institutes that can provide this kind of training since it is difficult for each company, particularly the small- to medium-sized ones, to have its own in-house facilities.

5 Japan's Financial Institutions

A distinguishing feature of the Japanese industrial scene is the high debt-equity ratio of its corporations. This has often been alleged in the West as giving Japanese firms an unfair corporate advantage over its U.S. and West European counterparts. For example, among a sample of 920 Japanese firms surveyed in 1981, debt as a percentage of total liability averaged 80.39 percent. This was substantially higher than that for U.S. companies (Kanabayashi 1982, p. 34). Given this phenomenon, financial institutions play a very important role in fueling the growth of the Japanese economy. This chapter examines the human resource development systems in two financial institutions, Nomura Securities Co., Ltd., the largest brokerage firm in Japan, and the Bank of Yokohama, a commercial bank.

Nomura Securities Co., Ltd.

The information here was obtained from several interviews with Yoshio Terasawa, chairman and CEO of Nomura Securities International, Inc., a wholly owned subsidiary of Nomura Securities Co., Ltd. Under the leadership of Mr. Terasawa, Nomura Securities International, Inc., became the first Japanese brokerage house to join the Boston Stock Exchange and the New York Stock Exchange *(Nomura Securities Co., Ltd., Annual report,* 1981). Mr. Terasawa is often described in the U.S. press as an "affable" Japanese who can work well with Americans and Japanese alike. When Sony became the first Japanese company to trade its shares publicly on the New York Stock Exchange, Akio Morita, chairman of Sony, Inc., lauded Mr. Terasawa as playing the "key role" in bringing about this historic event (Galante 1983, p. 34).

Overview

Nomura Securities Co., Ltd., was established in December 1925. The company currently has 104 branch offices and employs 8,386 people. In fiscal year ending 1981, the total value of customer assets held in its custody reached 13 trillion yen or $54.16 billion *(Nomura Securities Co., Ltd., Annual report*, 1981). In 1982, the revenue of Nomura Securities International, Inc., topped $20 million. Although this is small compared to the parent corporation's income, it has been expanding rapidly. In 1983, Nomura Securities, Inc., expects to increase its revenue to $30 million (Galante 1983, p. 34).

Recruiting

Nomura recruits primarily through the old boy network and recommendations by professors of business and economics. Every year, Nomura recruits between 200 and 300 college graduates and 100 to 150 high school graduates. Nomura is unique in this regard in that many of the other leading Japanese companies do not hire high school graduates as career staff. In the case of Nomura, Mr. Terasawa indicated that high school graduates who perform satisfactorily can be promoted to management positions. As in the United States, an undergraduate program in Japanese universities averages four years. If a college graduate and a high school graduate were to join the company at the same time, the former would always be four years ahead of the latter in terms of seniority.

Mr. Terasawa was asked whether there would be any difference in the rate of promotion between the college and high school graduates beyond the position of assistant manager. He replied in the negative. He indicated that in his company, some high school graduates have been promoted to a higher position than college graduates. He explained that while this is unique, it may stem from the nature of their business. Since Nomura is a brokerage firm, anyone who can generate high commissions for the company is highly regarded; however, he admitted, the "chances for a high school graduate to become the number one man, or president, are very minimal. He can be number 3 or 4, but not number 1." In most of the other large financial institutions, such as commercial banks, it is virtually impossible for a high school graduate to become a member of the board of directors. Mr. Terasawa explained that Nomura does not hire high school graduates from the big cities of Tokyo, Yokohama, Osaka, and Nagoya. Rather they are recruited from rural areas, such as Kyushu. The rationale behind this policy is that the Japanese believe that those who come from the rural communities may not be able to attend universities because of economic reasons, whereas those from the big cities who do not pursue a college education are "either very lazy or cannot go because of their poor academic performance." Mr. Terasawa contends that even if the high school graduates from the big cities are not financially well off, if they are ambitious and hard working, they could always "work and then go to college."

Staffing Policies

Nomura currently has 150 Japanese expatriates serving in its overseas offices worldwide and hires approximately 400 local nationals. About 85 percent of the latter are hired in clerical capacities; the remaining 15 percent occupy managerial positions. In the New York office, there are approximately 50 host country nationals.

The staffing policies of Nomura's overseas subsidiaries vary from one region of the world to the other. In Djakarta, Indonesia, the top position is occupied by a host country national in order to comply with the policies of the local government. Most developing countries permit foreign direct investment only if they fit in with national interests and priorities. In the case of Singapore, when Nomura first established its operation there, it could not do so on a wholly owned basis. There had to be equal or majority local equity participation in the initial phases. Consequently the top position was occupied by a Singaporean. After five or six years, when the government of Singapore became convinced "that the people from Nomura were all right and that they were not invaders, they allowed us to purchase other local interests." Currently only 2 percent of the equity of the Singapore operation is held by local nationals. In 1982, Nomura installed a Japanese as the president of the Singapore subsidiary.

When asked why Japanese multinationals tend to use parent country nationals more extensively than their U.S. and West European counterparts, Mr. Terasawa explained that there are several reasons. One is the problem of communication: "If there is an American executive who can read Japanese or Chinese characters as well as a Japanese, and can speak Japanese even though with a little bit of American accent (which I think is charming), we will start hiring Americans. Americans can go any place in the world without speaking the native language. They don't have to. But when we come to the United States, we have to learn English. Naturally, we speak Japanese at the head office. If we choose an American president in New York, it is perfectly okay if he doesn't understand Japanese in the United States; but when we hold the managers' meeting in Tokyo every year which is conducted in Japanese, he would not be able to participate." The Japanese are not unreasonable in this regard; most U.S. multinationals have similar requirements.

A second reason for the extensive use of parent country nationals could be attributed to differences in management practices. A distinguishing characteristic of Japanese firms is the policy of job rotation. Japanese companies, including Nomura, believe that by the time a person is promoted to the level of a director, "he must know a little bit of everything." In the United States, there is an emphasis on specialization. For example, if an American were to begin his career as a security analyst, even though he may eventually be promoted to the position of executive vice-president, he would usually be associated with the research end of the business. In Japan, by contrast, Mr. Terasawa explained, "If you are a security analyst, you also have to work as a salesman at one point as part of your career development. For example, I was a salesman. One day you may be a staff member of the personnel department. Another day, you may be the manager of a very small branch office in a rural community. On average, an individual experiences ten to fifteen different positions before he becomes a director. In Japan, we believe that it is necessary to give the person a total perspective on the business, rather than be too specialized in one field." Mr. Terasawa's assignment to New York is viewed as part of his career development. Consequently corporate headquarters can repatriate him to Tokyo "any time they wish. They can send another guy to head the New York office. Then I go home and may become the general manager in Osaka." Japanese companies can rotate Japanese nationals but not foreigners. For example, Nomura could not simply transfer an American president to head its branch office in Kyoto. If this were to occur, Mr. Terasawa is fairly confident that the American would leave the company. Although U.S. companies rotate American nationals from one region of the world to the other, they too do not generally transfer host country nationals. The chances that a Chinese manager hired in Hong Kong would be sent to head the London branch are virtually nil.

A third reason is that until recently, Japanese firms had difficulties in attracting highly qualified local nationals in the advanced nations to work for them. Mr. Terasawa recounted his experience on a discussion panel some ten years ago. A vice-president of Citibank posed the question, "In our Tokyo branch, we have 300 Japanese employees and only three Americans. How come the Bank of Tokyo in New York has 60 Japanese and 400 Americans? Why do you have so many Japanese?" Mr. Terasawa, the only Japanese on the panel, responded that Nomura's Hong Kong branch employed 200 Chinese and only 6 Japanese. "In other words, please do not compare Japanese with American style citing only one example because for Japanese business people, New York is considered a very advanced area. I am not with the Bank of Tokyo, but I presume that the Bank of Tokyo sends good candidates for future management positions to learn in New York for two to three years. The Bank of Tokyo does not send people to Hong Kong for two to three years for training purposes because there is not much to learn from Hong Kong. Similarly, American banks do not send their elite staff to Tokyo for training purposes because there is not much to learn. This is reason number one." Mr. Terasawa hypothesized that a second reason for the extensive use of parent country nationals by the Bank of Tokyo could be due to the "low quality of Americans who are hired as clerks—most of them have Spanish as their mother tongue and cannot speak good English. Citibank, on the other hand, is fortunate to recruit very well-educated, obedient, well-trained, and loyal Japanese. We do the same thing in Hong Kong—we have terrific Chinese people there. They speak English very well and they work very hard." Consequently, Mr. Terasawa noted, it is inappropriate to compare only New York with Tokyo. In the case of New York, London, and Paris, Nomura uses parent country nationals more extensively. But in cities such as Hong Kong and Seoul, Korea, where "the quality of labor is very high, we do not need to send that many Japanese there."

Mr. Terasawa believes that in order to internationalize, Japanese multinationals have to embark on a policy of localization. He would like to convert Nomura Securities International Inc. into a truly American institution. To attain this goal, the company is recruiting graduates from elite U.S. business schools who are then sent to Tokyo for six months' training where they are exposed to Japanese culture, the Japanese way of doing business, and Nomura's operations. He strongly believes that the CEO of the New York branch could be an American in a few years.

Overseas assignments for Japanese expatriates range from three to seven years; the individual is not informed in advance about the duration of his stay in a given country. Mr. Terasawa criticized this as a limitation in the existing system because the expatriates cannot plan for the future. "He may be here for seven years or he may be here for three years. It makes a big difference. He may have a mother and wife in Japan. They may plan to have a baby. If they are here for seven years, they may even plan to buy a house to save on taxes." Mr. Terasawa plans to change this by adopting a uniform policy of a five-year assignment, as practiced by Toyota Motors. An alternative approach would be to divide expatriates into two categories. One group, from the sales area, would stay for ten years to enable the individual to make more contributions to the overseas branch. These people will be interviewed and could consult with their spouse and parents about the assignment. The second category is for people from the personnel division who should be sent to the United States for two years to learn about new administrative procedures that are appropriate for Nomura. Mr. Terasawa noted that "major U.S. investment banking firms usually send Americans to Tokyo for two years and then recall them." Nomura currently does not have such a policy.

A Nomura employee cannot refuse an overseas assignment. Mr. Terasawa said, Nomura is "one of the most old-fashioned companies in Japan. We tell him that 'Today we had a board of directors meeting. You will be sent to New York.' That's it. That is the order. He says 'yes, sir,' goes home, tells his wife, and they start packing." The person has to be in New York in four weeks. The person cannot be excused for any reason. If an employee refuses an overseas assignment, he will either have to leave Nomura or be demoted." Mr. Terasawa notes that other Japanese companies are more lenient in this regard and consult the candidate. In the case of Nomura, an expatriate could not simply decide to return to Tokyo. If he does, he has to leave the company. Although he does not have the exact statistics, Mr. Terasawa believes that less than 1 percent of Nomura's employees leave the company for these reasons. The changing values among the younger generation may have some impact on Japanese organizations in the future in this regard. In the words of Tsueno Iyobe of the personnel development section at Mitsubishi Corporation, if an older person were asked to take an assignment in a hardship position, he would accept it "with pleasure. For the younger generation, they will say 'let me see.'"

Overseas experience is not considered a prerequisite for promotion to top management in Nomura. Mr. Terasawa explained that promotions are based entirely on the person's qualifications. Consequently a person who does not have overseas experience can become president. Conversely a person cannot "make himself president because he has lived in New York. It is entirely up to the person. If the person is suitable, he can become president regardless of his overseas experience." With the increasing internationalization of business, however, Mr. Terasawa, when asked whether it is important for the president to have an international perspective, noted that in the case of the general trading companies, "overseas experience is a prerequisite for promotion to the position of president. They must have lived at least four or five years in London or New York. In the case of commercial banks, more than half of the presidents have overseas experience, mainly New York. Usually, the president had been the general manager of the New York branch for two to four years. Other than that, it depends."

The percentage of income derived from international business is a critical factor here. In the case of Nomura Securities, the company currently earns 20 percent of its profits from overseas business, whereas Mitsui and Mitsubishi derive 60 to 70 percent of their income from international trade. In the case of many commercial banks, approximately half of their profits are derived from overseas operations. According to Mr. Terasawa, if Nomura begins to earn 30 percent of its profits from overseas business, "then the person who can speak English without an interpreter should be considered as one of the qualifications to be president of the company." He added that in five or ten years, Nomura's headquarters might be located in two cities, one in Tokyo and another in New York City. Since Nomura is in the service industry, the most important ingredients for success are "people and the most up-to-date and accurate information. As long as we have these, we can choose the most suitable place to do business. If that is not in Tokyo, we can go to London or New York." Consequently although the attitudes of the younger generation may be changing, the extremely competitive environment in Japan and the increasing internationalization of Japanese business are an incentive to serve abroad, even though it may mean temporary hardship and self-sacrifice.

Selection Criteria

A principal criterion that Nomura uses in selecting candidates for an overseas assignment is personality. Mr. Terasawa favors extroverts. In Nomura's experience, "99 percent of the time, those who are outgoing in Japan will be outgoing in New York." He believes that personality is more important that language facility. This is consistent with the findings of the Industrial Research Group that criteria such as "aggressive attitude to work; an ability to share the feelings of the local people" should take precedence over "language proficiency" (*Basic skills required of employees in international undertakings,* July–August 1978). In his opinion, the English-language capabilities of most Japanese are not as poor as many believe. If an individual can pass the aptitude test that is a prerequisite for entrance to the major Japanese companies, his language skills are "already quite good. It is a matter of practice. If one says English barrier, one thinks that he is so upset. He is upset because he was too good in Japan—he is a perfectionist. He used to be always number one in his class. It happens among students. Those who come to the Wharton School, for example, get so upset and sometimes become almost mentally ill and have to be sent back to Japan because they used to be top students in Japan. They expect to come to Wharton and become top students. When this expectation fails to materialize, they become upset. English language is terribly important, of course, but I now suggest to the personnel department that we should send people whose English is not necessarily perfect, but who have enough courage and are outgoing. We should not send people who are shy and always reserved, who have sad-looking faces and are not cheerful. I put more emphasis on one's personality and character. So I prefer people who are very healthy, charming, cheerful, likable, and aggressive. After all, we are stock brokers. Even if his English is not very good, in a matter of six months to one year of special tutoring in English, he will become proficient in the language." Consequently personality should take precedence over language capabilities for Nomura.

Because of the tough entrance examinations to Nomura, virtually anybody who is admitted to the company (putting language capabilities aside) is appropriate for an overseas assignment. Although a tour of duty overseas is considered part of one's career development, only 500 of the 4,000 career staff are selected to serve abroad.

Mr. Terasawa was asked whether the family situation is taken into consideration in the selection decision, such as the spouse's preference, education of children, and aged parents. Although the company does not explicitly take these into consideration, the personnel division has ample information on each employee. The personnel department in many Japanese companies uses computers for this purpose. Each employee's personal characteristics (such as habit, sports, when he got married, personality of his wife, and so on) are fed into the computer. When an overseas office needs two people with certain qualifications, the computer can provide a printout of suitable employees. Although Nomura does not use computers for this purpose, it does not generally make unreasonable assignments because of the close working relationships that exist between the superior and subordinate. In Mr. Terasawa's words, "People work very closely together and hence know each other. In Tokyo, we remain in the office beyond 5:00 P.M. After 7 o'clock, when three or five people [from a work section] are walking toward the subway, one will say 'It is very crowded at this time of the day. Why don't we have a nice, cold beer?' There are many bars, and after two or three glasses of beer and Scotch, at around 9, another person says 'I know of another nice bar which is not expensive.' They go. They talk and talk after work. So each person knows the other very well—they know what the other person's mother looks like, etc. It is very different in the United States.... In Tokyo, the boss knows your family situation. So the boss does not make any ridiculous decision. If I know you have a sick mother, I do not recommend you to the board of directors."

The company also takes into consideration special circumstances. For example, Nomura has an employee who married an American when he was studying language in the United States. The individual's supervisor told Mr. Terasawa that given the fact that this person's wife is American, "she may be happier living in the States because her parents are there, etc." So Mr. Terasawa assigned him to one of their U.S. branch offices.

Training

To prepare employees for overseas assignments, Nomura offers several kinds of training programs. The first category, initiated in 1961, involves sending employees to attend business schools abroad, primarily in the United States. Every year the company sends approximately ten people to study abroad. In the first five years, all the trainees were sent to U.S. schools, such as Harvard, Stanford, and Wharton. After that, Nomura also dispatched some people to England, France, Spain, and Canada. Currently the company also sends two employees to study in Beijing and one to Hong Kong. Those who are sent to France, Spain, Beijing, and Hong Kong attend language schools. In order to qualify under this program, they must fulfill the following three requirements: have an undergraduate degree, be male, and have at least two years of business experience with Nomura. The company pays for all the candidate's expenses plus his regular wages. The trainee may bring his wife along, but the company does not pay for the spouse's expenses.

In the case of Mr. Terasawa, after his graduation from Waseda University, an elite university in Japan, in 1954, he joined Nomura. He obtained a

Fulbright scholarship and attended a M.B.A. program at The Wharton School, University of Pennsylvania, from 1956 to 1957. This was an exceptional case, however. Mr. Terasawa was granted a leave of absence from the company and began his graduate education in the United States before the institutionalization of the study-abroad program at Nomura.

In the past, after the employee completed business school in the United States, he returned to Japan and worked for one year as a salesman in one of the company's branch offices where he was given on-the-job training. This one-year program served a two-fold purpose: it provided a testing ground to see how well the employee could perform in the field and provided apprenticeship training. This stems from the Japanese belief that certain management principles cannot be taught in the classroom setting. Rather, it must be learned on the job. In Mr. Terasawa's words, "This is one of the reasons why business schools do not exist in Japan. They do in the strict sense, but in Japan, people learn things on the job." While it is fairly common for the large multinationals to send some of their younger employees to pursue a M.B.A. program abroad, the more senior people in the company may not truly understand the purpose and functions performed by business schools. For example, according to Mr. Abe, who was sent by Mitsui Bussan to study business at Stanford, his colleagues congratulated him on being selected but asked him "What's an M.B.A.?" (Chase 1982, p. 1). While this might be an over-simplification in that most Japanese know what an M.B.A. stands for, it is true that senior management may not always know how to fully utilize the skills acquired by their younger staff from such programs. According to Dr. Jiro Tokuyama, executive director and dean of the Nomura School of Advanced Management, "Most of these executives do not know what their juniors have acquired in the two-year M.B.A. courses." Through the three-week program offered by the Nomura School of Advanced Management, the executives "begin to understand what (the younger employees) have learned, so they can more usefully utilize juniors who went through the M.B.A. courses."

Nomura has recently changed its policy of requiring those who have just completed a graduate degree in business administration to return immediately to Japan to work as a salesman for a year. The individual may now be assigned to one of the overseas operations or may be transferred to work in the international division of Nomura Securities in Tokyo.

A second category of training is an intensive three-month study program offered by the training department of Nomura Securities. Each of the one hundred branch managers nominates two employees; from these, thirty are selected to attend the three-month live-in program. They share the dormitory with Americans and British who are hired by Nomura for the purpose of aiding the Japanese trainees in improving their English-language skills and learning about foreign ways of life. The objective is similar to that of the IIST. The Japanese trainees must use English all the time. After the three-month program, they are sent overseas.

A third category of training was initiated in 1980 when Nomura began recruiting Japanese who have graduated from U.S. business schools. They are hired in Japan where they undergo training for one year and are then sent overseas. In Mr. Terasawa's opinion, in this third category, "there is no problem with the English language. Their problem is to learn the securities business." When asked how the third category of training differs from the first, Mr. Terasawa explained that the latter applies to Japanese born and raised in the country and have never studied or worked abroad before. These people join Nomura Securities immediately on graduation from a Japanese university. The third category is similar in many ways, except one: after graduation from a Japanese university, they work for another indigenous firm for two to three years and for whatever reason, they decide to pursue an advanced degree abroad on their own. After these individuals graduate, they desire to work for a Japanese firm. If they are capable, they will be hired by Nomura. Mr. Terasawa noted that "this is a revolutionary change" because in Japan, there is very little job hopping since the large companies do not hire people who have worked with other firms before. Under the third category, however, "We don't care whether they have worked with other companies before. If the person is very good, we hire him. We have hired between thirty to fifty people through this channel. They are very competent and they have some business experience other than at Nomura." People in this category are not recruited from competing brokerage firms; rather, all have business experience other than securities.

Besides in-house training, Nomura also sends employees to external agencies for language training. Every year, it sends one person to attend the IIST program and two to attend the Keio Business School in Tokyo.

The Nomura School of Advanced Management (part of the Nomura Group) was established in 1981. Every year, Nomura sends one of its senior management to attend this program. (The information on the Nomura School of Advanced Management is obtained from an interview with Jiro Tokuyama, executive director and dean of the school.) The Nomura School offers three courses annually. The first course is a three-week program in various aspects of management, including "internationalization, diversification, financial management, R&D management, and organizational theory." This is offered once a year in midsummer. In 1982, there were sixty-five participants including one representative from each of the top Japanese companies. The principal objective of the program is to develop the general management skills of the senior executives, with particular emphasis on strategy formulation, an area in which Japanese executives may be weak. The program is developed jointly with the Harvard Business School and uses the case method approach. The second course, of four weeks' duration, is the Wharton-Nomura portfolio money management program (cosponsored with The Wharton School). The third course in corporate financial management was introduced in fall 1983. When Dr. Tokuyama was asked why Japanese companies send senior executives to the Nomura School instead of the executive development programs at renowned universities abroad, he indicated that there were primarily two reasons. One is language: "Japanese is the sole language used in the classroom. We use interpreters for classes taught by English-speaking instructors. All the cases developed by the Harvard Business School are translated into Japanese accordingly." Two-thirds of the cases used are American or European, and the balance are Japanese company cases. In Tokuyama's words, "All the participants enthusiastically study the American and European company cases. When I asked them why, they say 'You never know when you will be assigned to be the head of the Japanese team of a joint venture.' How could they negotiate with American companies without knowing U.S. business strategy, skills and tools? Or they might be designated to manage their company's operations in New York, Los Angeles or Chicago one day. Who knows? One of our missions is to help them prepare psychologically for what they might encounter as Japanese expatriates at the new business sites." Given Japan's important international economic role and the rising number of joint ventures between Japanese and non-Japanese entities, many of the middle- and senior-management personnel of large Japanese multinationals could expect to have greater interactions with Americans and other foreign nationals in the future. Hence the information acquired through these case studies will be very useful later.

A second reason for using the facilities offered by the Nomura School of Advanced Management pertains to the duration of the program. Many of the executive programs offered abroad run for several months. For example, Harvard's Advanced Management Program (AMP) lasts for three months. Given time constraints, an executive could not afford to leave his job for such an extended period of time. According to Tokuyama, the Nomura School queried the personnel managers of several leading Japanese companies about the desired length of an executive program. "They all responded by saying that three weeks is an astonishingly lengthy period and having their senior management away from the office even for three days is hardly thinkable. So sending executives all the way to Boston for a long period of time is unrealistic in many Japanese companies."

Nomura does not provide any training for the spouses of expatriates. Mr. Terasawa noted that this is a limitation in their present system. He added, however, that "even though we may start to sponsor training programs for wives," it will most probably be some kind of environmental briefing. For example, "If the person is going to Indonesia, she should read this amount of literature on the history, the nature of the people over there, and that she should be careful with the maids there because they steal things, and so on."

Success and Reasons for Success

Mr. Terasawa indicated that less than 5 percent of Japanese expatriates at Nomura cannot perform abroad and have to be recalled back to Tokyo. He attributed the low failure rate to several factors. One is that the individual "endures and tries very hard." Besides the traditional sense of loyalty and commitment that the Japanese employee owes to his employer, in the case of Nomura, the individual could not refuse an overseas assignment or return to Japan without facing demotion or dismissal. This serves as a strong deterrent to poor performance abroad. Mr. Terasawa emphatically stated that an expatriate "has to endure. One feels rather uncomfortable in living in New York. So, there are two ways. If one can easily think of leaving his job, then of course he will say 'To hell with it, I will go back home.' Otherwise, one has to endure even though he finds it very hard to adjust to the life-style in New York." Less than 1 percent of the expatriates could not endure and had to leave the company. Of the remaining 99 percent, Mr. Terasawa estimated that approximately 10 percent of them "do not really enjoy living in New York, but still endure and try very hard to adjust to the foreign life-style."

A second reason for the low failure rate can be attributed to the overall quality of the career staff. Only the top graduates from universities are recruited into the major Japanese companies. Given the high quality of the recruits, Mr. Terasawa believes that disregarding language skills, virtually any of the 200 college graduates each year who join Nomura are suitable for a New York assignment.

A third reason for the low failure rate is that although Nomura does not systematically test the candidates for relational abilities prior to an overseas assignment, given the close working relationships in Japanese organizations, the supervisor has abundant information on the personality and family background of the individual. Hence, Nomura does not generally make wrong decisions in this regard.

A fourth reason for the low failure rate can be attributed to the longer time perspective adopted by Japanese multinationals with regard to the evaluation of performance. Mr. Terasawa normally allows the expatriate two years to adjust before he repatriates him: "I am being very patient. I will try to understand why he is not performing well here."

When asked whether the very few incidences of failure at Nomura could be attributed to culture shock, he responded that failure could be due to a combination of factors. "In some, it may be culture shock. In others, it may simply be due to chemistry—he doesn't like Americans and the latter don't like him." In Dr. Tokuyama's opinion, the younger generation in Japan are used to foreigners. "People know a lot about the United States through news media and many of them have experiences living in the United States as a student. Even personnel at the middle- and senior-management level are used to American surroundings during the Occupation. I don't know if it was true in cities like Tokyo and Yokohama, but I recall foreigners being either missionaries or English teachers at least in local towns in my young days. Now the population and variety of foreign residents have greatly increased." Consequently culture shock may not apply in the case of the United States but perhaps it does in Africa, Middle East, and Asia Pacific.

Mr. Terasawa was asked whether the family could have any influence on the expatriate's inability to perform overseas because it had been reported elsewhere that the wife of one of Nomura's employees in London committed suicide around 1981. Mr. Terasawa acknowledged that the story was true. But in general, he believes, Japanese wives are usually "more obedient and more dependent on their husbands. In my observation, she learns from her mother and grandmother that once she marries and the husband is sent to Djakarta, she should go with him and endure whatever hardship. That is her duty. If they get a divorce, it is not good for the children. We have divorces in Japan today, but they are fewer compared with the United States. Children are very important. I gather that an American wife who is sent to Tokyo gets frustrated and furious that nobody understands English and she does not want to learn Japanese because that is a language that is spoken only on a small island; so she always complains and complains and nags her husband; so they go back home. But the attitude of Japanese wives is different." Elizabeth Allan, assistant to Mr. Terasawa and a doctoral candidate in Japanese studies, added, "Japanese women perceive of their roles as wife and mother as jobs, not as emotional relationships. Of course, it is also an emotional relationship, but for her to go with her husband is to do her job well. So she is a failure if she cannot stand it. The American wife, on the other hand, thinks she has an independent life. The Japanese wife is not supposed to." Consequently the Japanese spouse has to endure whatever hardships may go along with her husband's career, but sometimes these may prove too much for her to bear.

Changes

Mr. Terasawa was asked to comment on changes he would like to make with regard to the human resource development system for expatriate assignments.

He believes that wives should be given more comprehensive training for living abroad. "Although I did say that they endure and they don't complain and they willingly or unwillingly do housekeeping, in a society like the United States, the wife plays a terribly important role in business. So it makes a lot of difference if Mr. Tanaka from Nomura has an obedient wife but does not speak a word of English, and there is Mr. Suzuki from our competitor, who has a wife that is obedient and who also speaks English fluently and makes friends easily with Americans. We will lose business, other things being equal."

A second change is to improve the language skills of the expatriates. In Mr. Terasawa's words, "We should seriously compel them to study English while in Tokyo. It is a waste of time if they come to New York and don't speak English, although they are very good businessmen. It is impossible to live in New York without a word of English."

A third area in which Mr. Terasawa hopes to see improvement is the availability of psychometric devices that could help determine whether a candidate has the appropriate chemistry to mingle with foreigners. He noted that although an employee may have an excellent command of the English language and is good looking, "He may not be successful. I don't know why. All I could say is that he does not have the chemistry which is acceptable to Americans."

A fourth area in which Mr. Terasawa hopes to see improvement is the problem of children's education. Mr. Terasawa is responsible for the thirty Japanese expatriates in New York, five each in Los Angeles and San Francisco, three in Honolulu, one each in Toronto and Sao Paulo, Brazil. Of these forty-five expatriates, approximately one-third have left their wives in Japan primarily because of their children's education and sometimes because of aged parents. "This poses a tremendous hardship. For example, I am very concerned about a few of our employees who live alone and who do not speak a word of English. They work like mad. So I always try to find some business excuse for them to visit Tokyo because it is too expensive if they have to pay their own way. I try to let them go home three or four times a year plus let their wives and children visit them in New York in the summer. I don't worry about single men." In September 1982 Mr. Terasawa joined the ranks of married expatriates who live abroad alone. His wife and their two youngest children have returned to Tokyo so that the latter could pursue an education back home. Their two older daughters are currently enrolled in private schools in New York (Galante 1983, p. 34). In Mr. Terasawa's words, "Language, reading, and writing must be acquired when they are young. It is the number one problem not only for Nomura, but for all other Japanese companies." When asked whether Japanese who are educated in elite universities in the United States are accepted by the well-established Japanese companies, Hiromichi Matsuka, deputy general manager of the Dai-Ichi Kangyo Bank Ltd., one of the largest commercial banks in Japan, noted that although it is "becoming easier as compared to ten or fifteen years ago, it is still a problem." While a number of the large Japanese corporations accept graduates from elite universities, such as Wharton and Harvard, they are still handicapped to a certain extent. "If they were employed, these would usually be assigned to positions in international business, regardless of the employee's preferences. So, their future is somewhat limited in that sense." Given the fact that a person's status in Japanese society is determined by one's position in a given organization, many Japanese are reluctant to place their children (particularly sons) at a distinct disadvantage by allowing them to be educated abroad. Given the increasing internationalization of Japanese business, it appears that the problem of children's education is one of the major issues that the Japanese government, business corporations, and society at large, have to address with some degree of urgency. Otherwise, it may result in a lot of unnecessary hardship for its people, and may have a negative impact on the expatriate's performance abroad.

Bank of Yokohama

The information on the Bank of Yokohama was obtained through an interview with Ken-Ichi Ozawa, general manager, planning section in the international department, and Susumu Yamada, deputy general manager of the same section. Mr. Ozawa previously worked for the personnel department of the bank.

Overview

The Bank of Yokohama, established in 1920, is the largest of the 63 regional banks in Japan. As defined by Japan's Ministry of Finance, a regional bank is one whose head office is housed in a provincial city and its principal area of operation is in the prefecture in which it is located. The provincial city here is Yokohama, one of the busiest seaports in the world. In terms of deposits, the Bank of Yokohama is almost on par with some city banks (brochure provided by Mr. Ozawa). In fiscal year ending 1980, the bank had assets over 4,470 billion yen ($18.625 billion) and deposits exceeding 3,722 billion yen ($15.51 billion). It has 167 domestic overseas offices and employs 7,198 people *(Bank of Yokohama: Annual report,* 1981). According to the *Nikkei Business* (May 17, 1982) survey of the most desirable companies to work for as perceived by graduates of elite Japanese universities, the Bank of Yokohama ranked sixty-third on the list of 225 companies, up from a position of seventy-second in 1981.

The Bank of Yokohama began its international operations in 1975 when it opened its first overseas branch office in London. Since then, it has established another overseas branch in New York and a wholly owned subsidiary in Hong Kong. Prior to 1975, the bank had only representative offices abroad. Today it still maintains representative offices in Singapore, Hong Kong, Mexico, Brussels, and Los Angeles. Currently there are some forty Japanese expatriates in its overseas operations. Over the past decade, the bank has sent sixty to seventy expatriates overseas.

Staffing

The senior management positions in most of the overseas operations are staffed by Japanese nationals, with the exception of London. The company employs two local nationals in senior management positions in the London branch. Since the bank began operations in New York only in 1979, all of the management positions are occupied by Japanese expatriates. This is in accordance with corporate policy that parent country nationals must be used in the start-up phase of an operation. The senior management positions in the representative offices are also staffed by Japanese. There are two expatriates in each of the representative offices. The head of the operation, similar to a CEO, is called the chief representative officer.

When asked why Japanese multinationals tend to use parent country nationals more extensively than their U.S. and West European counterparts, Mr. Ozawa pointed to several possible reasons. One, consistent with the observation made by many of the executives reported previously, is the problem of communication. Mr. Ozawa further noted that there could be "a psychological reluctance" among Japanese multinationals "to hire foreign people and let them into our management. I cannot say this for sure. Maybe we have such a psychological sentiment." When asked whether the psychological reluctance could stem from the differences in industrial systems between Japan and the West, he indicated that the systems of lifetime employment and seniority may be partially responsible. The Japanese style of management is followed in the bank's overseas branches, although bank tellers and clerks are not protected by the system of lifetime employment. The reluctance "may also come from racial traditions." Regardless of the reason for the general unwillingness to recruit foreigners, Mr. Ozawa admitted that "the fact remains that we are fairly reluctant to hire people from other countries." When asked whether this attitude will change in the future, Mr. Ozawa stated that it is already evolving. He noted the examples of other major corporations, such as the Bank of Tokyo, Mitsubishi Heavy Industries, and Nippon Steel, all of which are beginning to embark on a policy of localization, a trend motivated by two major forces: stipulations of local governments and the stage of evolution of Japanese multinationals. In order to make deeper inroads into foreign markets, the Japanese firms believe that it is imperative to localize their operations.

An officer at one of the leading banks in Japan explained that a reason for the extensive use of parent country nationals in Japanese financial institutions could be attributed to the fact that "most customers at our overseas branches and subsidiaries are Japanese firms." This applies to many Japanese banks. Hence, it is imperative to staff senior management positions with Japanese nationals so that they can relate to their major clientele.

Mr. Ozawa was asked to comment further on the two British nationals who have been hired as senior management personnel in their London branch. The first British national, Mr. Hill, was hired in 1973; he died in 1981. The second British national, Mr. Morgan, was hired to fill the position vacated by Mr. Hill. Mr. Morgan speaks only English and is a professional banker. Prior to joining the Bank of Yokohama, he was the general manager of the Westminster Bank. Although neither foreign national speaks Japanese, there have been no problems of communication because the English-language capabilities of the Japanese expatriates were high. Mr. Morgan serves in the capacity of an adviser, a common role relegated to foreign nationals recruited by Japanese multinationals. Given their understanding of the local culture and market, they are asked to provide market information to the Japanese corporations.

Language is not the only factor. Japanese employees are supposed to have an implicit understanding of corporate philosophy. Mr. Ozawa acknowledged that the bank did encounter some problems in this regard in the initial years of operation. After two years, however, the British national became quite familiar with the Japanese system. He was sent to Japan for two weeks to meet with top management in corporate headquarters and executives of Japanese subsidiaries of British-based firms. After staying in Japan for two weeks, he returned to London. Mr. Hill had visited Tokyo five times over the course of his career with the Bank of Yokohama. In Mr. Ozawa's words, "During that time, he learned. He was very smart, and at that time he was the expert in Japanese banking."

Selection

Mr. Ozawa explained that his bank exercises extreme caution in selecting employees for overseas assignments. In order to understand the selection process, he contends that it is imperative to delve into the evaluation system in the company.

The evaluation system is comprised of two major components: an interview and a written evaluation on standard forms. Both are conducted annually. The standard form is five pages long. The evaluation is done by three interviewers and the general manager. There are four columns, one for each assessor. The interview is conducted on a one-to-one basis. The first interviewer has only a few subordinates. The second interviewer is in charge of three or four sections and hence must make some adjustments to the score in the light of the evaluations for other sections. The most senior evaluator generally acts as a rubber stamp and gives his seal of approval after reviewing the evaluation sheet. The evaluation form provides information on the employee's personal and educational background and work experience. The four evaluators are asked to provide an overall assessment of the quality and quantity of work performed by the individual and comment on his general attitude toward work. The employee is then asked to provide a self-evaluation of the goals he attained over the past year and outline his aspirations and objectives for the following year. The interviewers then designate the positions they feel are most appropriate for the employee, providing reasons for their choices. Based on this information, the company gets some indication of the kinds of jobs the person would like to undertake. In Mr. Ozawa's opinion, the company tries to fulfill their aspirations as far as possible. The employee is then asked to describe his plans for self-enlightenment—how he proposes to develop his capabilities to the fullest. Each employee identifies the subjects he would like to study and whether he would like to attend graduate school abroad. Each evaluator finally provides an overall score based on an assessment of the employee's technical knowledge, his ability to implement organizational goals, and his general contribution to the firm.

The evaluation is divided into two parts: ability and performance. "We place a weight of 60 percent on ability and 40 percent on performance," said Mr. Ozawa. Knowledge of fundamental business principles and special skills is assigned a very low weight (approximately 10 percent) when evaluating the person's ability or performance. Based on these overall assessments, the evaluators are asked to recommend whether the person should be promoted. The evaluators are also asked to assess the employee on 110 personality traits, including aggressiveness, consideration of others, physical appearance (including an item on whether the individual is "bony" or "skinny"), sincerity, support for his superiors, participation in decision making and management, oral and written abilities, cooperative spirit, optimistic or pessimistic, docility, whether he is "fork-tongued," and so on.

This elaborate evaluation procedure is rather common among Japanese firms. In the case of Kobe Steel, Inc., ninety-eight observers are asked to assess each prospective candidate for overseas assignments on twenty-six criteria, including overall knowledge and perspective, ability to plan and develop, insight, ability to understand orders, and enthusiasm toward work (Yamanoue, 1982).

The annual interview for each employee at the Bank of Yokohama runs between forty-five and sixty minutes. All 7,500 employees are interviewed and assessed in this manner. Mr. Yamada explained that the company is willing to spend so much time and effort on the evaluation process because "that is the one chance for the employee." Of the 7,500 employees, half are male and the remaining half are female. Mr. Ozawa noted that while "we do not discriminate, we eventually place a greater emphasis on males." Mr. Ozawa stressed that under the lifetime employment system, the personnel department accumulates detailed information on each employee. Although all of these data are fed into a computer, each personnel officer "actually knows the person assigned to him. This is one of the greatest characteristics of Japanese personnel management. Personnel managers know each employee very well." Mr. Ozawa illustrated his point by citing the vital statistics on Mr. Yamada—"where he graduated from, how many years he spent in each status, what his performance was, his ability, and how many children he has (a boy and a girl). I know his career aspirations. His English is very good and he graduated from The Wharton School. He is very good as an economist right now."

Based on this detailed information that has been collected over a long period of time, the company selects those whom it believes are most suitable for an overseas position. In Mr. Ozawa's words, "The period of selection is very long—twenty-five or thirty years." When asked when an employee could expect his first overseas assignment, Mr. Ozawa replied that it varies. Under the system of lifetime employment, promotion is not based entirely on seniority but also on ability and performance. A general manager is generally selected from grade 10 (in Japanese organizations, employees are divided into various grades, number 1 being the lowest). The deputy general managers are selected from the four grades below grade 10. Mr. Ozawa explained that the company has to be careful in its assignments because "if we put the people from the same grade in the same branch, they may feel some sense of hostility because they compete with each other." Consequently, besides overall ability, seniority has to be taken into consideration in overseas assignments.

The duration of an overseas assignment is three to four years on average. The Bank of Yokohama has no fixed policy on how long the expatriate should remain in Japan before his next overseas assignment because its international business has been expanding very rapidly, particularly in the past six years. In 1982, for example, the bank had over $4 billion of its total assets invested in international business. In 1979, it was only $500 million. This rapid expansion, coupled with the company's policy of using parent country nationals in the start-up phase of the operation, implies a heavy demand for people who can perform effectively overseas.

When asked whether overseas experience is a prerequisite for promotion to top management positions, Mr. Ozawa's reply—"Maybe, but not yet"—is understandable because the company's international operations began only in 1975. In the case of Dai-Ichi Kangyo Bank, the president was formerly the general manager of the firm's New York branch. According to Hiromichi Matsuka, deputy general manager of Dai-Ichi Kangyo Bank, the former president of the company also had "long experience in international business. To become the top management of commercial banks, international experience is becoming an important factor." In the words of an officer of another leading Japanese bank, although overseas experience "is not necessarily considered as a prerequisite for promotion to top management, it is very important." Mr. Ozawa added that most people in his company believe that henceforth "international business will increasingly be more important."

Training

The company provides different types of training programs for all employees. In order to understand the various kinds of training programs, Mr. Ozawa believes that it is necessary to understand the personnel structure within the Bank of Yokohama, which is the same for most other large Japanese organizations. There are essentially two categories within the personnel structure: status and position. There are ten statuses or grades within the organization, with a high correlation between age and status. For example, high school graduates start at grade 1. They remain at that level for four years. They are promoted to grade 2 where they remain for three years and then spend another two years in grade 3, and so on. College graduates begin at level 2. The employee first works as a bank teller and is subsequently rotated through the various functional sections of marketing, finance, accounting, and so on. The number of years a person spends at each status is not fixed, but the higher the level of performance and the greater the capabilities of the person, the faster the rate of promotion. In Mr. Ozawa's words, if the career staff is "inferior in certain aspects, he must stay longer in each status."

Position, on the other hand, refers to the title given the individual, such as general manager. In the first ten years of employment, the employee generally does not have a title; he is simply referred to as a clerk. After ten years, the college graduate will receive his first position, such as assistant manager. When he is titled, he is referred to as an officer. The level above that is section manager. It generally takes a minimum of twenty years for promotion from entry level to the position of general manager.

Like Nomura Securities, the Bank of Yokohama hires high school graduates. Every year, the company recruits approximately 150 new employees, 20 to 30 of them high school graduates. There is no discrimination between high school and college graduates until middle-management positions. Beyond that, promotion for high school graduates becomes very difficult. When asked whether a high school graduate could take evening courses at the university so that when he eventually graduates, he could also be considered a university graduate, Mr. Ozawa said "no." Mr. Yamada explained, "It is very difficult to get a degree at night when the person is working in the daytime." This explains to a large extent why most Japanese place such a high premium on the acquisition of a college degree from an elite university; a person's status and position in life are determined solely by this factor.

The career development program at the Bank of Yokohama is organized according to this dual structure. There is a training program for each status. These training programs are divided into three categories: practical business knowledge, specialized knowledge (in this case, English), and overseas training and *shukko*. The last refers to an assignment outside of one's company to acquire special skills.

Under the practical business knowledge program, some courses are taught in a group setting, and others are acquired through self-education, correspondence, or evening courses. According to research reported by Harrari and Zeira (1978), "changing human behavior is most effective through group learning." The employees learn on the job and through books. The employees are supplied books, which they study at home. The functional knowledge in the banking field is divided into nine subjects: bookkeeping, general affairs, cash management, teller duties (such as window reception, handling deposits and withdrawals), loans, handling remittances and transfers, foreign exchange, and customer service. The company expects every employee to attain a certain level of competence in each of these subjects. The practical business knowledge courses are taught at four levels, rank 1 being the most elementary. Written examinations are administered for each subject at each rank. These tests are held annually. A person who fails a subject must repeat the entire program for the full year.

The employee is also given training in fundamental knowledge. These include subjects in economics, monetary policies, banking laws, legal affairs, tax laws, and corporate finance. The trainees acquire such fundamental knowledge through newspapers, magazines, books, and self-education. The employees are also examined on each of the subject areas. All employees have to master both practical and fundamental knowledge within seven years.

The second category of training program is specialized knowledge (foreign language, computers, and so on). Not all employees undergo this specialized knowledge program because participation is voluntary. The foreign language training is offered at four levels. At level 1, the employee is expected to master the skills of carrying out simple everyday conversation and writing simple letters. At the end of level 1 training, the employee takes the third-grade certified English examination. Under level 2, the employee is expected to write elementary reports using material from newspapers and magazines. At the end of level 2 training, the employee takes the second-grade certified English examination. Under level 3, the person should acquire greater fluency in expressing himself in both a social and business context. After completion of level 3 training, the person takes the first-grade certified English examination. Under level 4, the person should have no problem in conversing in a foreign language.

Mr. Ozawa was asked to comment on the various language training programs given expatriates prior to overseas assignment. The employee may use the language laboratory facilities in house. Every year the company sends several young employees to study English at an outside agency on a full-time basis for six months prior to departure. Every year it also sends six employees to attend M.B.A. programs in the United States. In addition, two employees are sent to attend executive development programs for middle-management personnel. Several employees are sent to study Chinese in

Taiwan annually. The senior-ranking officers who are assigned abroad are given private tutoring in English for three months. The company pays the expenses for these various types of training programs, in addition to the person's regular wages.

Two other kinds of programs are offered under the overseas training and *shukko* category. In *shukko* several employees are sent to attend training programs sponsored by their foreign correspondent banks for several months. In overseas training, a number of employees are sent to learn about international banking operations in one of the company's overseas offices for a year.

Besides these programs, the bank had previously sent several employees to attend the IIST program.

The company does not provide any training for the spouses of expatriates but offers them information about external agencies that sponsor such programs.

Success and Reasons for Success

Mr. Ozawa indicated that the failure rate for the Bank of Yokohama is below 1 percent. He attributed this to several factors. First is rigorous selection. The personnel evaluation system in the company is very comprehensive. Furthermore, employees are asked to describe their career aspirations. Consequently, only those who are bright, positive, and supposedly adaptive to foreign cultures are selected. A second factor can be attributed to the "close communication and mutual support among employees at each overseas office." Given the strong tradition of groupism, the Japanese who live abroad are very cohesive and provide mutual moral and material support. Third, in the words of Mr. Ozawa, "The International Department and Personnel Department always give mental and financial support to employees overseas." Thus, expatriates can rest assured that they will not be forgotten or passed up for promotion within the ranks of organizational hierarchy back in corporate headquarters. This reduces the amount of tension and stress that the expatriate may experience otherwise.

Both Mr. Ozawa and Mr. Yamada were asked how the Japanese try to cope with culture shock in foreign countries. Mr. Yamada believes that "most Japanese try to isolate themselves—they eat Japanese food, they speak Japanese in the office and family. So they are really not open to the American way of life. They see how Americans live, but they retain their own way of life. That can be a problem in the sense that they don't become localized." Mr. Ozawa hypothesizes that the reason why the Japanese may be able to cope with culture shock is that "psychologically, the Japanese have some sense of homogeneity as a nation. We know that we could always go back. At the same time, we respect the culture of European countries. That means that we observe the culture of the advanced countries. That is one of the reasons why we send our people to the United States to study. At the same time, we may have some kind of superiority complex with respect to the less developed countries. Even if we encounter problems when we are abroad, we think that someday we can go back home and we can meet with our own people." Mr. Yamada continued in this regard, "We know that we will be abroad for only several years, so we don't have any friction within ourselves."

Remuneration

In addition to the person's regular wage, the Bank of Yokohama pays a cost-of-living adjustment to the expatriate in local currency. This includes a portion of the rent on housing, purchase of furniture, family education, medical care, and so on. A percentage of the expatriate's base salary and the full amount of bonuses for the months of June and December are deposited in yen in the employee's savings account in Japan.

Changes

Mr. Ozawa was asked if he were given freedom to redesign the human resource development program with regard to selection and training for expatriate assignments, what kinds of changes he would make and why. He indicated that on the whole he is "satisfied with the present system." Some of the possible changes he would like to implement include embarking on a policy of localization, placing greater emphasis on the criteria of language and knowledge of foreign country in the selection of expatriates, and sending more people to attend M.B.A. programs in business schools abroad. Thus, although the priority assigned to language proficiency as a criterion for selection has declined relative to administrative and technical skills and certain personality traits, language is still important to successful performance overseas. It serves as a means to attain a desired goal: effective performance in a foreign country.

6

Manufacturers of Electrical Machinery

Over the past two decades, Japanese-manufactured electrical and electronic items have captured significant shares of the North American market. In television, transistor radios, and, more recently, videotape recorders (VTRs), the name *Sony* is a symbol of excellence and quality. In 1981 Sony had an 18 percent of the VTR market in the United States. This share decreased to 14 percent in 1982 because of tough competition. (Kanabayashi 1983, p. 33). In the field of 35mm cameras in the United States, the market share is largely in the hands of four Japanese camera manufacturers: Canon, Minolta, Nippon Nogaku (Nikon), and Olympus Optical. Canon alone accounts for nearly 40 percent of the total 35mm camera market share in the United States (*Business Week,* September 6, 1982, p. 61).

Although the success of Japanese manufacturers could largely be attributed to the quality of their products, which are highly suitable to the needs of U.S. consumers, the fervor and zeal with which the Japanese manufacturers have embarked on their marketing campaigns to capture the North American market are responsible in no small way for their astounding performance. The fervor characteristic of most employees of Japanese manufacturers is carefully nurtured through human resource development programs. As stated in Sony's corporate philosophy, a vital force behind the Sony spirit stems from its personnel, which is "to respect and foster each one's abilities—the right person in the right position—always striving to bring out the best in the person, believing in each one and constantly allowing the individual to develop his or her abilities" (*This Is Sony,* 1982, p. 1). Here we examine the human resource development programs at two of the leading Japanese manufacturers of electrical machinery and appliances.

Sony

The information on Sony Corporation is obtained through interviews with Nakao (Tom) Tawara, manager, Compensation, Sony Corporation of America, a wholly owned subsidiary of Sony Corporation, and Cnisato Uematsu, personnel manager of Olivetti Corporation of Japan. Mr. Uematsu previously worked for Sony Corporation in Japan.

Overview

Sony Corporation was established in May 1946 by Masaru Ibuka and Akio Morita, who now serves as chairman of the company, with paid-in capital of 190,000 yen ($785). From this humble beginning shortly after the war, the company has flourished. In 1972, domestic sales were almost on par with income from overseas sources. In 1973 domestic sales exceeded that of overseas revenues. Since then the company's net sales from overseas operations have expanded at a much faster rate than its domestic revenues. In 1981, Sony's overseas net sales amounted to 744.775 billion yen ($3.416 billion), compared to domestic sales of 306.266 billion yen ($1.404 billion), a 2.43-fold differential. In 1981, net sales in the United States alone accounted for 27 percent of the corporation's total sales (*Sony: Annual report,* 1981; *Sony Corporation: Consolidated financial summary,* 1981). In late 1982 and early 1983, the consolidated profits of the company took a 66 percent fall; however, some analysts believe that the company's earnings will regain much of its earlier strength gradually (Kanabayashi 1983, p. 33).

Most of Sony's operations overseas are on a wholly owned basis, although it sometimes enters into fifty-fifty joint venture arrangements with overseas distributors.

Staffing Policies

The Sony group employs over 60,000 people, including 10,000 employees in its overseas operations. Of the latter, 400 are Japanese expatriates. Japanese manufacturing concerns use local nationals more extensively in their foreign operations than do general trading companies. Sony Corporation of America (the company's largest overseas subsidiary), however, had an American who was installed as president in the early 1970s but was replaced by a Japanese national, Kenji Tamiya, in late 1981. Mr. Tamiya has worked with Sony for the past twenty years, fourteen of them in the United States. Although the question of why top management in the United States was returned into the hands of Japanese nationals was considered a sensitive issue, several people were able to shed some light on it.

Mr. Tawara explained that before going into some of the reasons for the reversal, it is important to understand the general evolution of Sony's operations overseas. The year 1982 marked the company's twenty-second year of operation abroad. These twenty-two years could be divided into three phases. In the initial decade, the start-up phase, Japanese nationals had to be used. The second decade (the 1970s), could be viewed as the "experimental stage where we witnessed the transition from Japanese to American management." Consequently an American president was installed as head of

Sony America, and most of the positions at the vice-presidential level were occupied by Americans. This situation persisted for six or seven years. In the words of Mr. Tawara, "Because of the sudden transition from Japanese to Americans, there were some problems, especially in terms of communication. Some of the employees who stayed during that period experienced the sudden change from one side to the other. This created some problems." There were also external problems between Sony America and Sony Tokyo. In the 1980s, the company has embarked on its third phase whereby Sony is "experimenting with mixing the two types of managers or creating a new system."

Mr. Tawara was asked whether the problems experienced in the second phase could be attributed to differences in objectives between Americans and Japanese. In general, U.S. corporations appear to be more short term oriented and demonstrate a greater concern for immediate profitability and return on investments, whereas Japanese firms are more preoccupied with growth and market share, both of which take years to develop. Mr. Tawara replied that in general there appears to be such a trend; however, he added, "This is not an individual difference but is based on societal differences. Most U.S. companies evaluate the person on a short-term basis, and the company itself is also evaluated on the basis of short-term earnings—quarterly, semi-annually, with the longest being a year. The stock market analyst, in particular, evaluates the quarterly performance of the company. When we enter into a new business, it takes years. This creates problems because the management has to be responsible for quarterly earnings. So they have to be short-sighted. I don't blame the individuals, but the society has such kind of a mechanism." On an individual basis, Mr. Tawara added that the senior vice-president of human resources at Sony America, Mr. John Stern, may have a longer-term orientation than himself.

In the opinion of another Japanese executive who is knowledgeable about Sony, there are two primary reasons for the reappointment of a Japanese to the position of president in Sony Corporation of America: differences in time perspectives between Americans and Japanese and differences in attitude. He noted, "Even for middle-management positions, Americans lack the love for the products of the company. I heard, but have not verified, that this is the main reason. For example, a Japanese is very enthusiastic about Sony products. An American in the United States is not very enthusiastic." This is an important difference. Due to the strong tradition of groupism in Japanese society, a Japanese associates very closely with his company. Although individual achievements are important, the overall accomplishments of the company or group are considered paramount and take precedence over individual goals. Consequently an employee identifies himself closely with the company's products and exhibits a genuine pride in them. This attitude explains the fervor the Japanese demonstrate in marketing their products, both at home and abroad, and accounts in large part for the competitiveness of Japanese manufacturers in overseas market.

When asked to elaborate on the external problems between Sony America and Sony Tokyo, Mr. Tawara again attributed these to societal or environmental differences. He explained that all industrial and management practices are developed within the milieu of the cultural environment of a given society. Since the company derives approximately three-quarters of its sales from its overseas operations, Tokyo is largely dependent on its subsidiaries. As such, "The Japanese have to change their way of thinking. We cannot change other people to accept our way of thinking. Both sides have to accommodate each other and find a happy medium. That is the target of the third stage of our business." Another officer at Sony concurred that a major problem between Sony America and Sony Tokyo was the differences in philosophy: "If we see a gap, it was a difference in philosophy between the Japanese and American styles of management. In those days, Sony's management style was too-much Japanese style and not too international." Consequently, to avoid possible tensions and frictions in the future, the company has decided to adopt a combination of American and Japanese styles.

When asked to identify some of the external problems that existed between Sony American and Sony Tokyo, Mr. Tawara indicated that, in his opinion, it was a problem of communication: "This was not merely the language spoken by either side, but rather a more fundamental misunderstanding of why and how each decision was made." Mr. Uematsu concurred that this was a major problem. The differences in attitudes and expectations between Japanese and Americans can lead to operational problems. To circumvent this difficulty, Matsushita (the manufacturer of items bearing the Panasonic brand name), which has over twenty years of experience in the United States, has established two separate personnel departments in its U.S. operation: one to manage its two thousand American nationals and the other to oversee the one hundred Japanese expatriates (Matsuno and Stoever 1982, p. 48).

In line with Sony's guiding philosophy to put "the right person in the right position," another officer at Sony Corporation contended that he did not believe that there was a deliberate attempt to replace the American president with a Janapese national. He indicated that when Mr. Morita "tried to find a suitable American as a successor, he could not locate one. Rather, it was easier to have a Japanese." Since Mr. Tamiya has extensive experience in the United States, he appeared to be a "very suitable person for the position." When Mr. Tawara was asked whether an American will be appointed as president in the foreseeable future, he replied that it "depends on the situation. We can't predict. The target for the third phase is some hybrid system." The candidates for the position of president could be selected from one of four major categories in the future: Japanese from Sony

America, Japanese from corporate headquarters, Americans in Sony America, and Americans from other companies. He added that Sony America has "no intention of sticking to one type of person. So every time there is an opening, we try to give equal opportunity to these four categories of candidates." This is in line with Sony's philosophy to appoint the best person for the position.

With regard to the staffing of senior management positions other than that of president of Sony Corporation of America, Mr. Tawara indicated that the majority of these were occupied by Americans. Sony Corporation of America (as distinguished from Sony Corporation in Japan, the parent company) has ten operating companies, six of them headed by Americans, none of whom speak Japanese. In addition, there are fifteen corporate vice-presidents, ten of whom are Americans and the remaining Japanese. Of the over 200 individuals who assume the position of managers in the operating companies, two-thirds are Americans and one-third are Japanese. Further down the organizational hierarchy, less than 10 percent of the positions at the middle- and lower-management levels are staffed by Japanese. There are only 170 Japanese expatriates in the United States, 50 of whom are associated with the manufacturing plants. These serve in the capacity of troubleshooters. Hence their durations of stay in the United States are short.

Sony's staffing policy varies from one region of the world to the other. In the developing nations, all top management positions are occupied by Jananese. In the industrialized nations, many senior management positions are occupied by local nationals. For example, host country nationals were appointed to top management positions in West Germany in 1975, the United Kingdom in 1977, and France in 1978; these subsidiaries are still headed by local nationals. An officer from Sony Corporation acknowledged advantages to the use of host country nationals: "Our sales improved and better local people joined us after we appointed local management." He conceded, however, that sometimes there are problems of communication between foreign nationals and corporate headquarters.

Mr. Uematsu hypothesized that there are other reasons for the extensive use of parent country nationals in the case of Japanese multinationals, in general (these may not apply to Sony). Besides possible problems of communication, Japanese firms have encountered serious difficulties in recruiting "good local talent." His reference was not to the educational levels of local nationals but to the emphasis placed on human relational skills in Jananese industrial society. Mr. Uematsu believes that "it is difficult for non-Japanese to have close relationships with external entities. In Japan, senior-management personnel have close relationships with officers in the government and competitive companies. So in that sense we place more emphasis on external relationships. Without such external relationships, they cannot perform their functions satisfactorily. We are not sure who would have such abilities in foreign countries. We are not sure how we could recruit such people. In that sense, we take the easy way" by using parent country nationals.

Mr. Tawara similarly noted that in recruiting local nationals for senior management positions, a principal criterion is not technical competence. Rather, "as a manager, the most critical factor is that his approach to management should coincide with Sony's concept and philosophy. We are looking for that type of person." For this reason, the company does not hire many M.B.A. graduates—only three to five out of the 200 to 300 applicants every year.

Some other Japanese firms, however, encounter problems in recruiting local nationals. In the case of the Bank of Tokyo, Mr. Terasawa of Nomura Securities International Inc. hypothesized that many of the clerical staff hired locally could hardly speak English. In the case of the smaller Japanese companies, there may be difficulties in attracting competent local nationals to work for them. Besides size of operations, the economic success of Japanese firms have gained the attention of the American public only fairly recently. Hence, until the recent past, there was a general reluctance among Americans to work for Japanese firms.

Mr. Tawara was asked whether there could be problems of credibility in using host country nationals. Mr. Nakajima of Mitsui Bussan, for example, observed that the Mitsui finance staff did not give serious consideration to proposals brought up by the British national hired by their London branch office. Mr. Tawara said that he had heard of another incident to the contrary. A Japanese-born professor in the United States "conducted an experiment several years ago. He sent a telex from New York to Tokyo by the name of an American using Japanese, and a similar telex by a Japanese using English. Next day, the American got the reply. The Japanese received the reply a week later. In this case, it depended on what language was used."

Mr. Tawara indicated that it is difficult to generalize from isolated incidences. He noted, however, that even among the Japanese themselves, "sometimes we have difficulty in talking to the new employees." This stems from the unique characteristics of the Japanese management system where control mechanisms are often implicit and where employees are expected to have an implicit understanding of corporate philosophy (Pascale and Athos 1981). Because of this distinguishing characteristic, Japanese firms invariably prefer to recruit graduates from college directly as "raw material," to borrow Mitsui's terminology, so that they can be molded to conform to the philosophy and objectives specific to each corporation. This sentiment explains the emphasis placed on human resource development programs in Japanese organizations because they serve as a principal vehicle for attaining organizational goals.

Mr. Tawara further noted that the size of the company is an important consideration in terms of communication. In large companies with annual sales of $5 billion or more and employing 30,000 to 40,000 people, an employee generally needs a number of years before he "knows exactly what the company is, where the company is heading, and what the corporate philosophy is. After they know, we can communicate. It is the same for everybody. For foreigners, more time will be needed. It may take a more extended period instead of a couple of years. We have to invest more time in order to get results. We try to hire students and teach them about the company's operations. After five or seven years, we can have better communication." Given this longer time perspective and the even lengthier period it takes non-Japanese to understand fully the internal workings of a Japanese corporation, three years was perhaps not sufficiently long enough for non-Japanese to assimilate Japanese management philosophy and practices completely. This highlights the need for those who intend to work for Japanese firms to adopt a longer time perspective.

Mr. Tawara observed that Sony Corporation of America plans to adopt a policy of promotion from within the company. In the past, the company hired senior management personnel from other companies. The policy of promotion from within appears to be more characteristic of the Japanese style of management.

Sony America Style of Management

Mr. Tawara has dubbed the management style practiced at Sony Corporation of America as the "Sony America" style. "Each company has its own management style. If we take the average, there is an American management or Japanese management style, but those do not apply to all companies. That is why we call it the 'Sony America style.' In other words, the management style is unique to each company." When asked whether American employees are covered by the system of lifetime employment, he noted that the latter "is not a system itself. If you look at the employment agreement, even in Japan, we do not guarantee the person for the whole life, nor do we put in a fixed period of employment in the contract, like three or five years. It depends on both sides. If the company wants to keep the employee, it can do so. If the employee chooses to remain, he will stay. If both sides agree to do it, then it is lifetime employment. That happens in Japan."

In the United States, the societal structure is different. If a service engineer wants to be promoted to upper management, his chances are fairly limited; consequently, he either leaves the company to take up a more senior position elsewhere or attends evening school and acquires an advanced degree and then requests promotion. Since Sony America operates in the United States, it has to conform to the peculiar characteristics of American society. "Of course, the orientation is to keep everybody, but sometimes that is not possible." When asked about the turnover rate among the local nationals, Mr. Tawara indicated that it is approximately the same as that for other U.S. companies, with the possible exception of engineers and blue-collar workers at the manufacturing plants, whose turnover rates are lower probably because of Sony's practice of promoting those who are capable to supervisory and sometimes managerial positions. This provides them with a major incentive to remain with the company, because, according to Mr. Tawara, "if they worked for the typical U.S. firm, their chances of promotion to managerial positions would be more limited." Mr. Tawara attributed a second reason for the lower turnover rate in the manufacturing plant to the greater cohesion among the employees—"everybody is in the same place." This facilitates communication. "In the offices, however, people are scattered around. In the branch offices especially, you have ten people here, and fifteen people elsewhere. So when we can operate successfully and show people that we are a firm with opportunities, then gradually the turnover rate will decrease."

Mr. Tawara was asked whether the American senior managers were involved in decision making. He replied, "It depends on the division of each company. Generally speaking, the decision is made by top management in the United States, with the broad consensus of others." Sony America has an operating committee, which "provides a forum where important topics are discussed." Through this committee, all of the operating companies become aware of each other's problems. The president of each operating company has the responsibility to make the decisions.

At the corporate level, the international operating committee (IOC) meets twice a year, attended by senior management from corporate headquarters and the various subsidiaries. The IOC provides a forum for senior management throughout the world to exchange information on a variety of subjects. The IOC is not a decision-making body. Its guidelines are established by Tokyo headquarters and are meted out at the IOC meetings. In Mr. Tawara's opinion, these guidelines are more "philosophical" rather than "concrete" in nature. The budget also provides guidelines to each subsidiary. Within the broad constraints of the general guidelines, the CEO in each subsidiary is responsible for implementing the plans.

Training for Local Nationals

Sony does not provide any formal training program to the local nationals hired at the management level, although they are sent to Tokyo to meet with the various levels of management and discuss Sony's business, particularly its worldwide operations. Somtimes corporate headquarters assigns a Japanese "who has a good mind and good contacts with foreigners" to serve in an advisory capacity or "as some kind of assistant" to the senior executives recruited in the United States in an effort to help them understand Sony's guiding philosophy.

Mr. Tawara was asked who would teach the American presidents who are hired to head six of the ten operating companies. He said that the "assistant to the president or the managers in Sony America or in Sony Tokyo" would be responsible for tutoring the president about how to conduct his job in accordance with Sony's philosophy. Mr. Tawara noted that there have been occasions where the local nationals were arrogant and would not learn from subordinates. Sony tries to avoid these situations by not "hiring that kind of people, even if they have the technical competence."

Japanese companies place a heavy premium on recruiting team players, not individuals, even in their overseas offices. For example, in Matsushita's eight manufacturing plants in the United Kingdom, all employees are referred to as members of the family. A motto of Matsushita is to "link the world with all our hearts and technology." Consequently, all employees are expected to "work together as a family of mutual trust and responsibility" (Taylor, 1982).

Selection Criteria for Expatriates

The selection criteria for expatriate assignments vary according to the job in question. For engineers, technical competence is considered the most important criterion, followed by ability to adjust to a new environment and then language. In administrative positions, the same criteria are used but here administrative ability is considered on a par with technical competence. Sales and marketing personnel are usually selected from those who are already working in the area sales department in the international division located within Tokyo headquarters.

After several years in Tokyo, some employees are transferred overseas. During their work in Tokyo, their supervisors have ample opportunity to observe their abilities, including human relational skills. Mr. Tawara noted that in the past, Sony used to stress language abilities; however, it now "realizes that it is not that essential." This is consistent with observations made by a number of Japanese executives interviewed for the study.

Although Sony does not administer a formal test to determine the candidate's ability to adjust to a foreign environment, the strong interaction between superior and subordinate in Japanese organizations provides a lot of information on the latter. According to another Sony officer, sales and marketing people have the opportunity to visit numerous countries. Many foreigners also visit Tokyo headquarters to attend conferences and so on. Through such business trips and conferences, supervisors observe their subordinates' skills in relating to non-Japanese. "These visits may be short, but if an individual receives hundreds of foreign visitors in a year, then I don't think it is a very short experience."

Sony does not officially solicit the employee's opinion about an overseas assignment but does so "semiprivately." Due to the emphasis on group work within Japanese organizations, the supervisor has the opportunity to observe closely the daily performance of his subordinates. In addition, most career staff socialize with their colleagues and immediate supervisors almost every evening. In the words of an officer of Sony, "During such social occasions, the manager informally inquires about the person's preferences."

Currently the family situation is not a major factor in the selection decision. With the changing values of Japanese youth, however, the officer at Sony was asked whether that would have any impact on the future practices of his company. He noted that Sony will be flexible and adjust procedures according to the changing times; however, he believes that "once the younger people are given positions of responsibility, they will become more company-oriented." (This appears to be a common sentiment among many Japanese executives.) Although employees theoretically can refuse an overseas assignment, they do not because the notice of transfer generally does not come as a surprise. "They realize that they will be transferred somewhere after several years of experience. The management always suggests vaguely at first: 'Do you want to go somewhere else? Any special place?' Day by day, and year by year, they have close contacts with their employees. Consequently, they are prepared to go to a special area." Mr. Uematsu indicated that in a company like Sony where overseas sales account for a substantial portion of total revenue and which has "a very aggressive marketing policy overseas," an employee who refuses an overseas assignment will be "treated unfavorably." Hence very few individuals will turn down an assignment.

Although the company does not explicitly consider the family situation, given the overall concern of the employer for the employee, the former does not generally make unreasonable assignments. Most of the expatriates go abroad with their families. Currently only 15 of the 400 married expatriates leave their families in Tokyo, primarily because of their children's education. In the case of Sony Corporation of America, only 1 or 2 out of the 170 expatriates leave their families behind. This figure is low compared with that of some other Japanese firms. Mr. Tawara noted that this lower percentage for Sony may be attributed to the age of the company: "We are still a young company."

There is no system as to how long an employee must be with Sony before he can expect his first overseas assignment. It depends on the needs of the overseas operations. Usually the candidate has to be at least thirty years old before he is sent abroad; however, if no suitable candidate can be found at a more senior level, a junior career staff with only two or three years of experience may be assigned abroad. The duration of an overseas assignment for engineers is between three and four years; that for sales and marketing people is between five and six years. In addition, there are the troubleshooters, whose duration of stay in the United States and other countries is much shorter. These are sent to assist the overseas plant in solving certain technical problems, and then they return to Tokyo.

Given Sony's extensive operations abroad, it is interesting to see whether overseas experience is considered a prerequisite for promotion to top management. An officer at Sony noted that although it is not a prerequisite at this point because of the relatively short history of its overseas operations (slightly over twenty years), he believes it may very well be the case in the future. He explained that because of the large number of staff in corporate headquarters, an employee seldom has the opportunity to meet with top management. However, top management tours the overseas subsidiaries several times a year and "during such visits, it is far easier for them to be recognized by the chief executive."

Mr. Tawara offered a different perspective on this issue. He indicated that there are both pros and cons to an overseas assignment, although he believes that the "drawbacks outweigh the merits." In his opinion, if a person accepts an overseas assignment for an extended period of time, say fifteen to twenty years, he may be out of the mainstream of corporate headquarters. This is particularly true for engineers; "if they leave pure engineering for three years, they have little or no room to go back to the engineering side." However, Mr. Tawara acknowledged that on the administrative side, from middle to top management, there are definite advantages to an overseas assignment: "They enjoy the longer period overseas. In most cases, they spend more than ten years in one country. They have the full responsibility. There are some merits in terms of knowledge and experience, but financially they suffer certain losses." The financial losses refer to the inability to purchase and maintain a house in and around metropolitan Tokyo, where prices have skyrocketed, the need to buy new furniture, and so on.

Given the problems encountered by the engineering staff, Mr. Tawara was asked why they would accept an overseas assignment. He cited three main reasons. First, given the fact that an overwhelming proportion of the company's revenues are derived from overseas operations, they have to know the international situation. Second, under the system of lifetime employment, a career staff implicitly agrees to accept whatever assignments and orders are given by the company. In Mr. Tawara's words, "They are assigned. They could not waive the order." Although another Sony officer stated that a person theoretically can refuse an overseas assignment, it is seldom done. Furthermore, Mr. Uematsu noted that the employee will be "treated unfavorably" if he disobeys the company's orders. A third reason for the engineers' willingness to accept an overseas assignment is personal interest. When Sony recruits engineers to work for the company, they hire only those "who have interest in a foreign assignment. So at school, they will have an interest outside of Japan." According to the 1982 rank ordering of firms by graduates of elite Japanese universities, Sony was listed 13 among the 225 companies (*Nikkei Business,* May 17, 1982).

Training for Expatriate Assignments

Sales and marketing people are not given any special training prior to departure because, in the words of an officer at Sony, "they are already specialized in the area of sales, and they also know the language." Most of these people also could speak English fluently. If they require some local language training, Sony offers in-house facilities For the production people, language skills are considered less important. Hence, a basic language course would suffice in most cases. Both the intensive and basic language courses are offered in Japan, supplemented by language courses in the foreign country on arrival. Sony offers a one-month intensive training course (ITC) in language to those who need them. The ITC runs during normal working hours so the person is exempted from routine duties.

The Sony officer was asked whether the company sponsors training programs to help employees relate to foreigners. He indicated that the company has recently started such a program. After the ITC (where necessary), the person is temporarily assigned to the area marketing division to familiarize himself with the operations of the country to which he has been assigned. This is followed by an environmental briefing program, which runs for several hours. In addition, the expatriate and his family are encouraged to discuss living abroad with those who have previously served in the foreign country. The spouse is given a brief orientation session. Sony uses in-house facilities for all training needs.

Sony also sends one or two employees to attend M.B.A. programs and several employees to attend technical schools abroad every year.

Culture Shock

When asked whether the Japanese experience culture shock, and if so, how they cope with it, the Sony officer indicated that sales and marketing people do not experience any culture shock because they "already have foreign experience from previous business trips that exceed a one-month duration. They have been sent overseas several times prior to the actual assignment." Engineering staff, however, tend to cluster in cultural enclaves. In San Diego, for example, there are some fifty engineers who form a small community. This same theme was echoed by Mr. Tawara. He noted that although some Japanese experience culture shock, they "don't think that it is culture shock. Instead the Japanese response it to try to live the Japanese way of life as much as possible. They try to speak to Japanese people only. They read Japanese newspapers, and so forth. They are physically located in the United States, but mentally they still live in a Japanese society." Mr. Uematsu added that "Oftentimes, the Japanese are criticized for isolating themselves by creating a Japanese society in a foreign environment."

Evaluation

Expatriates are evaluated on performance annually. The person is first evaluated by his immediate supervisor. Mr. Tawara noted, "In the case of expatriates, because they will eventually return to Japan, Tokyo's personnel division must have some kind of contact with that person." The expatriate is also evaluated by the general manager of the division and the president of the subsidiary company. These evaluations are forwarded to Tokyo where they are combined with Tokyo's assessment of the person's performance. Mr. Tawara admitted, however, that there could be problems in evaluating the performance of expatriates. In the case of Sony and other manufacturing companies where there are a combination of American and Japanese supervisors, "the evaluation could be different even though the person's performance is the same." This difference may stem from the varying criteria and values used by American versus Japanese supervisors and may also arise because of individual differences. Hence "the problem is how to adjust the evaluations between the American and Japanese supervisors."

Success and Factors for Success

The Sony officer indicated that the incidence of failures of expatriates is low. When asked to identify the reasons for failure abroad, he indicated three. One is language. Mr. Tawara concurred that there are problems in this regard, which is the reason for his recommending changes in this area. Second, a small proportion of expatriates "lose their common sense" while abroad. When asked to elaborate on the statement, he said that it could be due to culture shock because these people performed well in Tokyo. Third is status shock. In Tokyo the employee is only one member in a team and may have close interactions with members of his group and those of other departments and divisions. In Tokyo, decisions are made as a group. Once abroad, employees take on larger responsibilities and have to act on their own. This imposes a considerable strain on them.

Mr. Tawara attributed the low failure rate in Japanese multinationals to the system of evaluation. "In Japan, the evaluation is based on the person's capabilities, especially that in the long run, rather than on actual job performance. Of course, the company expects the person to do the job well. But there is some consensus that we usually allow at least a couple of years (minimum of two) before evaluation. So if we assign something to soneone, we wait three years for the results. In the first year it is very difficult to perform because the person does not know the situation and environment. So he is learning what is actually going on."

This system applies to positions in domestic corporate headquarters as well. Although many Japanese firms rotate personnel, when a person is assigned to a new position, "we expect that person to remain in the position for at least three years to achieve something, The first year is a learning period. We do not actually evaluate the person in the first year. The evaluation is based on whether the person is actually learning, not on whether the person is productive or not. In the second yar, the employee should be productive based on his experiences of the first year. In the third year, if the person has to rotate to other positions or other areas, he has to transfer the job to his successor. So, it is some sort of transition period. So, if we have a three-year assignment, the truly productive period is only one out of three." For this reason, many Japanese companies generally extend the overseas assignment to five years or longer.

There are several advantages to this longer time perspective with regard to evaluation. First, since a person is not quickly labeled a failure, his confidence in his abilities will grow and thus contribute to higher performance in the long run. Second, according to the findings by Harrari and Zeira (1978, p. 61), predeparture training is often inadequate to preclude culture shock. They stressed the need to exempt expatriates "from managerial responsibilities during the first several months of their stay . . . [to ease] their acculturation and help prevent mistakes they tend to make during this period."

According to Mr. Uematsu, a second reason for the low failure rate may be attributed to the employee's loyalty and dedication to his company. Mr. Tawara concurred and noted that in most Japanese companies, "people who are assigned to overseas positions have to stay for three years," except in developing nations. Given the limited job mobiity in Japanese society, the person has to endure. Consequently even if the expatriate and his family experience difficulties in adapting to a foreign country, they must be "patient until the three years is up." In such instances, they request repatriation to Tokyo "whenever the opportunity arises. We try to send them back to Tokyo in the shortest possible period of time. In those instances, it could be a failure. But most of the companies do not count them as failures. So the ratio is less than 1 percent. But if we count the other number of cases, even if they stayed for three or four years, the percentage would be around 20 to 25 percent."

Mr. Tawara provided some statistics. According to him, a quarter of the 120 expatriates in Sony Corporation of America are "really capable of doing the job in the United States and other foreign countries. They have the technical knowledge and relational abilities. More importantly, they know how to manage foreign people." In his opinion, the principles and dynamics of managing Japanese and non-Japanese employees are the same; however, Mr. Tawara lamented, only a quarter "know that people are people and that they are the same. The rest unfortunately think that foreigners are different. Among the remaining three-quarters, one-third try to find out how to get along with foreigners. They think that there is a different way to deal with foreigners—in fact it is really not that different. So it will take some time before they find out that people are really people. The other two-thirds (i.e., half of the total) just endure. They just wait until the period of assignment is over." These instances, however, could really not be counted as failures because even though the expatriates experience difficulty in living abroad, they endure and consequently try to be as productive as possible. This endurance stems from their loyalty and commitment to the company.

Remuneration

Sony divides the world into three geographic regions: the United States, Europe, and other. In the last category, there is no basis for comparison with the local salary. Consequently the company has established some general guidelines on cost-of-living adjustments and premiums for hardship positions. The former is designed to allow a Japanese expatriate to maintain the same standard of living that he enjoyed while working in Japan. In many instances, a portion of the salary is paid in yen and deposited in the person's savings account in Japan because some of these countries impose restrictions on the withdrawal of money from the banks and/or repatriation of foreign capital. The balance of the person's salary is paid in local currency.

For Europe, Sony tries to match the person's salary with those paid by other European companies for comparable positions. For example, if the president of a similar-sized company earns 50,000 pounds in London, the local national who is hired as president will be paid the same. If, however, the president were a Japanese, he would be paid 50,000 pounds "plus a certain percentage as foreign service premium," which would include a subsidy for cars and one for housing.

In the United States, the company pays the market price, "without any significant premiums," in order to comply with federal guidelines. If a president in a comparable U.S. company has three cars, the Japanese president will also be entitled to three cars. Sony Corporation of America is close to a $1 billion concern. If the salary of top management in Sony America is compared to a U.S. company of equal size, it may be less because if they had been paid an equal amount, the subsidiary president's salary may exceed that of the president of Sony Tokyo, when translated into Japanese yen. This is, inappropriate.

Changes

Mr. Tawara was asked if he were given freedom to redesign the selection and training procedures, what kinds of changes he would make and why. He offered several ideas.

The first recommendation pertains to the selection procedure. Mr. Tawara recommended that the human resources department should be involved in the preselection phase. Since the Sony group has some 60,000 employees, it is virtually impossible to single one person out of the 60,000. Consequently, under the current system, the selection is left almost entirely to each division or group, although the overseas offices have the opportunity to review candidates and occasionally refuse a person. In most cases, however, the overseas office accepts the recommended candidates. In Mr. Tawara's words, "If I were given the complete freedom, I would suggest that we add one more layer to provide input into the selection process, and thus eliminate the 25 percent that we talked about previously." Currently the human resources division acts almost as a rubber stamp. Under the proposed change, the overseas personnel department should be given the opportunity to interview prospective candidates and gather information from their supervisors and former supervisors so as to screen out misfits. The officer from Sony Tokyo independently made a similar recommendation. Under the current system, the management of each division is responsible for the selection and then informs the overseas personnel section within the human resources division in domestic headquarters. This means that in most instances, the management of the respective departments has already informally notified the individuals about such prospective assignments. Consequently, "it is rather difficult to reverse the respective management's decision."

A second recommendation is to include the family in the screening process because "the family is a major factor responsible for failure in most cases." Mr. Uematsu concurred. Mr. Tawara said that the evaluation of the candidate could be done by the immediate supervisor, while the assessment of the family should be performed by the human resources division.

A third recommendation pertains to language requirements and training. Although language proficiency is now no longer considered the most important criterion in selection, Mr. Tawara believes that it becomes "the major problem after they are assigned. It will take them about three to six months to feel comfortable, at the very minimum. There is really no way to improve the language skills after getting the assignment because in companies like Sony America, most of the Americans know how the Japanese speak English and they try to understand. In the business world, we use technical words. So if a person has a certain vocabulary, the person can communicate. But it is not communication in the true sense. It is a kind of business talk. Once we go out to see hockey or football, then it is entirely different. Most of the people cannot understand this kind of communication. My personal opinion is that this problem cannot be resolved by giving the employee an intensive English language course after the fact. The only solution is to get them to have experiences either at school age or right after graduation. These kinds of training could not be conducted in the business environment, but in the dormitory where there are no Japanese. That kind of technique is used, and I guess is still used, by the Foreign Ministry. They send the new recruits to the respective countries to learn the local language, like France for French." Although this training may be costly, Mr. Uematsu agreed that the best way to teach foreign language is to sponsor "four-week live-in programs. During these four weeks, the trainee has to forget about Japanese. From morning to night, he has to use English."

Another Sony officer recommended that changes should be made to the training program currently given to expatriates prior to their assignment. He would like to deemphasize the environmental briefing program because the younger Japanese usually know a lot about foreign countries from school, foreign travels, movies, and the news media. He suggested that the training should emphasize the development of management and communication skills, by which he means the ability to relate to people of a different culture. He added, however, that the "younger generation is more accustomed to communicating with people from foreign countries." With regard to management skills, he noted that although Sony currently sponsors many management courses, these are usually designed for the more senior people. These management courses are taught through a mix of lectures and case studies. He recommended that training programs of this nature be extended to the expatriates because one of the reasons for failure is status shock, or the inability to cope with the larger responsibilities of overseas work. Consequently, if the management skills of the expatriates could be improved, this would increase their ability to adjust to their new positions abroad. Mr. Uematsu similarly recommended that given the differences in decision-making and management styles between Japan and other nations, the expatriates should be taught the foreign style of management. "In most foreign countries, decisions are made from the top down. In Japan, we have the bottom-up approach. The other aspect of Japanese business style is *nemawashi*. *Ne* means 'root of plant,' *mawashi* means 'pushing into the ground.'

In other words, we try to make employees conform to one system and be involved in making a decision. This sort of concept may not exist in a foreign country. So the employees have to forget this style and learn a totally new style of decision making." This point is well taken. Although there are certain merits to the Japanese style of management, it is unique, and there may be problems of implementation in foreign countries, particularly if the firm is bent on a policy of localization.

Canon Inc.

The information presented here is based largely on an in-depth interview with Masaaki Kobayashi, general manager, International Operations, Canon Inc.

Overview

Canon Inc. was established in 1937. In 1955, when it opened an office in New York, its products were hardly known outside Japan, and the company's total sales abroad were below $150,000 per month. By 1976, its annual sales in North America reached $137 million. This figure increased another five-fold in the course of the next five years to reach $705 million. In the words of *New York Times* (March 30, 1980), Canon "transformed the 35-millimeter camera from a specialist's tool to an adult toy" that could be operated by almost anyone. In 1975, only 700,000 units of 35mm cameras were sold in the United States. In 1979, Canon sold more than 2 million units in the United States alone. The company projects its annual sales in North America to exceed $1 billion by 1984 (*Canon today, 1981/1982*). North America is by far the largest market for Canon products. In 1981, the consolidated sales of the company reached 470 billion yen ($2.14 billion), broken down as follows: North America, 33.1 percent; Japan, 30.6 percent; Europe, 27.7 percent; and Asia and others 8.6 percent (*Canon: Annual report, 1981*).

Today Canon is the world's largest manufacturer of cameras, with 25 percent of the world market (*Forbes,* March 31, 1980) and 34 percent of the Japanese domestic market (Lehner 1983, p. 38). Despite its success, photographic equipment no longer constitutes the largest product group in the company on a worldwide basis. In 1981, photographic equipment accounted for 42.9 percent of the company's consolidated sales; 48.5 percent was taken up by the business machines group, which includes calculators, electronic typewriters, and photocopiers. In 1979, for instance, over half of the 2 million photocopiers sold throughout the world (including well-known brand names such as Sharp, Savin, and Saxon) used technology licensed in part from Canon Inc. (*Business Week,* January 28, 1980). Other products manufactured by Canon include optical products and micrographics. In the North

American market, however, photographic equipment and products still accounted for the lion's share of the company's sales in 1981 (52 percent).

When Canon first marketed its products abroad shortly after World War II, the work was handled largely by distributors or contractors. In the past decade, however, the company has pursued a policy of establishing wholly owned subsidiaries abroad. These are referred to as the Canon group, which comprises some sixty operations worldwide, including Canon U.S.A. Inc., Canon Europa, N.V., Canon France, Canon U.K., Canon Germany, Canon Singapore, Canon Australia, and Canon Inc. Taiwan. Canon Europa distributes the company's products throughout Europe (except United Kingdom, France, and Germany), the Middle East, and parts of Africa. Today the wholly owned subsidiaries account for 95 percent of the company's annual sales abroad. The balance is sold through distributors. Since Canon manufactures several product lines, the policy is to appoint a distributor in each country for each product group. There are exceptions, however; some distributors may distribute as many as two to three different product lines. The wholly owned subsidiaries handle the entire Canon line of products.

Staffing Policy

In 1981, Canon employed approximately 25,000 people worldwide. Of these, 13,000 worked in its international operations in nearly 130 countries. Of the 13,000, only 300 were expatriate staff from Japan. In the early years Canon entered foreign markets by the route of exporting. Under that mode of entry strategy, it was not necessary to send its own staff abroad; however, when Canon began to establish wholly owned subsidiaries abroad, Japanese staff had to be sent overseas. This expatriation policy began in the late 1950s and early 1960s. The company deemed it necessary to use Japanese expatriates in the start-up phase of its foreign operations because of their greater familiarity with the company's products and its marketing strategy. This is common practice among multinationals, regardless of country of national origin. However, as the foreign subsidiaries became more well established, Canon (like Sony Corporation) began to pursue a policy of localization. According to Mr. Kobayashi, "As soon as we find host country nationals who are qualified to run the overseas operation, we will appoint them to be the manager or general manager there." The staffing policy for the position of president of the overseas subsidiary is not set. Some of Canon's overseas subsidiaries are headed by local people, while the top management positions in others are occupied by Japanese nationals from corporate headquarters. Currently the position of president in Canon's subsidiaries in the United States, France, United Kingdom, Germany, and a few other countries are occupied by Japanese expatriates. The majority of positions below the level of president in Canon's subsidiaries are staffed by local nationals.

In most of the Japanese multinationals examined here, a major reason for using parent country nationals at the top management level is to avoid possible problems of communication between corporate headquarters in Japan and the foreign nationals. Mr. Kobayashi was asked whether this could be a potential problem for Canon. He stated that it should not be because of the "unique system" Canon has implemented to facilitate communication between corporate headquarters in Tokyo and its subsidiary operations throughout the world.

In 1978, Canon converted its organizational structure into a three-dimensional matrix design. The first dimension, product groups, has three divisions: photo, business machines, and optical equipment. The second dimension of the matrix structure is area-grographic subsidiaries. The third is the functional organization, divided into marketing, production, and research and development. To facilitate the implementation of the third dimension, three committees were established in 1976: the Canon Production System (CPS), the Canon Development System (CDS), and the Canon Marketing System (CMS). These committees coordinate the marketing, production, and research and development functions of the company on a worldwide basis.

Through the matrix structure, Canon has succeeded in combining the positive aspects of centralization with the merits of decentralization. Although the functional activities are coordinated on a worldwide basis, the various product groups are organized as separate profit centers and hence are run as independent companies. "Each product group is ... responsible for its own decision making and revenue development. Yet all are tied together by a strong horizontal organization including the CDS, CPS, and CMS committees" (*The Canon story*, 1982; *Canon today, 1981/1982*). In 1979, a new International Operations Headquarters (IOH) was established. Headed by Mr. Kobayashi, the IOH coordinates the activities of the company's international operations. It thus constitutes an important arm of the organizational structure because international sales account for approximately 70 percent of the company's business. Besides the coordination of Canon's overseas operations, the IOH is responsible for preparing Japanese for overseas assignments and training and developing host country nationals who work for Canon throughout the world. (*Canon: Annual report*, 1981).

Although there are merits to the matrix structure, it is often difficult to implement. Canon apparently has done a remarkable job in this regard, as witnessed by its expansion in company sales since the implementation of the new organizational structure. The company's assets doubled from 231.926 billion yen ($996.35 million) in 1978 to 506.032 billion yen ($2.108 billion) in 1981. It was estimated that through the establishment of the CPS in 1976, which is designed to eliminate waste and promote efficiency in production, the company has saved 63 billion yen ($286 million) over a five-year period (*Canon: Annual report*, 1981).

Mr. Kobayashi elaborated on the operations of the matrix structure as it pertains to communication between the subsidiaries and corporate headquarters. Subsidiaries that are headed by Japanese nationals communicate directly with Tokyo headquarters. In subsidiaries headed by host country nationals, there is another "Canon central organization in that region to assist, support, and coordinate with the local presidents and Tokyo." In Europe, for instance, Canon Europa, N.V. is the central organization. This encompasses the subsidiaries in Norway, Sweden, Finland, and Denmark. Canon Europa "is responsible for sales, looking after and providing support to those subsidiaries that are run by local staff." The CEO of Canon Europa is a Japanese. In addition, the planning and decision-making committees are staffed by Japanese expatriates.

Japanese expatriates occupy staff but not line positions in each of these four European subsidiaries. The line positions are occupied primarily by host country nationals. The presidents of Canon's subsidiaries in Spain, Italy, and Belgium are also host country nationals. Each of these subsidiaries is responsible for the day-to-day decisions that affect its own operations. Major decisions, however, are made in conjunction with the central committee of Canon Europa.

Canon U.K., Canon France, and Canon Germany do not constitute part of Canon Europa N.V. but report directly to Tokyo because these three subsidiaries are headed by Japanese.

A frequent source of communication problems between corporate headquarters and non-Japanese staff can be ascribed to the differences in philosophy and objectives between Occidentals and Japanese. Mr. Kobayashi was asked whether Canon experienced problems in this area. In response, he said that such differences do not exist "because the local presidents have coordinated their plans very closely with the Canon Europa staff. The Canon Europa staff will then, in turn, coordinate them with Tokyo. Once the decision is made, the local presidents have the complete autonomy to implement the plans. This has worked beautifully in the past fifteen years. It is quite unlike what we read in publications that Westerners are very different from the Japanese. We give local nationals the complete autonomy to run the subsidiary once the policy is made. We do not interfere midstream. We have placed heavy emphasis on requiring the local presidents to make periodic reports—monthly, quarterly, and semiannually. Those reports are clearly defined by Canon to the responsible presidents." Like Sony, although Canon pursues a policy of localization and allows the overseas subsidiaries autonomy in their operations, the overall guidelines are set by corporate headquarters in Tokyo. This is not dissimilar from the practices of most U.S. and West European multinationals.

Since most of Canon's sales in Southeast Asia are handled through appointed distributors, there is no need for a central organization in that region. Canon has wholly owned subsidiaries in Hong Kong and Singapore, however.

Selection Criteria

When asked to identify the criteria Canon Inc. uses in selecting candidates for expatriate assignments, Mr. Kobayashi noted two. First is technical competence. Besides knowledge of the job, the individual "also has to know Canon—what Canon is." Given the diverse range of products manufactured by Canon, most employees specialize in one product line in Japan. Thus a person in camera has little knowledge about the products manufactured by Canon's other divisions. However, since the overseas wholly owned subsidiaries distribute the entire line of Canon products, the expatriate has to learn about all the product groups. Consequently, individuals selected for overseas assignment must familiarize themselves with the entire range of the company's products through a comprehensive training program. In the words of Mr. Kobayashi, the expatriate has to be "an expert in his field, but at the same time he must have a broader knowledge of all product lines handled by Canon."

Since the expatriates will take up positions at the managerial level abroad, they are selected from career staff who are on the threshold of promotion to the management level. Translated into years of service with the company, it will be slightly under ten years. Once abroad, the expatriate is initially assigned to a section in the overseas company where he will work under a manager who is a local national. After one or two years, the Japanese will have acquired expertise in the local operations of the overseas subsidiary and will most likely be promoted to a staff position as an adviser to the president in his area of specialization. In most instances, the expatriate is not promoted to the position of line manager but to an advisory capacity as a member of the president's staff.

A second selection criterion is language proficiency. Although Canon does not administer any test to determine the candidate's capabilities, given the rigorous training program provided the career staff coupled with the fact that prospective candidates are selected from those who have worked with the company for a number of years, the company has ample opportunity to assess their strengths and limitations. The recommendations for an overseas assignment are made by the chief of the respective divisions.

Mr. Kobayashi was asked whether a candidate can refuse an overseas assignment. He indicated that the company generally respects the individual's desires, "so before we make the final decision, we have to inquire." Most individuals accept an overseas assignment, however. One reason is "they think it is a challenge and it provides them an opportunity to become more experienced in different divisions overseas." In Japan the individual is engaged in one product line only; when he serves abroad, he has to deal with various product categories. Another reason is that because approximately 70 percent of the company's sales is derived from international business, overseas experience increases the chances of promotion in the organizational hierarchy within corporate headquarters. Although Mr. Kobayashi indicated that refusing an overseas assignment will not limit a person's chances for promotion, there is a real incentive for the individual to serve abroad because of the premium placed on international experience. Mr. Kobayashi added that if an employee refuses a particular assignment, he will be asked to specify the countries he would like to serve in. "We try to accommodate him, not immediately though. The personnel department makes a record of it."

The duration of an overseas assignment is generally five years, although it may be extended or shortened depending on the needs of corporate headquarters and of the subsidiaries. For those who accept extended periods of overseas assignments, say fifteen to twenty years, there are no problems with repatriation because of the frequent communication between corporate headquarters and its overseas staff. "From time to time, [the expatriate] will come back to Tokyo for very important meetings at corporate headquarters, such as reports on current market conditions, and projections of future market trends. On those occasions, he has an opportunity to meet with other managers, general managers, directors and the president." In the course of a five-year assignment, the expatriate returns to Tokyo at least once a year. The senior-ranking officers of overseas subsidiaries, such as general managers and presidents, visit Tokyo at least twice a year to attend international meetings to coordinate worldwide marketing activities, product planning, and development and to discuss market opportunities and the situation of its competitors. Furthermore, because of Canon's peculiar organizational structure, which emphasizes both centralization and decentralization, each overseas subsidiary maintains frequent contacts with corporate headquarters. Hence "there is no possibility of [the expatriates'] being forgotten while abroad."

Mr. Kobayashi was asked to comment on the subject of culture shock. He believes that culture shock is primarily a problem of the past. When Canon first began sending expatriates overseas in the late 1950s and early 1960s, there were problems because "everything [abroad] was so different from things in Japan. So there was bound to be some sort of culture shock in the first few months or first year." He contends, however, that the situation has greatly improved since then. "The young people whom we send abroad now do not appear to experience culture shock." He believed that the situation could be due in part to the fact that Japanese youth have much knowledge of foreign countries through books, the mass media, and foreign travel. Hence "the life-style and the way of thinking" of Japanese youth are quite similar to those in other countries. "So even if they go to New York, London, or Paris, they seem to overcome such differences, almost overnight." A second, and perhaps more important, reason for the general adaptability of Canon's employees could be attributed to the rigorous training program given by Canon prior to their departure overseas. "We teach them how to behave—manners, social etiquette, and so on. So they can act naturally."

Training

Like most other Japanese organizations, Canon places a heavy premium on human resource development in the company. In fact, a basic tenet of Canon's corporate philosophy is to help employees develop "a healthy body and mind" for the purpose of "personal development." Canon views personnel development as "the heart of a successful marketing operation" and the key to the company's phenomenal success (*Canon: Annual report,* 1981; material provided by Mr. Kobayashi). Given this awareness, the company devotes much attention to the human resource development programs within the company. These are divided into several categories: basic training for career staff, training for expatriates prior to assignment overseas, and training for host country nationals who work for Canon.

Basic Training for Career Staff: All college graduates who join the company attend an initial twelve-week training program. All new recruits, regardless of area of specialization at college, go through the same program, conducted on a full-time basis. In the first five weeks, they undergo a factory practicum to familiarize them with Canon's manufacturing facilities. During this time they are also given training in general administrative skills for three days. In the remaining seven weeks of the basic training, the new employee is assigned to one of Canon's sales companies to observe the marketing end of the company's business. During this period, they are taught about the operation of large mainframe computers for six days. During the twelve-week program, a boarding seminar is held to promote a spirit of camaraderie among the new employees.

After the basic training program, approximately half of the new recruits are assigned to work in one of the company's divisions on a full-time basis. The remaining half continue their sales training for an entire year.

After the first year of training, approximately 50 percent of those employees who underwent sales training will be assigned to a position related to sales in one of the company's divisions. The remainder (roughly one-quarter of the original recruits) are sent abroad to serve as trainees in one of Canon's overseas subsidiaries. The trainee could be assigned to any position in the overseas office—sales, accounting, and so on. The duration of the overseas apprenticeship program is at least one; sometimes it may be longer. On completion of the overseas training program, the individual returns to Japan and is assigned to a position in one of the company's divisions—perhaps in corporate headquarters in Tokyo or in one of the company's many sales offices or manufacturing plants through the world—where he will undergo on-the-job training. This on-the-job training will last another year.

Thus, the first three years of employment with Canon are devoted primarily to training. The recruits are given both classroom and on-the-job training. In Mr. Kobayashi's words, "We show and tell them the kind of work that is involved." In the initial three years, all the career staff are also given language training, which is offered at several levels. The regular course, which lasts for six months, is designed to improve the trainee's ability to communicate in English. A follow-up course is designed to improve the trainee's ability to make oral presentation in English. This program lasts for six months. There is a third course in English business correspondence and also an English-language program for people at the managerial level.

In the fourth and fifth year of his employment with Canon, the career staff will be assigned to "a responsible position under the manager." During this two-year period, his supervisors closely observe his performance. To improve organizational efficiency, the chairman of Canon Inc., Takeshi Mitarai, introduced a system of promotion on the basis of merit, a revolutionary change from the Japanese tradition of promotion primarily on the basis of seniority (*Fortune*, August 1980). This system of promotion primarily on the basis of merit is gaining popularity among an increasing number of Japanese firms.

Training for Overseas Assignments: The individual's performance is observed closely in his fourth and fifth years of employment. If he demonstrates suitability for an overseas position, the chief of his division will recommend him to the personnel department and the international operations headquarters. On selection, the candidate undergoes a broad range of training programs to prepare him for overseas work. These programs include both management and language training.

Since the expatriate will occupy a managerial position abroad, he must be given management training. It is essential to strengthen the administrative skills of those who are assigned overseas since a frequent cause of failure is status shock. Canon recognizes the importance of management skills to successful performance abroad and consequently devotes adequate attention to this area.

The management training program is conducted twice a week over a five-month period for a total of 158 hours. Several subjects are taught.

1. Canon's management objectives. This includes a description of Canon's medium- and long-range plans; Canon's technology—past, present, and

future; and Canon's objectives with regard to marketing, production, and research and development.

2. Principles of accounting and finance. As a management staff in an overseas operation, the expatriate has to be familiar with the various functional disciplines.

3. Principles of management. This includes a company simulation program held over a four-day, three-night period when the expatriate is asked to role play the president of a hypothetical company. He is asked to solve one or two crisis situations and turn in a profit for the company. "He will have an assistant vice-president and general managers and simulate the operation of an actual company. He is asked to prepare the financial statements—profit and loss, balance sheet, and cash flow."

4. Principles of marketing. Pricing strategies, advertising and promotion, distribution, and relationships with distributors are examined.

5. General knowledge of Canon's products. In Japan each individual specializes in one product line. Once abroad, the person has to handle the entire line of products manufactured by Canon. Hence the individual has to be exposed to the company's various product groups: cameras, office equipments, and optical instruments.

6. Basic preparations for international assignments. The trainee is taught about overseas personnel administration; management of overseas distributors; overseas business manners; social etiquette for living overseas (including how to behave at cocktail receptions and table manners); international business transactions; and "common sense for international businessmen," which includes instruction on the values and attitudes of foreigners, and how to cope with such differences.

Besides management training, the expatriate has to take language lessons (in addition to the regular language programs available to all career staff). The language training program extends for six months and is offered twice a week, for a total of 180 hours. All expatriates have to study English, regardless of country of assignment since English is the universal language of international business transactions. An individual assigned to a country where English is not spoken is also provided basic training in the local language.

The local language training programs other than English are about a month in duration. Canon uses both in-house and outside facilities for this purpose, although the latter are used more often. According to Mr. Kobayashi, on completion of these comprehensive training programs, the candidate "is quite qualified to become a manager or general manager."

Mr. Kobayashi was asked whether Canon uses the resources of other external agencies for their training needs besides local language training. He replied in the negative because he believes that Canon has adequate in-house resources to provide the necessary training. Most of the seminars are given by the managers and general managers of Canon Inc. In addition, they also invite prominent professors as guest speakers at the seminars. Mr. Kobaya-shi noted that Canon does not send any employee to attend business school abroad, although they are "presently thinking about it, but not yet."

Training for Wives: The spouses of expatriates are provided a one-day orientation session. This includes an introduction to Canon's products. In Mr. Kobayashi's opinion, "In Japan, the wives have very little opportunity to learn about Canon. They hear about it from their husbands or neighbors, but never directly. So we feel that they should be given a chance to visit Canon offices, factories, and meet some of the important people within the company, such as directors." In Japan, the wives are generally not involved in their husbands' work lives, including socializing in the evenings. Once abroad, however, the spouses are expected to play a more active role. In addition to the tour of Canon manufacturing plants, the company invites an outside speaker to brief them about what to expect in the country to which they will be sent. Each spouse is given a booklet printed in both English and Japanese that presents situations that may arise in a foreign country. For example, if the child becomes ill, "it tells them how to handle the situation." These orientation sessions are provided to the wives of expatriates who are sent abroad for the first time.

Canon does not provide language training for spouses. Although Mr. Kobayashi acknowledges that some of the spouses may have difficulty with a foreigh language, he believed that it should not create much of a problem because the younger women have been exposed to foreign ways of life since early childhood and the other Canon employees who are already living in the foreign country "will take care of them."

Training for Host Country Nationals: Given Canon's policy of localization and the company's overall dedication to education, foreign nationals who are recruited to work at the managerial level of Canon's overseas subsidiaries are also provided a two-week training, the Tokyo seminar for overseas local general managers. The Tokyo seminar, offered twice a year, is generally attended by five to ten managers from the various subsidiaries. In Mr. Kobayashi's words, only those "whom we think are qualified to be promoted to an executive position" will be selected to attend the seminar. The partici-pants at the Tokyo seminar must be recommended by the president of the respective foreign subsidiary to which he belongs. Some of the participants already occupy top management positions, such as that of president. In this case, they are selected by the Japanese president of the central organization that oversees the foreign operation. The objectives of the seminars are three-fold. First, the seminar provides host country nationals with a deeper under-standing of Japan and the Japanese. Professors from Japanese universities are invited to lecture on the subjects of Japanese history, culture, religion, and the country's political situation from the Tokugawa Shogunate, through the Meiji restoration, right down to the present period. According to Mr. Kobayashi, "We want them to understand that Japan's industrial development did not begin at the end of World War II, but that it began as early as the Tokugawa Shogunate era (1600–1867), when the country enjoyed nearly 300 years of peace and harmony. Education was much emphasized even back in those days. Then came the Meiji restoration (1868). During this period, the central government placed heavy emphasis on nationwide education by the central government. Primary schools were established throughout the nation, even in the rural areas. Today, the illiteracy rate in the country is virtually zero." This is supplemented with a tour to the historical sites in Tokyo and Kyoto. With respect to culture, the participants are taught about the need to "conform" in Japanese organizations and "the use of power in Japanese business." The participants also visit other manufacturing plants, such as Nissan Motor's Murayama factory, to give them a better understanding of the operations of the Japanese economy.

A second objective of the Tokyo seminar is to provide host country nationals with a better understanding of Canon, of what it means to be a Canon employee, and to imbue within the participants a greater enthusiasm for Canon's products. A distinguishing feature of the Japanese industrial system is the employee's close identification with the products and achievements of the company, which helps to foster an employee's willingness to endure whatever hardships required by the company and accounts for the fervor and zeal with which the Japanese sell their products. As one senior Japanese executive observed, a problem with local nationals is their "lack of love for the company's products." Consequently, through the two-week seminar, Canon hopes to incite the enthusiasm of host country nationals for the company's products.

A third objective of the Tokyo seminar is to assist host country nationals to acquire a greater understanding of their present jobs and thus improve performance. To promote this goal, they are given lectures on management policy, personnel policy (criteria for promotion and labor-management relationships), Canon's development system (the research and development activities within the company), Canon's production system (these are supplemented by visits to the manufacturing plants), Canon's marketing system, and corporate communications (the company's relationship to the broad societal environment, problems encountered in communications between Japanese and non-Japanese nationals, how to improve Canon's public image in the world, and so on). These lectures are given by managers and general managers at Canon's corporate headquarters and are supplemented by discussions with top management at Canon Inc. and a tour of Canon's Grand Fair, an exhibition of Canon business machines.

Each participant selects and attends seminars on one of the following nine professional subjects: production management, sales and marketing,

after-sales service, advertising and sales promotion, electronic data process-
ing, personnel administration, general affairs, accounting and finance, and
warehouse and transport operations.

Evaluation of Performance

Once abroad, the Japanese expatriate is evaluated annually. The evaluation
reports are sent to Tokyo. Like most other Japanese companies, there are
two kinds of titles within Canon: job and qualification. The former refers to
positions such as manager or general manager. There are more steps under
the qualification title category. An employee who wants to be promoted
under this category must take an examination. This is not compulsory. If the
individual passes the examination, his qualification title advances, and there
is a commensurate increase in salary. "His chances of promotion to a higher
position will also be increased. This procedure is followed up to the level of
managers. Managers and general managers are assessed on their job performance, not through examination."

   An expatriate is evaluated by the Japanese president of the subsidiary.
In places where the president is a host country national, the expatriate will
be evaluated by the Japanese president of a neighboring Canon subsidiary.
This system avoids the problem of how to adjust evaluations between Japanese and non-Japanese supervisors. While having its positive aspects, Canon's system may create other problems—for example, how much authority
does the non-Japanese supervisor actually have over the Japanese expatriate? However, in cases where top management is a host country national,
the Japanese expatriate generally occupies a staff, rather than line position.

Success and Factors for Success

Mr. Kobayashi indicated that in the early years when Canon began sending
its people overseas, "they were not able to get acquainted with the foreign
culture and operations. So, some were on the verge of nervous breakdown. I
think we had two cases in the past twenty-five years." These people were
transferred back to Tokyo or reassigned. Such incidences are virtually nonexistent today. In Mr. Kobayashi's words, "One reads about these in magazines, but it is not a problem with Canon. The reason for Canon's success is
that we carefully select only those who are highly qualified. Furthermore, we
give them very rigorous training." Canon provides comprehensive training
for its expatriate staff, and its phenomenal success in the world market is
testimony to its commitment in this area.

Remuneration

The salary structure for host country nationals is decided entirely by the president of the foreign subsidiary. Salaries are based on local wage scales. Tokyo allows each subsidiary complete autonomy in this regard.

In the case of expatriates, the remuneration policy is determined by corporate headquarters in Tokyo. The expatriate is generally paid a salary comparable to similar positions in indigenous corporations of roughly equal size. Although Canon does not specifically pay a premium for hardship positions, it is taken into consideration in the pay scales for different countries. According to Mr. Kobayashi, Canon has "a careful equation of what the pay should be for San Francisco, Melbourne, the Middle East, Africa, and so forth. The coefficient of the equation varies from city to city."

Changes

Mr. Kobayashi was asked if he were given the complete freedom to redesign the program, what kinds of changes he would make and why. He indicated, "I always try to improve the training program." Specifically, he would like to see changes in two areas. The first pertains to the attitude of the younger generation in Japan. In his words, "The youngsters nowadays are too well off. They live in an affluent society." Hence, their attitudes and work ethics are somewhat different from those of their forefathers. In Mr. Kobayashi's opinion, the younger generation appears to be "a little bit lacking in perseverence and seriousness of purpose. I don't know what kind of training we can give them in this regard. This involves spiritual or mental training." A second change pertains to language training. "The Japanese, unlike other nationalities, are poor in foreign languages. We live next to Korea, the Philippines, and China. Almost none of us are able to speak their languages. I have lived in the United States and Europe, and I find that the people there speak other languages besides their own. For some reason, the Japanese are very poor linguists. This is also true with our staff." He faulted the way in which foreign languages are taught in Japanese schools. "Admittedly, the structure of Japanese language is very different from that of other foreign languages, but I don't think that is the main reason. I think it is due to the way in which language is presently taught in Japan."

7

The Heavy
Industrial Sector

Besides electrical machinery and appliances, Japanese manufacturers have also attained dominance in the steel and automobile industries. In steel, Japan's production increased from 7 million tons per year prior to World War II to a record high of 119 million tons in 1973, a seventeen-fold increase over a thirty-year period. Today, the world's largest manufacturer of steel is Nippon Steel Corporation (*Nippon: The land and its people,* 1982). Another industry in which Japan has gained world dominance is automobiles. From a production of 38,490 units in 1951, it overtook the United States as the world's largest manufacturer of automobiles in 1980 (Tung 1982b). Nissan Motor Company, manufacturer of Datsun cars, is the second largest producer of automotive vehicles in Japan, after Toyota Motor Company. This chapter describes the human resource development programs at Nissan Motor Company and Nippon Steel Corporation.

Nissan Motor Company

The information presented here is obtained through interviews with Yoshi-kazu Hanawa, general manager, Technical Services, Nissan Motor Company, and Katsuhiko Satoh, senior staff personnel at Nissan. Mr. Hanawa is also a vice-president of the Nissan Motor Manufacturing Corporation, U.S.A.

Overview

Nissan is the second largest manufacturer of automobiles in Japan, with total sales of 3,016.2 billion yen ($14.36 billion) for the fiscal year ended March 31, 1981 (*Nissan Motor Co., Ltd.: Annual report,* 1980). In 1980, the company exported 1,665,140 units of automotive vehicles, 58.5 percent of them to North America and Europe (*Nissan: Annual report,* 1980). In response to increasing pressures from foreign producers, Japanese auto-mobile manufacturers have imposed restraints on their annual exports of automobiles to the United States to 1.68 million units per year until the end of March 1984. Furthermore, in anticipation of the passage of the domestic-content bill with regard to automotive parts in the United States, a number of Japanese producers have begun to establish manufacturing facilities in this country. By early 1983, the domestic-content bill had passed the House of Representatives in the United States but had yet to be reviewed by the Senate. If enacted into legislation, the bill will require that automobile manufacturers that export over 900,000 units per year to the United States have a 90 percent domestic content in the final product beginning in 1986. For manufacturers exporting 700,000 units per year to the United States, the domestic-content requirement is 70 percent. This legislation would not affect auto manufacturers exporting 100,000 or fewer units per annum to the United States (*U.S. news and world report,* February 7, 1983, p. 47).

To protect their market shares if such legislation passes, the leading Japanese automobile manufacturers have adopted precautionary measures. In early 1983, Toyota entered into a fifty-fifty joint venture agreement with General Motors to build compact cars in Fremont, California. Honda Motor Company has established a manufacturing plant in the United States that produces its Accord cars. Nissan Motor has constructed a $500 million plant in Smyrna, Tennessee, which began production in August 1983. The Smyrna plant is expected to produce 15,000 light pickup trucks per month (Sheller 1982). Besides the Smyrna plant, Nissan has over 25 assembly and manufacturing plants in some twenty nations throughout the world (*Nissan: Annual report,* 1980).

Staffing Policies

In 1982, Nissan employed some 60,000 employees, 20,000 of them career staff. Of the latter, 200 serve as expatriates in the company's overseas operations. The company has been sending Japanese expatriates to manage its foreign operations for the past twenty years. Most of these occupy positions at the presidential and vice-presidential levels in the company's overseas subsidiaries. A striking exception is the Smyrna plant; its president and four of the six vice-presidents are Americans. None of the American senior executives speak Japanese. There are two Japanese vice-presidents. When asked why Nissan took exception in the Smyrna plant, Mr. Hanawa posited two primary reasons. One is that the company is located in the United States, which has a very large pool of "talented managers who are experienced in the field of automobile manufacturing." The president of Nissan Motor Manufacturing Corporation, U.S.A. is Marvin Runyon, a former executive at Ford Motor Company (Sheller 1982). As such, he is thoroughly familiar with the workings and operations of the U.S. automobile industry, and Nissan Motor could certainly benefit from his expertise and experience. A second reason for hiring host country nationals at the top management level is "to raise the morale of the employees." Mr. Hanawa believes that if all senior positions were staffed by Japanese expatriates, Americans might be discouraged from joining Nissan for fear they may not have the opportunity to rise to the top of the organizational hierarchy.

Since none of the American executives speak Japanese, Mr. Hanawa was asked whether Nissan anticipates problems in terms of communication between the U.S. subsidiary operation and corporate headquarters in Tokyo. He acknowledged that there are many barriers between Americans and Japanese, including language and cultural differences; however, he added, through frequent communications, Nissan hopes to overcome these possible barriers. Another way in which Nissan plans to surmount this potential problem is to teach American employees about Japanese management practices.

The Smyrna plant will adopt a modified version of the Japanese style of management. Thus far, Japanese industrial practices have been well received by the 2,650 Americans hired to work in the Smyrna plant. Some such practices include greater job security, a closer working relationship between leader and subordinate, emphasis on training, and optional calisthenics (Sheller 1982). Although lifetime employment is not guaranteed, most employees know that they can retain their jobs as long as they are productive and they decide to remain. This is, in essence, the practice of lifetime employment, which is not explicitly guaranteed; rather, it is an implicit agreement entered into between employer and employee.

The human relations aspects of management are also emphasized in the Smyrna plant, reflected in the close working relationships between superior and subordinate. In the words of a twenty-six-year old employee at the Nissan plant, "My boss is my friend" (Sheller 1982, p. 84). A third aspect of Japanese management practice adpoted by the Smyrna plant is the emphasis on training. Since the operations in the plant are highly mechanized, it is imperative to provide adequate training to all levels of employees to ensure the smooth functioning of the organization. Furthermore, in line with the principle of cross-functional rotation, Nissan believes it is necessary for each production worker to possess a wide range of technical skills. For these reasons, Nissan has allocated $63 million to train workers at the Tennessee plant. This amount is supplemented by a $7.3 million grant by the state of Tennessee. Each of the 2,650 workers employed in the plant is referred to as a manufacturing technician. Each will undergo several hundred hours of training. Besides teaching the workers about the technical aspects of the job, each employee is also taught the proper attitude toward "jobs, supervisors, and company" (Sheller 1982, p. 85). This is similar to the indoctrination or orientation provided Japanese recruits when they join the parent company in Tokyo. To provide American employees with a better understanding of how Japanese factories are managed and run, 425 Americans (including 125 hourly workers) have been sent to Japan for a ten-week on-the-job training at Nissan's manufacturing plants there (Sheller 1982).

Selection Criteria

In selecting a Japanese for an overseas assignment, several criteria are taken into consideration. Knowledge and experience are deemed the most important requirements. A second criterion is personality and adaptability, and a third is language. Mr. Hanawa noted, however, that these are his own personal guidelines; Nissan does not have a written policy in this regard. Thus each manager can use his own set of criteria in selecting candidates for overseas positions.

The candidate's knowledge and experience can be gauged from the annual evaluation forms. Although there is no specific test to determine the candidate's adaptability and suitability to living and working in a foreign environment, Mr. Hanawa contends that because of the unique system of Japanese personnel management, the superior has much information on which to base his selection: "We know each other very well, much more than an American company. When we graduate from university, we join the company. For example, I joined the personnel/human resources division, and my boss trained me for ten, twenty, or twenty-five years. Mr. Satoh [a senior staff personnel], for instance, joined the company fifteen years ago and I know him very well because I have contacts with him for ten years or more. I know his work experience, his strong and weak points, his personality, his family situation, almost everything. I know many people in the human resources division, so I can select a suitable person very easily." This theme was echoed by almost all the Japanese executives interviewed for this study.

Mr. Satoh supplemented Mr. Hanawa's remarks by noting that although the company does not conduct a specific interview to determine a candidate's suitability for a particular overseas assignment, it was not necessary because "my superior, Mr. Hanawa, has interviewed me for a long time, ever since I joined Nissan. Every day is an interview." An employee must be with Nissan for at least ten years before he can expect his first overseas assignment. Thus, his supervisor has ample opportunity to observe his performance and personality. Consequently the supervisor generally does not make unreasonable assignments.

With regard to the issue of personality and adaptability, Mr. Hanawa was asked whether Japanese expatriates experience culture shock while abroad and, if so, how they cope with it. He believes that "it is very difficult for Japanese to adapt to a foreign culture." But because of their overall commitment to the company, they endure. Mr. Hanawa noted that the United States generally does not pose much of a problem for most Japanese because many of them "have adopted certain aspects of American life-styles, such as food, clothing, certain characteristics, speaking, discotheques, and so on. We learn many things from the United States, so there is less difficulty there." The situation is very different in Europe. "In England or Europe, especially in France, we feel a tremendous difference in terms of culture."

Unlike some of the other Japanese multinationals, Nissan does not consult with its employee about a prospective overseas assignment. The company just issues a command: "You should go to United States" or some other place. Mr. Hanawa recounted his own experience. In April 1980, the personnel division office phoned him at his residence and asked him to report to their office the following morning. "I knew that he would give me some kind of assignment, but I had no idea what kind of assignment. Next morning, I went to his office. The chief of the personnel division said: 'This afternoon, I will give you one assignment, that is to go to the United States and be the advisor of the new company.' I went to his office at 10 o'clock and he gave me one-hour notice." Mr. Hanawa indicated that it was "very natural" for him not to question the assignment. Given the close working relationship between superior and subordinate, coupled with the fact that the personnel department has abundant information on each employee's personality and family background, the company generally will not make unreasonable assignments.

Mr. Hanawa was asked whether a person could refuse an overseas assignment. He indicated that although it is possible, the company has to discuss with the individual the reasons for refusal. A person who refused an overseas position might find that this decision limits his chances of future promotion in the company because "in Japan, it is common practice that we should obey the company's wishes as much as possible."

Because a substantial portion of Nissan's revenues is derived from foreign sales, Mr. Hanawa was asked whether overseas experience was considered necessary for promotion to top management. He indicated that it may be, although promotion is based largely on the person's performance within the company. Consequently, even if a person has extensive overseas experience but his performance is not good, he will not be promoted.

The duration of an overseas assignment is generally five years, but this varies from one region of the world to the other. In countries such as Kuwait and Saudi Arabi, the assignment is usually for two years. In industrialized countries, such as the United States, the duration may be as long as ten years. After a person completes an overseas assignment and is repatriated, there is no fixed policy as to how long he should remain there before his next tour of duty abroad. Some Nissan employees have been assigned to the United States three times over the past twenty years. This is consistent with the finding by *Japan Economic News* (June 24, 1982) that three out of four expatriates have lived in one country only.

Mr. Hanawa was asked whether extended periods of overseas assignments could lead to problems of repatriation for Nissan expatriates. He indicated that it should not because the personnel division, which is the power center in Japanese organizations, closely monitors the performance of its expatriates. The division wields considerable power with regard to the "transfer, promotion and control of the company's employees. There is a division within Nissan, which is referred to as the Overseas Personnel Section of the Human Resources Division, which oversees the interests of employees sent to other countries." That division is always on the alert as to who is in the country and what kind of person he is. Every year, they check the performance, working conditions, the family situation and salary.

Training for Expatriates

Nissan offers a variety of training programs for prospective candidates for an overseas assignment. These include study-abroad programs, in-house training, and educational programs provided by external agencies in Japan.

Every year, Nissan sends approximately twenty-five employees to attend universities in various countries. The schools are primarily business and technical. The employees selected to attend the study-abroad programs are generally between the ages of twenty-five and thirty-five. The procurement of an advanced degree is viewed as part of the person's career development. On successful completion of the work for the degree, the person may be immediately assigned to work in the subsidiary office of that foreign country. When asked whether an overseas graduate education will increase the person's chances of promotion within the company, Mr. Satoh replied that it depends entirely on the person's performance. Nevertheless those who are selected to undertake an advanced degree program at a foreign university are considered elite trackers.

Prospective expatriates who do not undergo an advanced degree program abroad are trained through alternative means, such as in-house training, courses at external agencies within Japan, and the process of self-enlightenment.

Nissan sponsors a special training program for senior management personnel who are to be sent overseas, the International Management Development (IMD) program, which is offered in-house. This program consists of 450 hours of English-language instruction and 180 hours of lectures and seminar discussions in various aspects of international business. Some of the subjects taught are international finance, international marketing, labor law and practices in major economies in the world, European economic history, and evolution of the world automobile industry. These courses are taught by people from within Nissan and supplemented by lectures given by university professors. In addition, the IMD program provides prospective candidates a forum to discuss different aspects of doing business abroad with executives who have previously served in the company's foreign operations. The program extends over a six-month period, and the participants attend eleven three-day live-in programs. For the live-in programs, the participants stay in a hotel so that they could be totally immersed in language training and learning about international business.

In 1981, Nissan started a training program in language and international business for lower-management personnel. In addition, Nissan offers English-language conversational classes to all career staff, offered at three levels: elementary, intermediate, and advanced. Those who work in the export department and those who have been selected for an overseas assignment must attend special language training programs. They undergo ninety hours of training in English and also take courses in international business.

Nissan also uses the services of external agencies, such as the IIST. Mr. Hanawa is very satisfied with the quality of the IIST program.

Nissan provides training for the wives of expatriates conducted by an external agency, the Hatano Family School, located in Tokyo. The spouses undergo a forty-hour program on how to adapt to a foreign environment. In addition, a short language course is offered. While a forty-hour program may be inadequate to teach a spouse to cope with all of the contingencies of living in a foreign country, it is more comprehensive than the training provided wives by many other Japanese multinationals. The children of expatriates are not given any training.

Evaluation of Performance

Expatriates are evaluated annually by the general manager of the foreign subsidiary or their immediate supervisor. Because of the considerable power wielded by the personnel division in corporate headquarters with regard to transfer and promotion, it may gather information on an expatriate's performance from independent sources to verify the evaluation provided by the general manager. If the evaluation is fairly negative, the supervisor has to pinpoint the person's limitations and specify in detail how he, the supervisor, plans to help the subordinate improve his performance. This information is then transmitted to the personnel division in Tokyo.

Mr. Hanawa explained that under the personnel system in Japanese companies, the human resources division has abundant information on each employee from various sources. If a general manager gives a negative evaluation of a particular employee, the personnel division may check with general managers of other divisions "to see whether the evaluation is accurate. We have the cooperation of many departments. All of us have been at Nissan for a very long time, so we know each other. So even though a person may not be the general manager of the person being evaluated, they may have a close relationship. Mr. Satoh, for instance, has worked here for fifteen years and many, many people in our company know his ability, experience, and personality. The human resources division can get much information about him from many sources. It is very easy. This is information gathering, Japanese-style."

Mr. Hanawa elaborated on the role of the personnel division by referring to the example of Mr. Satoh. Mr. Satoh has worked with the human resources division for the past fifteen years; "he has close contacts with people from many departments, such as export and domestic sales. In Japan, we have contacts not only with one's superior, but with numerous people from various departments. This is very different from U.S. companies. So people from many divisions know him." Mr. Satoh explained that in order to perform well in Japanese organizations, a person has to work closely with people from other divisions. This explains why human relations skills are paramount in Japanese organizations and why the ability to probe the positions adopted by people from other divisions and to negotiate issues diplomatically with other departments is considered a prerequisite for promotion to the managerial level.

Mr. Satoh elaborated on the notion of why extensive contacts with personnel from other divisions are a key to efficient operation in Japanese organizations. In U.S. companies, for instance, if one were employed in the human resources department and one's boss requested the person to recruit ten people, the subordinate would proceed accordingly. Mr. Satoh explained that this is inadequate in the Japanese context. The subordinate "has to check whether ten people is appropriate or not—should it be five, ten, or fifteen? He has to check the number even if it is provided by the boss. His boss expects him to check. If he finds that ten is too much, he will tell his boss that ten is perhaps too much, and that it should be seven or some other number. We will then discuss. If I agree, we will hire seven. In that case, my subordinate has done a good job. If he does not check and hires ten people, I think his performance is not satisfactory. So he has to contact various departments. For example, if he has to hire two for the finance department, three for domestic sales, and five for the export division, he has to contact the finance department and inquire why they need two people. Next, he has to ask domestic sales how they propose to use the three people. He should ask whether it is sufficient to hire two." Although the final decision is made by his boss, if the subordinate could "show a clear-cut reason, supported by data and the opinion of top executives in the respective departments," his boss probably will concur with his recommendation and then commend him for doing a thorough job.

Remuneration

A primary consideration in the determination of the amount of remuneration for an overseas assignment is the cost of living in the foreign country.

Nissan does not pay any premium for hardship positions, but the company pays special attention to such employees to ensure that their tenure abroad is satisfactory. In Mr. Hanawa's assignment to the United States, for example, Nissan believes that he should enjoy the same standard of living as an American vice-president. Thus, the company will provide adequate compensation to ensure that this is possible. Mr. Satoh elaborated that since Mr. Hanawa occupies a position equivalent to that of a vice-president in the United States, if the average vice-president in America has three cars, Mr. Hanawa will also be provided with a similar number of automobiles, even though he may have only one car in Japan.

Success and Factors for Success

Over the past twenty years that Nissan has been sending its people overseas, Mr. Hanawa indicated that the incidence of failure is under 1 percent. A person's failure will probably have a negative impact on his chances of promotion within the company.

Mr. Hanawa indicated two reasons for the low failure rate. One is the family and its attitude. "The employee does not say that 'I am a failure' or 'I feel bad in this country.' Their family would not complain that they don't like a particular country. In a U.S. company, the wives raise many complaints. Japanese wives and children don't voice their complaints very often. Even in Japan, the family may have complaints, but they don't voice them often." In the words of one Japanese executive, approximately 75 percent of American wives of expatriates of U.S. multinationals do not enjoy living in Japan and would openly express their feelings. This is in contradistinction to Japanese wives. Mr. Hanawa admitted, however, that although the employee may not openly express his feelings, discontent may negatively affect his job performance. A second reason for the low failure rate can be attributed to the system of evaluation. If the expatriate is not performing up to his usual standard, corporate headquarters will "ask his immediate supervisor in the foreign country to encourage him." Also, given the longer duration of an overseas assignment, the supervisor will generally allow the expatriate one to two years to adjust to the foreign country before adopting any drastic action.

Mr. Hanawa was asked whether changing values among the younger Japanese, whereby the family may be considered more important than the company, may influence the future performance of Japanese multinationals. Although Mr. Hanawa concurred that the attitudes of some youth are changing, he did not believe that it will negatively affect Nissan's future performance because "we have more talented people in our company now than in the past. So we can select the most suitable people very easily. In the past, we did not have that many talented people. So sometimes even if I thought a person was inappropriate, I still had to appoint him. Today, the situation has improved greatly—we have very many talented young people. So the chances for failure are minimized."

Changes

Mr. Hanawa was asked whether there was any aspect of the current selection and training procedures he would like to modify or redesign. He indicated that the company does not need "any drastic change" because the system at Nissan has evolved gradually over the past thirty years in response to changing conditions. The overseas section within the personnel division reviews the system annually to determine whether modifications are needed. For example, a training program for lower management was introduced in 1981 in response to changing needs. An area in which Mr. Hanawa expects modification in the future is the issue of compensation and remuneration for expatriates.

Nippon Steel Corporation

The information provided here is obtained from interviews with Yoshiro Sasaki, general manager, and Makoto Haya, manager, Personnel Department of Nippon Steel Corporation.

Overview

Nippon Steel Corporation is the world's largest manufacturer of steel with a production of 32.93 million tons of crude steel in 1980. The world's second largest manufacturer of crude steel is United States Steel Corporation with an output of 21.13 million tons in the same year.

Japan enjoys the distinction of housing four of the ten major manufacturers of steel in the world, including Nippon Steel Corporation. This is all the more impressive considering that Japan is largely dependent on foreign sources of raw materials for the production of steel. Approximately 80 percent of the iron ore and coking coal are imported (*This is Nippon Steel,* June 1981). Shortly after World War II, iron and steel was designated as one of the key industries in Japan. Under the protection of the Japanese government, huge outlays in capital investment, and adoption of innovative technology, the industry flourished and "became a model for technical progress in Japanese industry as a whole" (*Nippon: The land and its people,* 1982, p. 103).

Nippon Steel Corporation was formed in 1970 as a result of a merger between the two largest steel manufacturers in Japan, Yawata Iron & Steel Co., Ltd., and Fuji Iron & Steel Co., Ltd. Yawata's origin dated back to 1901. Despite the economic recession in the early 1980s and increasing pressure from other advanced nations on Japanese manufacturers to restrain their export of steel, Nippon Steel Corporation boosted its revenues by 267,777 million ($1,271 million) to reach 3,112,603 million yen ($14,776 million) in 1980. The company attributed much of this increase to the rapid expansion of the firm's engineering and construction division, which was established in 1974. The latter division capitalizes on the company's vast experiences in manufacturing steel and its abundant human resources to engage in construction and engineering projects throughout the world, such as building of offshore oil drilling platforms, overland pipelines, and bridges (*Nippon Steel Report,* April 1, 1980–March 31, 1981).

Staffing Policies

In fiscal year ended March 31, 1981, the company employed over 69,500 people, 20,000 of them career staff. The company operates wholly owned subsidiaries in major cities throughout the world, including New York, Los Angeles, Houston, Dusseldorf, London, Rio de Janeiro, São Paulo, Rome, Sydney, and Singapore.

Mr. Sasaki indicated that the people whom Nippon Steel sends abroad can be classified into one of three major categories. The first category includes expatriates who are sent to manage the overseas subsidiaries. In 1982, there were approximately seventy expatriates from Japan. The company began this policy of expatriation in the early 1950s. The second category consists of employees who undertake advanced degree programs in the United States and European nations. Every year the company sends approximately fifty employees to study business, engineering, and other technical subjects. The third category comprises people who travel abroad on business trips. These trips vary in duration and are usually undertaken by senior executives in the company. In recent years, however, the company has begun sending younger employees, including those at the managerial or assistant managerial level, abroad to engage in international business negotiations.

With regard to the staffing of its overseas subsidiaries, Japanese expatriates occupy all the senior and middle management positions. The company has hired fifty local nationals at the lower management level. In the United States and Western Europe, host country nationals are employed only at the clerical level. In Brazil, host country nationals have been hired as lower management personnel and accounting staff. The reasons for the differences in staffing policy in the case of Brazil are primarily two. One is that Brazil has the largest settlement of Japanese outside of Japan itself. Consequently there are a lot of *niseis* (second-generation Japanese) who are fluent in Japanese and familiar with the Japanese way of dong things. Second, the functions performed by the various subsidiary offices differ. In the case of Brazil, the subsidiaries are responsible for sales promotion and the purchase of raw materials. In the U.S. and West European subsidiaries, the primary function is that of liaison with Tokyo headquarters. Hence, it is imperative that this coordination function be performed by Japanese nationals who speak Japanese and thoroughly understand corporate policies and objectives.

When asked why Japanese multinationals in general tend to use parent country nationals more extensively than their U.S. and West European counterparts, Mr. Sasaki put forth two primary reasons. The first pertains to the function of the overseas office. In the case of Nippon Steel, except for the Brazilian subsidiaries, which are engaged in sales and purchase, the other overseas branches serve as liaison offices only; thus their principal purpose is to facilitate communication between the overseas subsidiary and Tokyo headquarters. "This means that the employees in the branches should know in detail the conditions, situations, or people in the head office." This is possible only with parent country nationals. This situation holds true for many overseas offices of Japanese general trading companies. A second reason for the extensive use of Japanese nationals could be atrributed to language differences. Many Japanese who were born in the 1930s or earlier may not be fluent in a foreign language. Since most non-Japanese do not speak Japanese, it is difficult for foreign nationals to communicate with senior management in corporate headquarters in Tokyo. Mr. Sasaki noted, however, that it may be necessary to embark on a policy of localization in the near future.

Selection Criteria

Mr. Sasaki indicated that Nippon Steel does not have a fixed set of criteria in selecting people for an overseas assignment. Moreover, these criteria vary for the three categories of people sent overseas. In the case of expatriates who are sent to manage the overseas subsidiaries, their present career paths are taken into consideration. "For example, if the New York office needed people to liaise in the area of steel exports, we will send people from the export department in corporate headquarters, not people from the raw materials division." A second criterion is "the general ability of the person to pursue the job in the overseas office," or technical competence. A third criterion is personality, such as ability to adjust to living and working in a new cultural environment. Mr. Sasaki pointed out, "Most Japanese people are very shy and reserved." Consequently, the company has to select those who are outgoing, persuasive, and aggressive.

Nippon Steel, like most other Japanese companies, views the study-abroad program as a major investment in its employees' future. Consequently the company selects only those who have the potential to make major contributions to the organization. This is used as a principal criterion for selection. *Potential* refers to the person's "general competence in the future rather than his actual performance in the present stage of his career development." This criterion is consistent with the evaluation system used in most Japanese organizations at the premanagerial phase. A second criterion for selection under the study-abroad program is personality, "especially aggressiveness, the ability to communicate with faculty and friends, and the capability to assimilate new knowledge." A third criterion is proficiency in a foreign language so that the individual can enroll in a foreign university.

When asked how the company assesses an employee on the criterion of aggressiveness, Mr. Sasaki explained that this is made possible by the unique practices of Japanese personnel management. The personnel system at Nippon Steel, like that of most other Japanese corporations, is "very different from that of U.S. companies. Personnel functions are centralized and the personnel department reports directly to the office of the president. Every year, the employee has to write a self-evaluation of himself and then the boss evaluates him. The evaluation forms are then submitted to the personnel department. The personnel department also gathers information about the employee from his boss and colleagues through daily conversations. Through this system, the personnel department has very complete information about the character of each employee."

An employee can generally expect his first overseas assignment after he has been with Nippon Steel for ten years. Only those who have attained a minimal level of assistant manager will be sent abroad to manage the overseas subsidiary. In Mr. Sasaki's words, "It takes ten years before the employee has an understanding of the company in Japan."

When asked about the criterion of adaptability to a foreign cultural environment, Mr. Sasaki observed that there are not many problems in this regard because "generally speaking, it is easy for Japanese people to adapt to foreign cultures and foreign people. For example, if you look at the history of Japan, the Japanese have learned from the Chinese and Koreans. Of course, there are some people who could not understand or speak a foreign language fluently. But it is very rare." Mr. Sasaki's comments in this regard are a marked departure from those made by the majority of Japanese executives interviewed for this study. Mr. Sasaki, however, was focusing primarily on the Japanese attitude of acquiring useful knowledge from other nations. This is consistent with the theme expounded in Chapter 2.

When asked whether language is important in selecting Japanese expatriates, Mr. Sasaki noted that although it is taken into consideration, it is not a principal factor because the company provides candidates who are not fluent in a foreign language an opportunity to study the language in the foreign country. In the case of Dusseldorf, West Germany, for instance, the Japanese expatriate will study for three to four months in a language institute in Germany prior to his assumption of responsibilities in that country.

Besides acquiring language skills, such postdeparture training also provides the candidate an opportunity to observe and interact with local nationals. As Herrari and Zeira (1978, p. 61) noted, if expatriates are exempted from managerial duties in the first several months after arrival, it "will ease their acculturation and help prevent mistakes they tend to make during this period [which are] usually detrimental to both the expatriate and his organization." Thus, language training in the country of assignment appears to serve several important objectives.

Mr. Sasaki was asked whether the company consults with the employee prior to an overseas assignment. Before actual assignment, the personnel division staff discusses the situation with the prospective candidate's immediate supervisor. All subjects pertaining to the person's career, performance, and family are carefully reviewed. Consequently the company seldom makes unreasonable assignments. Mr. Sasaki was asked whether an individual can refuse an overseas assignment. He responded, "In the strict sense, the employee has the right to refuse an assignment. In the final analysis, there has been no such cases. When we join the company, we make an implicit commitment that we will be transferred through our entire career." If the person has a good reason, such as aged parents, illness in the family, or the problem of children's education (all of which could be verified by the company), he may turn down an overseas assignment without incurring any penalty or negatively affecting his chances of future promotion. Mr. Sasaki recounted that a friend of his turned down an assignment to Brazil some thirty years ago; nevertheless he was eventually promoted to the position of general manager.

The company encourages expatriates to bring their families with them, and those with young children generally do so. All of the seventy current expatriates are accompanied by their spouses. Those with children in high school may leave them behind in Japan, however. When asked whether the wives' opinions were consulted prior to an overseas assignment, Mr. Sasaki replied in the negative; "in comparison to American or European wives, Japanese wives do not raise many objections." He added, however, that many spouses have to undergo a major adjustment and some undertake outside classes to prepare them for living abroad.

Given Nippon Steel's extensive operations throughout the world, Mr. Sasaki was asked whether an overseas assignment was considered a prequisite for promotion to top management. The company does not have such a policy now, but he believed that "in the near future, overseas experience will be an important criterion for promotion to top management positions." Mr. Eishiro Saito, now the chairman of the board of Nippon Steel, introduced a policy of requiring all managers to learn a foreign language when he was president of the company several years ago.

The average duration of an overseas assignment is three to four years. There is no fixed policy as to how long a person should remain in corporate headquarters after repatriation before his next tour of duty abroad. Mr.

Sasaki indicated that there is no problem with repatriation at Nippon Steel because the maximum duration of an overseas assignment is five years, after which the person is repatriated. Furthermore, he added, "It is very good for the Tokyo office to have an employee who knows the overseas market."

Training Programs

Like many other Japanese companies, Nippon Steel Corporation emphasizes the importance of human resource development, which is supposed to extend beyond the mere scope of education and training. Shortly after the formation of Nippon Steel Corporation in 1970, the company president issued two directives to all employees emphasizing the importance of human resource development. The first was sent to all employees and included the following five objectives: "One, work happily in cooperation with many people; two, persevere in your tasks; three, become experts in your field; four, create something better, while considering your actual circumstances; and five, become a sensible member of society." The second directive was circulated to all management-level personnel and included the following two guidelines: "One, to become, through self-study, an example to subordinates; and, two, to make unselfish efforts toward the personnel development of subordinates who will be the future managers of the company" (material provided by Mr. Sasaki). The objectives laid down in these two directives are similar to the personnel development programs of most other Japanese companies.

To implement these directives, Nippon Steel has established four-year plans for personnel development. Under the current and third personnel development program (extending from fiscal years 1980 to 1984), the company seeks development in the areas of technical, engineering, and international business skills. To accomplish these objectives, the training programs are divided into several categories: the study-abroad program, in-house training (general and specialized), and external facilities within Japan.

Study-Abroad Programs: Every year Nippon Steel sends twenty-five young employees to attend graduate programs at foreign universities, including business and engineering schools. Since the average duration of these programs is two years, this means that in any given year, approximately fifty Nippon Steel employees are studying abroad. Every year, the company recruits 250 Japanese college graduates as career staff. This means that roughly 10 percent of all college recruits have the opportunity to study abroad.

The primary criterion for selection for the study-abroad program is the person's potential. Consequently only potential high performers are selected.

Mr. Sasaki noted that very few senior executives are sent abroad to attend management development programs, primarily because of language problems. However, given Mr. Saito's emphasis on foreign language training, Mr. Sasaki believes that in the future, more senior managers will be sent abroad to participate in executive development seminars.

In-House Training: The in-house personnel development program at Nippon Steel is divided into two major categories: those for managers and white-collar workers and those for blue-collar workers. Under each category, there are general and specialized training programs.

The general training portion for managers and white-collar workers includes a week-long live-in orientation session for new college recruits to develop group consciousness and to help them understand the correct attitude as members of an enterprise and society. This is followed by a nine-month theme training in which the recruits are exposed to the fundamentals of performing their duties. Some recruits are dispatched to the Iron and Steel Junior College; before they leave, they undertake a three-month live-in program to sharpen their skills in English, mathematics, chemistry, and physics.

On advancement to middle-level career staff without title, after they have worked with Nippon Steel for several years, the employees undertake a three-day, two-night program to develop their analytical skills and foster a team approach to problem solving. On promotion to the level of assistant manager several years later, the employees are provided a week-long training session to develop their management capabilities. After the person has served as an assistant manager for three years, he is exposed to a six-month subject training program for assistant managers, conducted both during and after office hours, which seeks to develop problem-solving skills and improve their "mental horizon...and comprehensive judgment" (material provided by Mr. Sasaki). On promotion to level of manager, the employee takes a six-month program to hone the skills developed under the six-month subject training program for assistant managers.

The specialized programs include training in language, technical subjects, control procedures, patents, and computers. With respect to language training, English is taught at three levels: elementary (nine months), intermediate (five months), and advanced (five months). These are conducted both during and after office hours. In addition, there is a six-month program on how to write technical English. Chinese, French, Spanish, and Portuguese are also taught at both the elementary and intermediate levels. The elementary- and intermediate-level training in each non-English language extends for nine months and is conducted outside of office hours. The technical training is divided into two levels: elementary (five months) and applied (five-day, four-night program). The former consists of an introduction to the technology involved in the manufacture of iron and steel and lessons on quality control. The latter involves company-wide discussions on the application of certain techniques. The training on control procedures is divided into three segments. The first and second segments consist of fifteen and a half days of full-time study on control procedures, operations research, and the application of statistical procedures. The third segment revolves around theme training in control techniques. This is a ten-day, full-time course in which the employees solve actual problems using control procedures. In addition, there is another ten-day training on the use of computers. At the assistant manager level, there is a ten and a half hour training in patent systems (material provided by Mr. Sasaki).

External Agencies: Every year Nippon Steel sends one employee to attend the IIST's three-month program. Mr. Sasaki added, however, that his company prefers to send employees to attend educational programs abroad. In the past, it used the IIST quite extensively. In recent years, however, since Nippon Steel (like many of the larger Japanese firms) has established its own in-house training programs, it naturally tends to use its own facilities more.

For those who do not have the opportunity to attend the advanced-degree programs, Nippon Steel provides language training both prior to departure and immediately after arrival in a foreign country. The average duration of an overseas language training program is three months. Every year Nippon Steel sends twenty-four or twenty-five employees to attend language institutes in the United States and United Kingdom in an effort to improve their proficiency in English. An employee sent to attend an advanced-degree program abroad is allowed one year of language training followed by two years for the advanced degree. Besides English, Nippon also sends employees to study Spanish, Portugese, and Chinese in the respective nations. The average duration of a non-English-language program is one to one and one-half years. The company pays for all expenses incurred for the language training. In addition, all expatriates receive general guidance on the country to which they are assigned.

Nippon Steel does not provide formal training for the spouses of expatriates, although it gives them literature about a foreign country. In addition, the wives are encouraged to take the free week-long training program sponsored by Japan Air Lines.

Success and Factors for Success

To the best of Mr. Sasaki's recollection, over the past thirty years that Nippon Steel has been sending its people abroad, there was only one single incident of failure—an employee sent to study in the United States got into trouble with local nationals.

Mr. Sasaki attributed the extremely low failure rate at Nippon Steel to three primary reasons. One is "the general character of the Japanese. The

Japanese are very moderate. They don't like to make trouble." A second reason can be attributed to the overall quality of the people recruited to work for Nippon Steel. This point is similar to the one made by Mr. Terasawa that putting language abilities aside, almost any college graduate recruited into Nomura Securities is suitable for an overseas assignment. In the case of Nippon Steel, as far as nonengineering graduates are concerned, the company selects the top eighty university graduates from over one thousand applicants. Thus, only the elite are chosen to work for the company. A third reason for the low failure rate can be attributed to the system of lifetime employment. Given low job mobility in Japan, a career staff knows that it is in his best interest not to create disturbances. Consequently, he should endure whatever assignments are given him by the company and do his best under the circumstances.

Mr. Sasaki was asked whether the low failure rate in the past could also be attributed to the general attitude of Japanese employees with respect to their employers; that is, they tended to place the company above their family. With the younger generation, however, the trend may be changing in that the family is considered more important. In response, Mr. Sasaki indicated that he did not "see a *basic* [emphasis added] change in the mentality of the Japanese people. The differences between the older and younger generations are not that great. If people perceive a change, it could perhaps be due to the fact that young people nowadays are more open in expressing their opinions. So some people think the younger generation has changed. I think that more direct and open expressions of opinions will help the company. So I see it as a positive change." Consequently, in Mr. Sasaki's opinion, it should not negatively affect the future performance of the company.

Remuneration

The remuneration policy at Nippon Steel is fairly similar to that of other large Japanese corporations. Remuneration is based on the cost-of-living index in a given country. In assignments to developing nations, such as Africa and the Middle East, the company pays a hardship premium. Because of the generally lower cost of living in these countries, however, the actual amount paid the employee may be less than that paid an individual assigned to New York, which has a higher cost of living.

Changes

Mr. Sasaki was asked whether there are any modifications he would like to make to the existing program. He offered three. The first pertains to the heavier emphasis on overseas assignment as part of one's career development. Under the present system, overseas experience is not considered a prerequisite for promotion to top management positions; however, with the increasing internationalization of Japanese business, Mr. Sasaki believes that it is necessary for all top mangement personnel to have overseas work experience. A second suggestion pertains to the need to update and improve the selection and training procedures used in the company. This second suggestion perhaps reflects the Japanese commitment to overall progress and development, a cornerstone of zen philosophy. A third suggestion is for non-Japanese to have a better understanding of the Japanese way. This is essential if the company embarks on a policy of localization. Currently only *niseis* in Brazil who speak Japanese are hired as low-level management and accounting personnel in the company's overseas subsidiaries. If the company were to recruit host country nationals in other countries, it may have to sponsor programs similar to the ones offered by Canon Inc. and Nissan Motor Corporation so that foreign nationals can become better acquainted with Japanese industrial practices.

8 Conclusion

This book first compared the human resource development programs with regard to selection and training of expatriates between a sample of U.S. and Japanese multinationals and subsequently examined the human resource development programs at a number of Japanese multinationals. In general, it appeared that the Japanese multinationals send abroad individuals who are more adept at living and working in a foreign environment, as evidenced by substantially low failure rates. Throughout the book, the contention is made that although the international competitiveness of U.S. multinationals may be weakening because of the narrowing technological gap between the United States and Japan, a more important reason perhaps could be attributed to the fact that since Japanese multinationals traditionally place heavier emphasis on international markets, they devote considerably more attention to selection and training of their people for overseas assignments, which in turn translate into better performance abroad. Because of its large domestic market, U.S. corporations have often relegated international sales a secondary position in the overall corporate picture. This attitude is often reflected in its staffing policy—an effective manager in the United States will perform well in a foreign environment, regardless. In this day of increasing global competition, this strategy does not fare well and there are many tales of misadventure among U.S. multinationals that have pursued this policy.

In contrast, Japanese multinationals have done an excellent job in this regard, all the more remarkable considering that the Japanese, by culture and history, do not readily mix with *gaijins* (foreigners). Because of the homogeneity of Japanese society and its relative isolation from the outside world until the mid-nineteenth century, its people are less adept at living and working in a foreign environment. However, through self-discipline and meticulous preparation, the Japanese who have been sent abroad to establish and manage foreign subsidiaries have succeeded in making Japan a formidable global economic force. Although much of this success can be attributed to the quality and competitiveness of its products, the ingenuity of its work force also plays a pivotal role in ensuring that its products are effectively marketed in foreign countries. As Jiro Tokuyama, executive director and dean of the Nomura School of Advanced Management, said, there appears to be a general thirst or quest for global information on the part of many Japanese executives: "Many of the Japanese executives not only follow many Japanese magazines and newspapers, but read at least a few of the following periodicals: *Newsweek, Time,* the *London Economist,* the *Wall Street Journal,* the *New York Times,* and the *Financial Times.* We are making such an effort to understand the global market. As you know, we live in an information oriented era when countries with valuable pieces of information or intelligence win. So-called industrial policy is not necessarily the cause of our competitive position in world markets. The economic 'miracle' of Japan is attributable in part to our eagerness to gather and analyze available information on world markets. I recommend that American executives do the same if they want to remain intact in the highly competitive global market." This is where the human factor comes into play. Without a highly developed and trained core of internationally oriented human talent, the competitiveness and indeed the viability of a multinational are greatly jeopardized. Throughout the chapters, the reasons for the lower failure rates among Japanese multinationals were alluded to. These are now summarized and discussed.

Reasons for Lower Failure Rates among Japanese Multinationals

Overall Qualification of Candidates

In Japan, there is a heavy emphasis on education. The report of the U.S. National Commission on Excellence in Education released in early 1983 found that the average high school graduate in Japan receives an equivalent of four years more of education than his or her American counterpart. The entrance examinations to the elite universities in Japan are tough, and admission is based entirely on the results of scholastic aptitude tests. According to a 1981 finding by the Japan Ministry of Education, Japan has the second highest proportion of students enrolled in higher education. The United States ranks first, followed by France, the United Kingdom, and West Germany in third, fourth, and fifth places, respectively (*Human resource development in industry,* 1983, p. 7).

Since a person's status in Japanese society is determined to a large extent by the company to which he works, college graduates exercise extreme caution in selecting the company that they would like to work for. Stated Mr. Terasawa of Nomura Securities International Inc., "To choose a job is almost as important as selecting a woman for his wife. In fact it is more important." In the event of an inappropriate spouse, divorce is an option. But in the case of a job, it is difficult to quit and seek another position elsewhere unless "one sacrifices himself, both financially and status-wise."

The well-established companies meticulously choose prospective employees from among the large pool of new college graduates every year. The hiring decision is based primarily on performance in the aptitude tests administered by the respective companies. Nippon Steel Corporation chooses the top 80 candidates from nearly 1,000 applicants. They are recruited as career staff and are protected under the system of lifetime employment. Consequently only the elite are selected. The same procedure holds true for other well-established Japanese companies.

Once inducted into the company, these candidates are given an extensive training program that spans several years. Hence, in the opinion of Mr. Terasawa of Nomura Securities, barring language proficiencies, "practically anybody that is admitted into the company is qualified for an overseas assignment." This may be an overstatement because technical competence alone does not necessarily guarantee high performance abroad; however, when technical competence is combined with other factors, it can become a very powerful force and in turn account for high performance overseas.

This emphasis on quality is reflected in the change in criteria for promotion up the organizational hierarchy. Until recently promotion within Japanese organizations was largely based on seniority, although the overall performance of the individual was weighed. Consequently, those who demonstrated exceptional talent were assigned more responsible tasks. In recent years, an increasing number of Japanese firms have espoused the policy of promotion primarily on the basis of merit. According to a finding by the Japan Institute of Labor, "Today the notion of using examinations as the primary means of assessing ability is fast gaining currency" among an increasing number of Japanese organizations (*Human resource development in industry*, 1983, p. 12). This trend reflects a greater commitment to education and performance and undoubtedly will raise the overall quality of employees.

Commitment to One's Company

Given the traditional Japanese loyalty to one's company and low job mobility in Japanese society, the expatriate has to endure and do his best even if he does not like the assignment. Poor performance abroad would constitute a loss of face, and given the importance of face saving in the Japanese context, the expatriate will do his utmost to uphold his track record in a foreign country. Furthermore, given the system of lifetime employment, a Japanese career staff knows that he should not cause trouble for the organization. As the Japanese maxim goes: "The nail that sticks out will get hit with the hammer." Consequently, a Japanese expatriate feels that he must not disrupt the foreign operation because it will not be good for his future career in the company.

The values of the younger generation may be changing. A 1979 survey by the Public Opinion Research Institute in Japan found that respondents voiced a greater need to distinguish between their work and personal lives, coupled with a greater emphasis on striking a "balance between work and private life" (*Human resource development in industry,* 1983, pp. 9-10). But Mr. Sasaki of Nippon Steel Corporation believes that these findings can be attributed in part to a greater willingness on the part of the young to voice their opinions. Perhaps another more compelling reason to believe that this trend may not have too great an impact on the future performance of Japanese organizations could be ascribed to the projections by the Japan Ministry of Labor that in the years ahead, senior management positions in Japanese companies will become more competitive. In 1978, it was found that approximately 60 percent of Japanese university graduates in the fifty to fifty-four age category had attained the position of departmental or divisional head. By 1988, it is projected that only 30 percent of university graduates can expect to reach senior management positions (*Human resource development in industry,* 1983, pp. 6-7). Given the more limited chances of upward mobility and the overall competitiveness of the Japanese people, it is unlikely that as the younger generation matures, this overall dedication, loyalty, and commitment to their organizations will slacken.

Longer Duration of Overseas Assignments

Although the exact duration of an overseas assignment varies according to position and country, the average span is five years. Most overseas assignments of U.S. multinationals are for two or three years. This variation stems from the overall difference in time perspective between U.S. and Japanese' multinationals. The former are generally more short-term oriented and tend to focus on immediate profitability and return on investments. Japanese firms tend to be longer-term oriented and are more concerned about market share and growth.

This difference in time perspective has often been a source of friction between joint cooperative agreements between U.S. and Japanese firms (Tung 1984). Americans are unique in this regard in that their West European counterparts also tend to possess longer time perspectives in decision making and planning. In general, the performance of European managers is judged not so much by short-term fluctuations in the company's earnings but by long-term profitability. Hence, they can concentrate more on courses of action that are beneficial to the long-term interests of the company (Ball, 1980). The pursuit of long- vis-à-vis short-term goals may often be in conflict—for example, reducing expenditure in R&D will result in increased short-term profits, but may be detrimental to the long-term goals of the company. Because of the system of evaluation used in most U.S. firms, many managers tend to focus on short-term objectives at the expense of long-term goals.

The longer duration of overseas assignments means that the Japanese expatriate has more time to adjust to a foreign country. Most of the Japanese multinationals interviewed for this study indicated that they do not expect the expatriate to be performing to full capacity until the third year of assignment. In the first year, they allow the individual to adjust to the foreign culture. In the second year, the expatriate "tries to be active" (Mr. Miyazaki of Marubeni Corp.), but corporate headquarters make allowances because this is still viewed as part of the basic period of adjustment. In the third year, the expatriate begins to function at his usual capacity. Some Japanese executives feel that the duration of certain overseas assignments should be extended to ten years because the company could then have a full seven years to enjoy the fruits of their labor.

In contrast, the frequent rotation of personnel in the overseas operations of U.S. multinationals often does not give the expatriate sufficient time to get acquainted with a foreign environment. For example, it was reported that when a U.S. food manufacturer sent its marketing manager to Japan for eighteen months, the individual spent the first six months in adjusting to Japan and the last six months planning for his reentry back to the United States. Consequently there were only six months in which the individual was really contributing to the subsidiary operation in Japan. Given his preoccupation with the problems of entry to and exit from Japan, the company lost approximately 98 percent of its market share to a major European competitor over the eighteen-month period.

Support System in Corporate Headquarters

Another possible reason for the generally briefer duration of overseas assignments can be attributed to the fact that the expatriates themselves are anxious to return to corporate headquarters as soon as possible for fear that they may be forgotten and hence passed up for promotion. These fears are justified to a large extent because of the revolving-door policy at the top management level in U.S. corporations. An expatriate who has been away for an extended number of years may find himself a stranger to the members of the board. Although some Japanese expatriates express a similar concern, it is only infrequently mentioned.

Most Japanese multinationals provide a comprehensive support system or network for the expatriate that covers a fairly broad spectrum of activities. Many of the larger multinationals have a division whose sole purpose is to look after the needs of expatriates. For example, Nissan Motor has an overseas section within the company's human resources division. Similarly, two divisions in the Bank of Yokohama provide both "mental and financial support" (Mr. Ozawa of the Bank of Yokohama) to their expatriates. The superior-subordinate relationship or mentor system in Japanese organizations involves certain obligations and responsibilities on the parts of the leader and the led. In the words of Mr. Tsuneo Iyobe of Mitsubishi Corporation, "My boss will continue to be my boss for a long time. I know he will take care of me." Not many American expatriates can speak with such certainty. Also, due to the Japanese organization's greater concern for the total person, the company will try to find excuses for expatriates who leave their families in Japan because of their children's education to make frequent business trips to Japan. And at any time there is usually a fairly large contingent of Japanese expatriates in a given country. Because of the strong group feeling among the Japanese, Japanese who have already lived in the foreign country for several years help the new arrivals.

Evaluation of Performance

Given the longer-term orientation of most Japanese firms, their criteria for evaluation of an individual's performance are different from that used by many U.S. companies. In Japanese organizations, evaluation generally is based on a person's capabilities in the long run, and Japanese managers are usually more understanding of circumstances that may temporarily affect an employee's level of performance. For example, in the first one to two years of an expatriate's assignment overseas, even though the individual is not performing up to his usual capacity, most managers make allowances for such behavior.

Selection for Overseas Assignments

Although a Japanese multinational might not administer specific tests to determine the candidate's relational abilities and adaptability prior to overseas assignment, it would carefully review every aspect of the employee's qualifications before making a final decision. This is possible because of the unique system of personnel management in Japan.

Recommendations for an overseas assignment are generally made by the division chief in consultation with the personnel department in corporate headquarters. In Japan, the personnel department wields considerable power, is highly centralized, and reports directly to the office of the president. Because of the strong group orientation and the regular after-hours socializing among the male career staff, the immediate supervisor in a Japanese company is thoroughly familiar with an individual's family background, general preferences, qualifications, and so on. Given such knowledge, the Japanese supervisor would generally not make unreasonable recommendations.

Most Japanese companies keep detailed personnel profiles or inventories on their career staff compiled from the annual or semiannual performance evaluations completed by the individual, his immediate supervisor, and the chief of his division. Every year, the employee is asked to write a self-description detailing his aspirations and career plans on how to attain this goal. Furthermore, the personnel departments of some companies conduct forty-five- to sixty-minute interviews with each career staff as part of the annual evaluation.

Most candidates considered for an overseas assignment (excluding those who have been selected to study abroad) have generally been with the company for ten years. During this time they have been carefully indoctrinated with the company's philosophy and overall objectives, and the company has had ample time to assess their capabilities and qualifications. Consequently, although Japanese multinationals may not administer specific tests prior to selecting an individual for an overseas assignment, they generally have sufficient information to assess the candidate's suitability.

Although the values of the younger generation may be changing in the direction of striking a greater balance between work and private life, given the strong team orientation in Japanese society, the phenomenon of groupism (as distinguished from individualism in the United States) will continue to be emphasized. Consequently the interaction among members of a work group will continue to be strong.

Training for Overseas Assignments

Because of the system of lifetime employment and the longer-term perspective of most Japanese firms, the firms feel safe in investing in their employees' future by spending huge sums of money to train them for an overseas assignment. Tung (1982a) reported that 57 percent of the Japanese multinationals surveyed sponsored some formal training program to prepare expatriates for overseas assignments. This is consistent with the findings of *Japan Economic News* (June 24, 1982), which showed that 70 percent of the 267 largest companies in Japan offered some preparatory courses for their expatriates. The human resource development programs differ in content and emphasis, but they often have similar components.

Language Training: Language was cited by virtually all the Japanese companies as an important criterion for selection, although its rank ordering has decreased since the mid-1970s. Practically all of the companies interviewed for this study sponsored intensive language training programs for their expatriates. Prior to intensive language training, the average career staff already has eight years of education in English in high school and at the university. Knowledge of a foreign language enables the individual to communicate in the host country and helps the person gain insight into the host nation's way of thinking and nuances in the foreign culture. To promote fluency in a foreign language, many Japanese companies invite Caucasians to share the same dormitories so that the Japanese trainees will have ample opportunity to practice their language skills and to gain a better understanding of the foreign country.

General Training for Career Staff. A career staff in a Japanese company typically does not receive his first major promotion until ten years after he joins the company. Thus, the initial ten years can be viewed as one extensive training period in which the individual is inculcated with the various aspects of the company's operations. This extended training period allows the career staff time to acquire technical competence in the various functional disciplines and at the same time provides the company with ample opportunity to assess the person's capabilities.

Field Experience. Many of the Japanese multinationals surveyed send select members of their career staff to serve as trainees for one year in their overseas subsidiaries. As trainees, their primary mission is to observe closely and learn about the company's foreign operations. In the overseas trainee program, the Japanese employee tries to acquire as much information as possible about the foreign country, including noneconomic variables. This kind of training prepares them for an eventual overseas assignment, which is viewed as part of one's career development.

While the Japanese employees serve in the capacities of consumers rather than producers in the one-year overseas job training programs, the companies do not feel that this is a waste of money because of the Japanese belief that in order to become better producers later in their careers, the employees need to have an adequate understanding of all factors (both economic and noneconomic) that could influence a society's functioning.

A small but growing number of U.S. executives are beginning to share this sentiment. In the summer of 1983, Williams College sponsored a five-week program for fifteen middle-management executives on a number of subjects, ranging from film criticism, politics, art, classical music, and literature to human behavior. The participants were slated as fast-trackers by their respective companies, among them International Business Machines, Polaroid Corporation, and General Electric Corporation. These companies were willing to invest $5,200 in the program because they believe that candidates for top management positions must sharpen their powers of inquiry and reflection and have a deeper understanding and awareness of social issues. These skills may not be adequately conveyed through business or technical courses. In order to become a successful CEO, Irving Shapiro, former chairman and CEO of Dupont, believes that it is imperative for the person to have a broad understanding of world issues "beyond the provincial limits of his own business" (Louis 1983, p. 38). This sentiment is similar to that espoused by Japanese executives who contend that in order to become better businessmen, it is necessary to understand the social, economic, and cultural factors that make up a society.

Graduate Programs Abroad: Every year, many of the Japanese multinationals surveyed send ten to twenty career staff to attend graduate business, law, and engineering programs overseas. The company pays tuition and all expenses in addition to the employee's regular salary. These graduate programs may sometimes take as long as four years. In the first year, the trainee is immersed in intensive English-language training in the foreign country. This is followed by two years of the M.B.A. program and a fourth year in field experience. While attending graduate school, the Japanese employee is exposed to foreign principles of management. Furthermore, during the two years' duration, the Japanese employee gains a better understanding of the broad functioning of other societies. Thus, the study-abroad programs serve a function similar in many ways to that of the overseas job training program.

In-House Training Programs: Besides language training, expatriates take courses in international finance and economics and are given environmental briefings about the country of assignment.

In the past, the emphasis was on language training. Many Japanese companies are now beginning to realize the importance of developing the management or administrative skills of their expatriates. A principal reason for failure is the inability of the expatriate to cope with the larger responsibilities of overseas work. Many Japanese expatriates may initially encounter status shock when they have to operate pretty much on their own, isolated from corporate headquarters. Although they maintain daily contact through the telephone or other means of telecommunication, they cannot have the kind of close interaction that they were accustomed to at home. The expatriates suddenly find themselves burdened with added responsibility as overseas representatives, a status or role they are generally not used to performing, on a singular basis. To a Japanese who has been used to working in a group, the adjustment problem may be tremendous. Consequently a number of the Japanese executives interviewed for the study feel that it is imperative to develop the management skills of expatriates to prepare them for the added responsibilities as overseas representatives of a Japanese firm.

As Dr. Jiro Tokuyama of the Nomura School of Advanced Management noted, a principal objective of their program is to develop the skills of senior management with respect to strategy making, an area in which Japanese executives are presumably weak. The purpose of the three-week program at the Nomura School is to prepare senior management personnel to take on "general management responsibilities including the development and implementation of corporate strategies and the determination of the range of operations." Apparently, these are skills required of an expatriate while serving as the company's representative or liaison person abroad.

Outside Agencies. A number of institutes in Japan prepare expatriates for overseas assignments. One is the IIST, established under the auspices of MITI. The institute offers a three-month program designed for specialists and covering courses in English and international business transactions and a one-year program designed to "foster generalists and internationally-minded businessmen." Trainees enrolled in the longer program have to master English plus one other foreign language, and they receive intensive training in area studies. Besides the use of visiting professors from foreign countries, there is an exchange program so that students from other nations live under the same roof as the Japanese trainees. The purpose here is to provide ample opportunities for the trainees to practice their language skills and learn more about a foreign country.

Role of the Family

In the case of U.S. multinationals, and indeed in the case of most European multinationals, a principal reason for failure is the family situation; the expatriate's spouse and children are unable to adjust to a foreign country, which may in turn affect the person's performance overseas (Tung 1982a). In Japan, wives are generally more "obedient and dependent," according to many Japanese executives interviewed. In the words of an American who is a student of Japanese history, "Japanese women perceive of their roles as wife and mother as a job. So she is a failure if she cannot stand it. An American wife, on the other hand, thinks she has an independent life." Given the emphasis on face saving, a Japanese woman would not want to fail in her role as a wife by constantly complaining about the problems encountered in living in a foreign country.

From the foregoing, it appears that a multitude of factors has accounted for the lower failure rates among Japanese multinationals, which in turn contribute to the increasing competitiveness of Japanese firms in the international context. However, this is not to suggest that Japanese multinationals are not without their problems. Throughout the chapters, the issues confronting Japanese multinationals with regard to expatriate assignments were alluded to. These are now summarized and discussed.

Problems Facing Japanese Multinationals

A major problem facing Japanese expatriates is that of children's education. All Japanese executives interviewed for this study were unanimous in this regard. The average Japanese male graduates from college at age 22 and gets married at age twenty-seven or twenty-eight. Since a career staff generally gets his first overseas assignment ten years or more after he has been with the company, many of those assigned overseas may have children in junior or senior high school. At these critical junctures, Japanese parents are reluctant to allow their children to be educated abroad. Consequently many leave their children in Japan. Since the wife's first responsibility is to her children, she generally stays in Japan, a situation that creates hardship for the expatriate.

Although the Japanese government has tried to improve the plight of expatriates by establishing special schools for Japanese children who were educated abroad, these youngsters nevertheless may have difficulty catching up. Furthermore, the entrance examinations to Japanese universities emphasize knowledge of factual information, not the forte of many children who received a high school education abroad. Even if the children were to attend elite universities in advanced nations abroad and were admitted to the well-established firms, according to Hiromichi Matsuka, deputy general manager of Dai-Ichi Kangyo Bank Ltd., their careers are limited to a certain extent because they are generally assigned to positions in the international division regardless of personal preferences.

Many Japanese parents are unwilling to place their children at a distinct disadvantage by allowing them to be educated in high schools abroad. The number of Japanese expatriates going abroad alone was as high as 50 percent in a number of the companies interviewed, as in the case of Toray Industries, which has 220 Japanese expatriates, and Furukawa Electric Co., Ltd., which has some 150 expatriates. According to Masakazu Mizutani, general manager of general planning, Overseas Operations Division, Furukawa Electric Co., Ltd., expatriates assigned to industrialized nations bring their families along, while those assigned to the developing countries go abroad alone. According to another Japanese executive, 75 percent of the Japanese expatriates in New York City are living alone because their wives and children have returned to Japan for the reason of children's education. This is an area that deserves immediate attention by the Japanese government, industry, and society as a whole. If the problem remains unresolved, it may negatively influence the morale, and hence performance, of Japanese expatriates.

A second problem pertains to the changing value system of Japanese youth. According to the findings of the Public Opinion Research Institute in 1979, 51 percent of the respondents indicated that they would not undertake "difficult assignments" to increase their chances of promotion. Only 16 percent said they would do so unquestioningly, and another 29 percent indicated that they would if "that's the only way" (*Human resource development in industry,* 1983, p. 10). If the problem of children's education remains unresolved, more and more Japanese employees may consider an overseas assignment an undue hardship. This would severely affect the number of people willing to accept an overseas position. Other factors that compound the difficulty of an overseas assignment pertain to the increased standard of living in Japan and the soaring prices of real estate in Japan. Because of the former, an overseas assignment has lost much of the attraction it held for many Japanese in the early years after the war when the standard of living in the country was still very low. Due to the rising prices of real estate in Japan, expatriates may find it difficult to buy a house in Japan. If they have already bought one, they are reluctant to sell or rent it out for extended periods of time.

Another problem that Japanese industry has to face in general is the aging of the work force. According to the National Census Bureau in Japan, the number of people aged sixty-five and over will increase from 8.9 percent in 1980 to 11.0 percent in 1990 and 14.3 percent in the year 2000 (*Human resource development in industry*, 1983, p. 6). In terms of expatriate assignments, this will mean a general decrease in the number of career staff in the younger age brackets who could be assigned abroad. Although the Japanese government and industry are trying to cope with the problem on the domestic front, a possible solution in terms of staffing overseas operations would be greater use of host country nationals. This would also help develop better public relations abroad. While there are still difficulties in incorporating foreign nationals into the overall structure of a Japanese firm, it appears that through greater understanding by non-Japanese of the Japanese way of doing business and through careful restructuring of the organizational system of communication, these problems could be surmounted, as attested to in the case of Canon, Inc.

Implications for U.S. Multinationals

Based on the comparative analysis of the human resource planning programs between U.S. and Japanese multinationals and the cursory review of the reasons for the lower failure rates among Japanese multinationals, several implications for U.S. firms can be drawn.

In the U.S. sample (Tung 1982a), it was found that the more rigorous the selection and training procedures used, the lower the rate of poor performance in a foreign country. Given the recognition that lack of relational skills is often responsible for failure overseas, U.S. multinationals should emphasize this criterion in their selection decisions for certain categories of overseas job assignments and certain countries in accordance with the contingency paradigm proposed by Tung (1981). Furthermore, U.S. multinationals should sponsor training programs to prepare expatriates for overseas assignments. While U.S. multinationals may contend that their Japanese counterparts can afford to invest in their people because of the system of lifetime employment, an argument could be made that the high failure rate among U.S. multinationals is also very costly. The cost of sending an average U.S. family overseas is estimated at $150,000 to $250,000 per annum. This includes base pay, cost-of-living differentials, and other adjustments. When these salary and fringe benefits are combined with lost market opportunities, they could be equally as staggering as the costs borne by Japanese multinationals to train expatriates.

U.S. firms should develop a longer-term orientation with regard to overseas assignments. Short stints abroad are not conducive to high performance because the expatriate barely has time to adjust before transfer to another location. Because of the concern among U.S. expatriates that prolonged absence from corporate headquarters may negatively affect their chances of promotion within the corporate organizational hierarchy, the implementation of some supportive mechanisms (similar to those found in Japanese companies) may alleviate these fears.

A longer-term orientation among U.S. companies may also engender a greater commitment and loyalty among employees and hence increased willingness to sacrifice temporary inconvenience in order to advance the company's overall goals.

While it may be difficult to change the attitudes of spouses and children with regard to overseas living, U.S. multinationals could try to cope with the situation by including the spouse in the selection procedure and providing training programs for the spouse and children. Tung (1982a) found that U.S. multinationals that interviewed both candidate and spouse to determine suitability for an overseas position experienced significantly lower rates of failure among their expatriates. The family situation may, of course, be compounded by several factors. One, the wife may feign preference for a foreign country because she feels that the assignment has a positive effect on her husband's future career. This problem may be partially overcome through rigorous training programs. Two, the provision of training programs for the spouse and children is costly. Here again the argument could be made that the cost of failure to the company is also very high. Furthermore, the training program provided the family need not be as rigorous as the one given the expatriate. This will help reduce costs. Three, with the increase in the number of dual-career families, U.S. wives are becoming less mobile. This problem does not apply to overseas assignments only but to relocations within the United States as well. Consequently, U.S. firms should develop procedures to deal with this issue.

In conclusion, U.S. multinationals that emulate the positive aspects of the human resource development programs of their Japanese counterparts may find that the failure rate of expatriates will fall, and thus U.S. international competitiveness may be maintained. Given the narrowing technological gap between the United States and Japan, U.S. multinationals can no longer rely solely on technology to gain a competitive edge in international markets. Rather, their focus should be shifted to the area of human resource planning because companies and technology are, after all, managed and operated by humans. The international competitiveness of U.S. multinationals has to depend on the ingenuity of its people and, more important, the people sent overseas as representatives of corporate headquarters.

Bibliography

Abegglen, J.C., Kato, T., Mulkern, L.J., Kawata, K., Hoadley, W.E., and Narusawa, K., eds. 1980. *U.S.-Japan economic relations: A symposium on critical issues.* Berkeley: University of California.

Abegglen, J.C., and Stalk, G. 1983, "Japanese trading companies: A dying industry?" *Wall Street Journal,* July 18, p. 19.

Adams, T.E.M., and Kobayashi, N. 1969. *The world of Japanese business.* Tokyo: Kodnsha International.

Ball, R. 1980. "Europe outgrows management American style."*Fortune,* October 20, pp. 147-148.

Bank of Yokohama: Annual Report. 1981.

Bartholomew, J. 1981. "Cultural values in Japan." In B.M. Richardson and T. Ueda, eds. *Business and society in Japan,* pp. 244-280. New York: Praeger Publishers.

Basic skills required of employees in international undertakings. 1978. Survey conducted by the Industrial Research Group. In *Survey of Employee Education in International Corporations.* Tokyo: July-August.

Borrmann, W.A. 1968. "The problem of expatriate personnel and their selection in international business." *Management International Review* 8, 4-5, pp. 37-48.

Business Week. 1980. January 28.

————. 1981a. August 31, pp. 68-72.

————. 1981b. September 16, pp. 61-64.

Campbell, R.D. 1969. "United States military training for cross-cultural interaction." *Office of Naval Research,* June 4.

Canon: Annual Report. 1981.

Canon Today. 1981-1982.

Celebration of Canon's first twenty-five years in America. 1955-1980.

Chase, M. 1982. "Japanese still think there is something to learn in the U.S."*Wall Street Journal,* October 20, p. 1.

Cole, R.E. 1981. "Labor in Japan." In B.M. Richardson and T. Ueda, eds. *Business and society in Japan,* pp. 29-36. New York: Praeger.

Correspondence from Namiji Itabashi, International Education Center. 1982. November 16.

Daicel Chemical Industries, Inc.: Annual report. 1980.

"Dentsu, the world's largest ad agency." 1982. *Fortune,* November 1, pp. 66-74.

Deutsch, S.E. 1970. *International education and exchange: A sociological analysis.* Cleveland: Case Western Reserve University Press.

Doing business in Japan. 1982. Tokyo: Japan External Trade Organization.

195

Drucker, P. 1954. *The Practice of management.* New York: Harper.

Fiedler, F.E., and Mitchell, T. 1971. "The culture assimilator: An approach to cross-cultural training." *Journal of Applied Psychology* 55, no. 2, pp. 95–102.

Forbes. 1980. March 31. p. 25.

Fortune. 1980. August. pp. 22–23.

Furukawa Electric: A brief survey. 1981.

Goodwin, C.D., and Nacht, M. 1983. "Foreign students still flock to the U.S." *Wall Street Journal,* July 21, p. 26.

Harrari, E., and Zeira, Y. 1978. "Training expatriates for managerial assignments in Japan." *California Management Review* 20, no. 4, pp. 56–62.

Harris, P.R., and Harris, D.L. 1972. "Training for cultural understanding." *Training and Development Journal* (May): 8–10.

Harrison, R., and Hopkins, R.L. 1967. "The design of cross-cultural training." *Journal of Applied Behavioral Science* 3, no. 4, pp. 431–460.

Haitani, K. 1976. *The Japanese economic system.* Lexington, Mass.: Lexington Books, D.C. Heath.

Hays, R.D. 1971. "Ascribed behavioral determinants of success-failure among U.S. expatriate managers." *Journal of International Business Studies* 2: 40–46.

_____. 1974. "Expatriate selection: Insuring success and avoiding failure." *Journal of International Business Studies,* 5, pp. 25–37.

Henry, E.R. 1965. "What business can learn from Peace Corps selection and training." *Personnel* 41 (July–August).

Hill, R. 1977. "East is still East." *International Management* (May): 15–18.

Howard, C.G. 1974. "Model for the design of a selection program for multinational executives." *Public Personnel Management* (March–April): 138–145.

Human resource development in industry. 1983. Japan Industrial Relations Series 10. Tokyo: Japan Institute of Labor.

Inohara, H. 1982. "Japanese subsidiaries in Europe: Promotion of local personnel." *Business Series* 8. Tokyo: Sophia University.

Institute for International Studies and Training Brochure. 1980–1981. Tokyo/Fujinomiya.

Institute for International Studies and Training. 1982. *IIST: Regular Program—Outline of Trainee Recruiting.*

_____. 1982a. *IIST: Practical Trade—Outline of Trainee Recruiting.*

International Education Center Brochure. 1982.

Itabashi, N. 1978. "Adult education: English teaching at a language school." In *The Teaching of English in Japan,* pp. 169–186. Tokyo: Eichosha Publishing Co.

Ivancevich, J.M. 1969. "Selection of American managers for overseas assignment." *Personnel Journal* 18 (March).

Japan Economic Journal, February 28, 1982.

Japan Economic News, June 24, 1982.

The Japanese consumer. 1980. Tokyo: Japan External Trade Organization.

Japanese corporate decision making. 1982. Tokyo: Japan External Trade Organization.

Japanese corporate personnel management. 1982. Tokyo: Japan External Trade Organization.

The Japanese market in figures. 1980. Tokyo: Japan External Trade Organization.

Johnson, C. 1982. *MITI and the Japanese miracle.* Stanford: Stanford University Press.

Journal of Japanese Trade and Industry. 1982. September, pp. 24–26.

Kanabayashi, M. 1982. "Japan's latest corporate advantage." *Wall Street Journal,* September 16, p. 34.

———. 1983. "Sony's profit will rise only gradually due to VTR competition, analysts say," *Wall Street Journal,* June 27, p. 33.

Kawaji, K. 1982. "Selection of personnel for a long-term overseas assignment." Tokyo: Mitsubishi Electric Co. Ltd.

Keys to success in the Japanese market. 1980. Tokyo: Japan External Trade Organization.

Lehner, U.C. 1983. "Canon takes No. 1 position from Nikon in the battle of Japanese camera giants." *Wall Street Journal,* September 16, p. 38.

Louis, E.T. 1983. "Williams College summer course for executives stresses liberal arts, shuns job-related subjects." *Wall Street Journal,* August 26, p. 38.

Lublin, J.S. 1983. "Overseas work appeal to more U.S. managers as a wise career move." *Wall Street Journal,* July 19, p. 1.

Lynton, R.P., and Pareek, U. 1967. *Training for development.* Illinois: Dorsey Press, 1967.

Marubeni: Human resource development system. 1981.

Marubeni: Annual report. 1981.

Marubeni America Corporation: Annual report. 1982.

Matsuno, S., and Stoever, W.A. 1982. "Japanese boss, American employees." *Wharton Magazine* (Fall): 45–48.

Miller, E.L. 1972. "The selection decision for an international assignment: A study of the decision maker's behavior." *Journal of International Business Studies* 3, pp. 49–65.

Mitsui Group: Yesterday, today, and tomorrow. 1982. Tokyo: Mainichi Newspapers.

Mitsui & Co., Ltd.: Annual report, 1981.

Musashi, M. 1982. *The book of five rings.* Translated by Nihon Services Corporation. New York: Bantam Books.

Naitoh, M. 1980. "American and Japanese industrial structures: A sectoral comparison." In D. Tasca, ed., *U.S.-Japanese economic relations,* pp. 61–75. New York: Pergamon Press.

Nakane, C. 1972. *Japanese society*. Berkeley: University of California Press.

New York Times. 1980. March 30.

Nikkei Business. 1982. May 17, pp. 59–65.

Nippon: The land and its people. 1982. Tokyo: Nippon Steel Corporation.

Nippon Steel Report, April 1, 1980–March 31, 1981.

Nissan Motor Co., Ltd.: Annual report. 1980.

Nomura Securities Co., Ltd.: Annual report. 1981.

Ouchi, W.G. 1981. *Theory Z*. Reading, Mass.: Addison-Wesley.

Pascale, R.T., and Athos, A.G. 1981. *The art of Japanese management*. New York: Simon and Schuster.

Patrick, H., and Rosovsky, H., eds. 1976. *Asia's new giant*. Washington D.C.: Brookings Institute.

Productivity and quality control. 1981. Tokyo: Japan External Trade Organization.

Richardson, B.M., and Ueda, T., eds. 1981. *Business and society in Japan*. New York: Praeger.

Roberts, J.G. 1973. *Mitsui: Three centuries of Japanese business*. New York: John Weatherhill.

Robinson, R.D. 1978. *International business management*. 2d ed. Hinsdale, Ill.: Dryden Press.

Robock, S.H., and Simmonds, K. 1983. *International Business and multinational enterprises*. 3d ed. Homewood, Ill.: Richard D. Irwin.

Role of trading companies on international commerce. 1982. Tokyo: Japan External Trade Organization.

Rubin, I. 1967. "The reduction of prejudice through laboratory testing." *Journal of Applied Behavioral Science* 3, pp. 29–50.

Schein, E.H. 1981. "SMR Forum: Does Japanese management style have a message for American managers?" *Sloan Management Review* (Fall): 55–68.

School of International Studies Brochure. 1982.

Seward, J. 1975. "Speaking the Japanese business language." *European Business* (Winter): 40–47.

Sheller, J.L. 1982. "A tale of two worlds in Tennessee." *U.S. News and World Report,* December 20, pp. 84–85.

Sieveking, N., Anchor, K., and Marston, R.C. 1981. "Selecting and preparing expatriate employees." *Personnel Journal* (March): 197–202.

Sony: Annual Report. 1981.

Sony Corporation: Consolidated financial summary. 1981.

Sony Voice. 1982. Publication of Sony Corporation of America. January–February.

Summary of recruitment survey: Personnel training within a corporation. 1980. Tokyo: Japan Recruitment Center.

Tasca, D., ed. 1980. *U.S.-Japanese economic relations*. New York: Praeger.

Taylor, R. 1982. "Sony's real secret." *Observer* (U.K.), October 31.

Textor, R.B., ed. 1966. *Cultural frontiers of the Peace Corps.* Cambridge, Mass.: MIT Press.

This is Nippon Steel. 1981. June.

This is Sony. 1982. February.

Tokuyama, J. 1982. "Turning strength into weakness." *Newsweek,* January 25, p. 4.

Toray Industries, Inc.: Annual report. 1980–1981.

Toray: The corporation that walks with the age. 1982.

Training program for spouses. 1982. Tokyo: Japan Overseas Educational Services.

Treece, J.B. 1983. "Japanese inch toward 5-day workweek as banks take one Saturday a month off." *Wall Street Journal,* August 24, p. 28.

Tung, R.L. 1981. "Selection and training of personnel for overseas assignments." *Columbia Journal of World Business* (Spring): 68–78.

_____. 1982a. "Selection and training procedures of U.S., European, and Japanese multinationals." *California Management Review* 25, no. 1, pp. 57–71.

_____. 1982b. "The rise and rise of the Japanese automotive industry?" *Academy of International Business Proceedings,* pp. 668–679.

_____. 1984. *Business negotiations with the Japanese.* Lexington, Mass.: LexingtonBooks, D.C. Heath.

Unique world of the sogo shosha. 1978. Tokyo: Marubeni Corporation.

Useem, J., Useem, R., and Donoghue, J. 1963. "Men in the middle of the third culture." *Human Organization* 22, pp. 169–179.

U.S. News & World Report. 1983. February 7, pp. 47–48.

Van Zandt, H. 1970. "How to negotiate in Japan." *Harvard Business Review* (November–December): 45–56.

Wall Street Journal. 1983a. February 1, p. 4.

_____. 1983b. March 23, p. 34.

White paper on international trade. 1981. Tokyo: Japan External Trade Organization.

Yamanoue, M. 1982. "Selection of personnel for long-term overseas assignments: Case of Kobe Steel Co." Tokyo: Kobe Steel Company.

Yearbook of U.S.-Japan economic relations. 1980. Washington, D.C.: Japan Economic Institute of America.

Appendix

UNITED STATES

When completing the items contained in this questionnaire, please note the following:

(1) For purposes of this study, the word "affiliate" includes branches, subsidiaries, joint ventures and minority investments.

(2) Some of the information requested pertain to regions of the world in which your company may not have foreign operations. Please omit those items or sections. Only answer those items or sections that are relevant to the regions of your company's operations abroad.

(3) If the information requested on relevant regions is not available, please provide some approximate estimates.

---

1. Your affiliate operations are located in:

( ) Western Europe
( ) Canada
( ) Middle and Near East
( ) Eastern Europe
( ) Latin and South America
( ) Far East
( ) Africa

The questions in this section are aimed at obtaining information regarding positions at different management levels in your affiliate operation(s) abroad and how they are staffed. For this purpose, the following terms mean:

(1) "Parent Country Nationals":   these refer to personnel who are
                                    U.S. citizens.

(2) "Host Country Nationals":   these refer to personnel who are
                                    citizens of the country of foreign
                                    operation.

(3) "Third Country Nationals":   these refer to personnel who are
                                    neither citizens of the U.S. nor
                                    country in which the foreign oper-
                                    ation is located.

PART I

Please indicate your response by a (✓). Limit your answers only to those regions that are relevant to your company's operations abroad.

WESTERN EUROPE	CANADA
a. Senior management positions in this region are primarily staffed by:	a. Senior management positions in this region are primarily staffed by:
( ) parent country nationals.	( ) parent country nationals.
( ) host country nationals.	( ) host country nationals.
( ) third country nationals.	( ) third country nationals.
b. Middle management positions in this region are primarily staffed by:	b. Middle management positions in this region are primarily staffed by:
( ) parent country nationals.	( ) parent country nationals.
( ) host country nationals.	( ) host country nationals.
( ) third country nationals.	( ) third country nationals.
c. Lower level management positions in this region are primarily staffed by:	c. Lower level management positions in this region are primarily staffed by:
( ) parent country nationals	( ) parent country nationals.
( ) host country nationals.	( ) host country nationals.
( ) third country nationals.	( ) third country nationals.

MIDDLE AND NEAR EAST	EASTERN EUROPE
a. Senior management positions in this region are primarily staffed by:	a. Senior management positions in this region are primarily staffed by:
( ) parent country nationals.	( ) parent country nationals.
( ) host country nationals.	( ) host country nationals.
( ) third country nationals.	( ) third country nationals.
b. Middle management positions in this region are primarily staffed by:	b. Middle management positions in this region are primarily staffed by:
( ) parent country nationals.	( ) parent country nationals.
( ) host country nationals.	( ) host country nationals.
( ) third country nationals.	( ) third country nationals.
c. Lower level management positions in this region are primarily staffed by:	c. Lower level management positions in this region are primarily staffed by:
( ) parent country nationals.	( ) parent country nationals.
( ) host country nationals.	( ) host country nationals.
( ) third country nationals.	( ) third country nationals.

LATIN AND SOUTH AMERICA	FAR EAST
a. Senior management positions in this region are primarily staffed by:	a. Senior management positions in this region are primarily staffed by:
( ) parent country nationals.	( ) parent country nationals.
( ) host country nationals.	( ) host country nationals.
( ) third country nationals.	( ) third country nationals.
b. Middle management positions in this region are primarily staffed by:	b. Middle management positions in this region are primarily staffed by:
( ) parent country nationals.	( ) parent country nationals.
( ) host country nationals.	( ) host country nationals.
( ) third country nationals.	( ) third country nationals.
c. Lower level management positions in this region are primarily staffed by:	c. Lower level management positions in this region are primarily staffed by:
( ) parent country nationals.	( ) parent country nationals.
( ) host country nationals.	( ) host country nationals.
( ) third country nationals.	( ) third country nationals.

AFRICA

a. Senior management positions in
    this region are primarily staf-
    fed by:

    (   ) parent country nationals.

    (   ) host country nationals.

    (   ) third country nationals.

b. Middle management positions in
    this region are primarily staf-
    fed by:

    (   ) parent country nationals.

    (   ) host country nationals.

    (   ) third country nationals.

c. Lower level management positions
    in this region are primarily
    staffed by:

    (   ) parent country nationals.

    (   ) host country nationals.

    (   ) third country nationals.

PART II

A. Check one or more of the applicable reasons below for staffing overseas
operations with parent country nationals (i.e., personnel who are U.S.
citizens):

(   ) a. The foreign enterprise is just being established (start-up phase).

(   ) b. The parent firm wishes to develop an internationally oriented
management for the headquarters (foreign assignments are seen
essentially as management development).

(   ) c. No adequate management is available from other countries.

(   ) d. The parent firm has <u>surplus</u> managerial personnel toward whom
it feels responsible.

(   ) e. Virtually no autonomy is possible for the foreign enterprise
because it is integrated so closely with operations elsewhere.

(   ) f. The foreign enterprise is seen as short-lived.

(   ) g. The host society is multiracial or multireligious, and a
local manager of either racial origin or religion would make
the enterprise potentially vulnerable or lead to an economic
boycott.

(   ) h. There is a compelling need to maintain a foreign image.

(   ) i. It is felt desirable to avoid involving particular local nationals
or families (former distributors or agents) in management, and
the use of other local nationals would create dangerous animo-
sities.

(   ) j. Local nationals are not mobile and resist assignment elsewhere.

(   ) k. A parent country national is simply the best man for the job,
all things considered.

(   ) l. Control is weak, particularly in cases where local nationals are
highly nationalistic (patriotic) and more responsive to government pressures than would an expatriate.

(   ) m. Technical expertise.

(   ) n. Many times our clients request U.S. nationals.

(   ) o. Other (specify)_____

B. Check one or more of the applicable reasons below for staffing overseas
operations with third country nationals (i.e., personnel who are neither
citizens of the U.S. nor of the country of foreign operation):

(   ) a. Reduced costs.

(   ) b. Technical expertise.

(   ) c. The host society is multiracial or multireligious , and a
local manager of either racial origin or religion would
make the enterprise politically vulnerable or lead to an
economic boycott.

(   ) d.   It is felt desirable to avoid involving particular local nationals or
            families (former distributors or agents) in management, and the use
            of other local nationals would create dangerous animosities.

(   ) e.   U.S. personnel are generally less interested in overseas assign-
            ments, particularly in out-of-the-way locations.

(   ) f.   A third country national is simply the best man for the job,
            all things considered.

(   ) g.   No adequate management is available from other sources.

(   ) h.   Language skills that parent country nationals do not possess.

(   ) i.   Other (specify) _____

C.   Check one or more of the applicable reasons below for staffing overseas
operations with host country nationals (i.e., personnel who are citizens
of the country of foreign operation):

(   ) a.   Reduced costs.

(   ) b.   Denial of entry of aliens.

(   ) c.   Denial of work permit to aliens.

(   ) d.   Knowledge of language.

(   ) e.   Greater familiarity with the local culture.

(   ) f.   Good public relations.

(   ) g.   A host country national is simply the best man for the job,
            all things considered.

(   ) h.   No adequate management is available from other sources.

(   ) i.   Other (specify)_____

PART III

> In selecting "parent country nationals" to fill overseas assginments,
> you may base your selection decision on a set of criteria. You may or may
> not use the same set of criteria for selecting people to fill overseas mana-
> gerial positions. For purposes of this study, we will classify overseas
> managerial assignments according to four general categories. These are:
>
> (1) Chief Executive Officer: whose responsibility is to oversee and
>   direct the entire foreign operation.
>
> (2) Functional Head: whose job is to establish functional depart-
>   ments in a foreign subsidiary.
>
> (3) Trouble-Shooter: whose function is to analyze and solve
>   specific operational problems.
>
> (4) Operative: rank-and-file members.

For each of the four categories, please identify the criteria that you may use for selecting people by checking appropriate boxes.

Criteria	Chief Executive Officer			Functional Head			Trouble-Shooter			Operative		
	Criterion Not Used	Use, Not Important	Use, Very Important	Criterion Not Used	Use, Not Important	Use, Very Important	Criterion Not Used	Use, Not Important	Use, Very Important	Criterion Not Used	Use, Not Important	Use, Very Important
Experience in Company												
Technical knowledge of business												
Knowledge of language of host country												
Overall experience and education of candidate												
Managerial talent												
Interest in overseas work												
Initiative, creativity												
Independence												
Previous overseas experience												
Respect of laws and people of host country												
Sex /Gender												
Age												
Stability of marital relations												
Spouse and family's adaptability												
Adaptability, flexibility in new environmental settings												
Maturity, emotional stability												
Communication												
Same criteria as other comparable jobs at home												
Other (specify)_____												

PART IV

Please identify the steps that you may go through in selecting a candidate for a foreign assignment.

a. Are tests administered to determine the candidate's technical competence?

Yes (   )   No (   )

b. Are tests administered to determine the candidate's relational abilities i.e., ability to empathize with different cultural values and norms?

Yes (   )   No (   )

If yes, briefly describe the nature of the tests used to determine the candidate's relational abilities.

_____

_____

_____

_____

_____

c. For management positions, are interviews conducted with the candidate? Please check one.

Yes, with both (   )   Yes, with (   )   No (   )
candidate and   candidate
spouse   only

d. For technical positions, are interviews conducted with the candidate? Please check one.

Yes, with both (   )   Yes, with (   )   No (   )
candidate and   candidate
spouse   only

Every year, some managers may have to be recalled to their home country or their employment terminated because of their inability to function effectively in a foreign environment. Below are a list of possible reasons for such failures.

In your opinion, how often are such failures (in your company and other companies you are familiar with) attributable to each of the reasons given below? Please indicate your response by placing a (✓) in the appropriate columns.

REASONS FOR FAILURES	This reason does not apply	To a very little extent	To a little extent	To some extent	To a great extent	To a very great extent
Inability of the manager to cope with the larger responsibilities posed by the overseas work.						
Lack of motivation to work overseas.						
Manager's personality or emotional maturity.						
Manager's lack of technical competence for the job assignment.						
The manager's inability to adapt to a different physical or cultural environment.						
The inability of the manager's spouse to adjust to a different cultural or physical environment.						
Other family-related problems.						
Other (specify) _____						

B. What percentage of overseas personnel have to be recalled to their home country or dismissed because of inability to function effectively in a foreign assignment? Please check one.

      ( ) Between 0 - 5%
      ( ) Between 6 - 10%
      ( ) Between 11 - 15%
      ( ) Between 16 - 19%
      ( ) Between 20 - 39%
      ( ) Between 40 - 59%
      ( ) Between 60 - 80%
      ( ) Over 80%

C. In your organization, after a candidate from corporate headquarters has been selected for a foreign assignment, does he/she have to undergo a special formalized training program to prepare for the overseas work?

      ( ) Yes   ( ) No

If "no," what are the reasons for omitting formal training prior to overseas assignment? Please check one or more of the following reasons:

      ( ) Temporary nature of many assignments.
      ( ) Lack of time because of the immediacy of the need for the employee overseas.
      ( ) Trend toward employment of local nationals.
      ( ) Doubt effectiveness of existing training programs.

PART VI

Companies may sponsor formal training programs to prepare their candidates for overseas assignments. Please indicate by a (✔) the type of training program that your organization has for candidates who would be taking up overseas managerial positions in each of the four categories.

	Categories
(1) Chief Executive Officer:	whose responsibility is to oversee and direct the entire foreign operation.
(2) Functional Head:	whose job is to establish functional departments in foreign subsidiary.
(3) Trouble-Shooter:	whose function is to analyze and solve specific operational problems.
(4) Operative:	rank-and-file members.

Type of Training Program	Chief Executive Officer	Functional Head	Trouble-Shooter	Operative
Language Training				
Cultural Orientation--information about the cultural institutions, value systems of host country.				
Environmental Briefing--information about the geography, climate, housing, schools, etc.				
Culture Assimilator--brief episodes describing intercultural encounters.				
Sensitivity Training--to develop attitudinal flexibility.				
Field Experience--wherein trainees are actually sent to the country of assignment or a "micro culture" nearby, where they could undergo some of the emotional stress that they would expect in living and working with people from a different sub-culture/ culture.				
Other (specify) _____				

B. Is there any evaluation of the effectiveness of the formal training programs currently utilized by your company? Check one:

            Yes (   )   No (   )   Don't Know (   )

If "yes," please indicate the procedures used to evaluate the effectiveness of such training programs.

(   ) Trainee's subjective evaluation of the usefulness of training programs.

(   ) Supervisor's subjective evaluation of trainee's performance after formal training.

(   ) Objective tests (e.g., aptitude tests, etc.)

(   ) Others (specify) _____

_____
_____
_____
_____
_____
_____
_____

                              THANK YOU VERY MUCH FOR YOUR COOPERATION

                              Name of firm (Optional):

                              _____

Index

path, 29–30, 34, 40–41, 46, 73, 74, 79,
80, 86, 93, 97, 108–110, 125, 126,
137, 138, 157, 159, 163, 166, 176,
184, 188; -oriented, 33, 34, 191
Proposed changes. *See* Human resource
planning, proposed changes to
Psychological appraisal, 10; *see also*
Psychometric devices
Psychological makeup, 9, 14, 15; *see
also* Adaptability; Culture shock
Psychometric devices, 104, 120; *see also*
Psychological appraisal
Public Opinion Research Institute, 183,
184, 191

Quality of career staff, 118, 159, 178,
182, 183; *see also* Aptitude; Talent
Questionnaire, 201–212
Questionnaire survey, 3–21, 65, 66

Recruitment, job, 31, 32, 48, 73, 108,
116, 178, 182, 183
Regular program, 57–60, 190
Relational skills, 10, 13, 19, 23, 24, 41,
49, 56, 57, 65, 80, 83, 88, 93, 100, 118,
139, 145, 168, 173, 174, 186, 192
Remuneration, 41, 87, 101, 102, 129,
145, 146, 160, 168–170, 178; *see also*
Wages; Bonus; Company benefits
Repatriation, 67, 68, 86, 87, 95–97, 102,
103, 144, 153, 165, 166, 174, 175, 193
Retirement, 30, 192
Reward system, 35, 40, 41, 84
Ringi-sho. *See* Consensus decision
making
Runyon, Marvin, 162, 163

Saito, Eishiro, 174, 175
Samurai, 27
Sanseis, 91
Sasaki, Yoshiro, xiii, 170–179, 184
Satoh, Katsuhiko, xiii, 10, 161–170
Savin, 148
Saxon, 148
School of International Studies (SIS),
64, 65
Schools: business, 9, 28, 29, 73, 83, 99,
100, 104, 111, 114, 115, 127, 129,
142, 157, 166, 171, 175, 189; elite, 27,
28, 31, 36, 41, 48, 76, 96, 97, 111,
114, 120, 126, 191; for children of

returned expatriates, 96, 97, 191;
han, 27; limitations in system, 96; *see
also* Education of children; temple,
27; terakoya, 27; weekend, 67, 68
Selection of employer, 31, 32, 182
Selection procedures, expatriate,
10–11, 23–25, 146, 179, 186, 187; *see
also* Criteria for expatriate selection
Self-appraisal, 37, 38, 82, 95, 123, 124,
187
Self-confidence, 39
Self-development, 30, 45, 78, 80, 98,
104, 127, 175, 179
Self-enlightenment, 30, 45, 84, 98, 124,
127, 166, 175, 179
Seniority, 16, 32, 34, 40, 41, 47, 80, 97,
108, 122, 155, 183
Senpai-kohai. *See* Employer-employee
relationship
Sensitivity training, 12, 16, 21
Sex. *See* Gender of candidates
Shapiro, Irving, 188
Sharp, 148
Shukko, 48, 49, 78, 84, 126
Simulation, use of, 65, 156
Sloan School of Management, 99
Smyrna plant, 162, 163
Sogo shosha. *See* General trading
companies
Sony Corporation, xiii, 18, 32, 107,
131–149
Special assignments, 48, 49; *see also*
Shukko
Specialists, 55, 190
Spouse: adaptability of, 11, 14, 15, 59,
77, 114, 119, 157, 174, 190, 193;
assessment of, 11, 16, 19, 59, 77, 94,
113, 146, 174; role of, 11, 33, 62, 63,
66, 96, 104, 113, 169, 174, 190, 191;
training for, 62, 63, 65–68, 77, 82, 83,
100, 117, 119, 142, 157, 167, 177, 193
Staffing policy, 2, 5–8, 71–74, 90–93,
109–112, 122, 123, 132–137, 149–152,
162–164, 171, 172, 192
Stanford University, 104, 114
Status in society, 28, 32, 44, 62, 120,
121, 126, 182, 191
Status shock, 14, 15, 19, 49, 50, 143,
147, 155, 189
Steel, 161, 170–179
Stern, John, 133

About the Author

Rosalie L. Tung received a Ph.D. from the University of British Columbia and is now an associate professor of management at The Wharton School, University of Pennsylvania. She was formerly on the faculty of the University of Oregon and has taught at the University of California, Los Angeles, and the University of Manchester Institute of Science and Technology (England). She was invited as the first foreign expert to teach management at the Foreign Investment Commission (now the Ministry of Foreign Economic Relations and Trade), the highest agency under the Chinese State Council that approves all joint ventures and other major forms of foreign investment. She has been included in *The International Who's Who of Intellectuals, Who's Who in the Frontier of Science and Technology, The World's Who's Who of Women, Who's Who of American Women,* and elsewhere for outstanding contributions in her field.

Dr. Tung is the author of four other books: *Management Practices in China; U.S.-China Trade Negotiations; Chinese Industrial Society after Mao;* and *Business Negotiations with the Japanese.* She has also published widely on the subjects of international management and organizational theory in leading journals such as the *Columbia Journal of World Business, Journal of International Business Studies, California Managment Review, Academy of Management Journal, Academy of Management Review, Journal of Vocational Behavior, Journal of Applied Psychology, Pacific Basin Economic Review,* (a publication of the Wharton Econometric Forecasting Associates), *The Business Graduate* (U.K.), and *Multilingua.*

Dr. Tung is a reviewer of peer proposals for the National Science Foundation and the U.S. Department of Education. She sits on the editorial board of several academic journals. She served as 1983 program chairperson for the International Management Division, National Academy of Management. She is a member of the Academy of International Business, Academy of Management, American Management Association, American Economic Association, American Psychological Association, and International Association of Applied Psychology.